Cuckoo Too

Nancy Allen

Kay Bruce

Fran Fauntleroy

Pat Glauser

Isla Reckling

Mary Whilden

Cover and illustrations by
Laura Bailie

Back cover photograph by
Heinz Kugler

Distributed by
Peanut Butter Publishing
Mercer Island, Washington

This book is a collection of recipes written by six housewives who have learned, in the midst of solid confusion, to be creative cooks for their families. The book is divided into six sections with each one devoted to a particular family's favorite dishes. So, refer to the index often.

There is no such thing as an original idea. However, many of these recipes are our own, while others are adaptations of recipes from friends, families, and cookbooks.

Some of these recipes are what we call "put togethers." They are dishes that have been tried by many, for our group is famous for exchanging and sharing a bowl of this and a bite of that. When you create something that isn't half bad, you have to get another opinion. Our cookbook is unique—with six cuckoos in six kitchens, you hatch a different product. However, we all have two things in common—we love to cook—we love to eat! We hope you love it too!

BETA
APPLE

Auntie's Egg Nog

3 tbsp sugar
4 eggs, separated

1 pint whipping cream
1 c of bourbon (Old Forester)

Put 1 tablespoon of sugar in each of 3 bowls. Put the whites of 4 eggs in 1 bowl, the yolks of 4 eggs in a second bowl and the whipping cream in a third bowl. Beat the whites with an electric beater until quite stiff, then place in the refrigerator. Add 1 cup of bourbon to the bowl with the egg yolks and beat slightly. Put in the refrigerator. Beat the whipping cream until fairly stiff and put in the refrigerator about 20 minutes. Mix the egg yolks and bourbon with the whipping cream then fold the egg whites into this mixture. Pour off the juice in the bottom of the bowl with the whites before folding into the whip cream mixture. This is delicious as well as nutritional. Serves 5.

Whiskey Sours
for Sunday Brunch

2 cans (6 oz each) frozen
   lemonade concentrate
1 quart water

1 fifth bourbon

Combine ingredients and pour over crushed ice. Add a cherry, a sliced orange to decorate each glass.

Spritzer

⅓ glass of white wine
soda (splash)

lemon peel
Serve over ice.

Wine Cooler

⅓ glass of white wine
7-Up or Shasta Lemon Lime
  Soda

large squeeze of lemon juice
Serve over ice.

Mimosa

champagne (domestic)
1 jigger light rum
orange juice

squeeze of lime juice
sprig of mint

To make one glass, put 1 jigger of rum over ice. Add orange juice almost to the top of glass. Add champagne, a squeeze of lime and a sprig of mint. This is a light drink and gets the conversation flowing.

Tea Punch

2 family sized tea bags
1½ c, or more sugar
1 6 oz can frozen limeade

1 42 oz can pineapple juice
sprigs of mint
2 qts hot water (boiling)

While tea is steeping 5 minutes in 2 qts hot water add sprigs of mint. In gallon container add tea and sugar. When tea mixture is room temperature add limeade and pineapple juice. Pour over block of ice in punch bowl. Serves 20.

Iced Tea

1 large family tea bag
1 Constant Comment tea bag
½ can frozen lemonade

½ c sugar
1 quart of water

Bring water to a rolling boil in a pot. Turn heat off and add tea bags. Steep the tea bags in the boiling water 5 minutes. Take tea bags out and add lemonade and sugar. Tea is ready for the day. Keep it out of the icebox. The icebox makes tea murky.

Proper Tea

Boil water in a pot. Scald an earthenware or china teapot to pour the boiling water into. Use 1 teaspoon of tea for every cup of water. Steep the tea for 4–5 minutes. Do not boil tea or make a pot of strong tea and dilute with hot water.

Salted Nuts

white Karo
2½ lb pecans

½ stick melted butter
salt

This recipe is my grandmother's and there is just one ingredient that makes it very special—white Karo. In a baking pan cover carefully picked fresh pecan halves with melted butter. Toss in pan until all pecans are coated. Place in 400° oven for 12–14 minutes. Take out of oven when brown. While pecans are browning, tear open a large paper bag so you can lay it flat on the counter. Drip a tiny stream of white karo up and down on the paper bag. Pour browned pecan halves out on the paper. Salt generously and toss with hands or spoon. When room temperature, put in containers.

Wild Duck Hors d'Oeuvre

wild duck
parsley

hot mustard
pumpernickel bread

Place duck breast side up in a 500° oven for no longer than 15–20 minutes—as little as ten minutes. Remove from oven, place on a tray with parsley in the neck and tail. Cut meat in ¼ inch strips and leave in place on duck. Serve with buttered pumpernickel bread and a little hot mustard. Cut pumpernickel in strips a little larger than the slices of duck.

Cheese Tray

One of our favorite appetizers is a cheese tray. We also use a cheese tray with fruit for dessert. Our choice of cheese depends on how elegant the occasion. Some of our favorite cheeses are Baby Swiss, cheddar, Bel Paise and Brie. We use all types of crackers—a plain wafer, saltine, Ritz or Rye Crisp. I usually place one or several large hunks of cheese on a tray with slices of apple intermittently spaced between the crackers and a large whole apple in one place. If I have parsley, I add a sprig here and there. I add more fruit to the tray when using this for dessert.

Hot Cheese Squares

2 loaves unsliced bread,
  no crust
½ lb English cheese
½ lb American cheese
¼ lb soft butter

3 whole eggs
1 tsp worcestershire
1 tsp onion juice
paprika
cayenne pepper, shakes

Cream butter and cheese over low heat on the stove. Add well beaten eggs, worcestershire, onion juice and cayenne pepper. Slice bread 1½" thick. Cut each slice into 4 cubes. Cover each square with cheese and sprinkle with paprika. Refrigerate overnight. Toast at 350° for 10 minutes. Average loaf makes 16 squares.

Crabmeat Dip

1 c mayonnaise
½ c sour cream
1 tsp lemon juice
1 tsp worcestershire
shake of Tabasco

salt and pepper to taste
1 6½ oz can well picked
  crabmeat
1 tsp sherry (optional)
cayenne pepper, several shakes

Combine all ingredients and chill. Before placing in a bowl, pour crabmeat into a strainer to drain off extra juice. Decorate with a couple of sprigs of parsley and serve with melba rounds.

Barbequed Sausage

We use Echrich sausage, but any good link sausage is delicious barbecued for 10 minutes on each side and cut into bite-size pieces. Sometimes we put the Echrich sausage in the oven under the broiler and serve in larger portions with cheese grits for a fast dinner.

Fresh Beluga Caviar

Fresh caviar is the most special hors d'oeuvre. Beluga caviar comes in a tin and must be kept on ice. It is very expensive, but a great way to celebrate anniversaries or New Year's Eve or any occasion that calls for a special treat. I have never served caviar when the party was not a success. This is how we serve it:

1 (14 oz) can fresh Beluga caviar
toasted buttered bread rounds,
 3 loaves
sour cream, 1 pint
1 onion, finely chopped

2 lemons, sliced and halved
3 hard boiled eggs,
 finely chopped
1 lb of butter

On a silver tray, place 5 round bowls. In 1 bowl, place caviar tin on top of ice. In each of the other bowls, put lemon, sour cream, onion and egg. We use our Blue Bristol bowls and the setting is very elegant. To the side, put buttered bread rounds in biscuit box or bread tray. Drink ice cold vodka with this. Remember to chill the vodka and the glasses.

To prepare buttered bread rounds, cut out circles of soft bread with biscuit cutter. Each slice of bread should make 2 rounds. In a pot, melt 1 lb of butter. Dip bread rounds in butter and fry on both sides. This can be done early and the bread rounds can be placed on a cookie sheet and run under broiler before serving. Serves 10.

Tamales and Chile

This is an easy, filling dish that can be done ahead of time. Our boys like it and we fix it for neighborhood entertaining. Serve this with rice, guacamole salad and pralines for dessert.

3 cans tamales, shucked
1 can chili with beans (24 oz)
1 can chili without beans (24 oz)
1 large onion, chopped
½ lb Monterrey Jack cheese,
   shredded

1 tsp oregano
1 tsp cumin seeds
1 tsp chili powder

Heat about ⅓ cup oil in the casserole over direct heat. Add chopped onion. Cook until tender, about 10 minutes. Remove casserole from heat. Put ½ of the shucked tamales over onions, add the chili with beans and the plain chili. Sprinkle 1 teaspoon of oregano and 1 teaspoon of cumin seeds and 1 teaspoon of chili powder over this. Top with remaining tamales. Cover and refrigerate until 1 hour before serving time. Sprinkle cheese over top and bake in preheated 350° oven, uncovered, for 30 minutes or until bubbly. If entertaining and guests are not ready to eat, turn oven to warm and serve at your convenience. Serves 6–8.

Instant Chalupas

1 14½ oz can refried beans
1 10½ oz can Fritos bean dip
4 large ripe avocados
1 c mayonnaise
1 pkg taco seasoning mix

4 tomatoes chopped
1 bunch green onions chopped
lemon juice
green chiles

Place the above ingredients in a large casserole (13½ × 8¾) in 7 layers. Mix refried beans and Frito bean dip and spread on the bottom of the casserole. Peel, mash and season the avocados with lemon juice and green chiles. Place on top of the beans. Mix sour cream and mayonnaise and taco seasoning and put on top of the avocados. Next place chopped, *drained* tomatoes, followed by chopped onions, grated cheese and black olives.

Variation: Make avocados into guacamole for avocado layer, season sour cream mixture with picante sauce and top with jalapenos instead of black olives.

Quick Chili for 5

2 lb ground beef
1 medium chopped onion
1 (15 oz) can tomato sauce
2 cans Van Camps Kidney Beans
   (New Orleans style)
1 tsp chili powder

garlic salt
salt
pepper
cayenne
several shakes of Tabasco

Brown beef and onion. Add tomato sauce and kidney beans. Season with chili powder, salt, pepper, Tabasco, garlic salt and cayenne to taste. We prepare this chili only when we are in a big hurry. This is a bland chili that small boys like.

Bambe's Chile Rellenos

3 (4 oz) cans green sliced
   chili peppers, drained
1 lb cheddar cheese,
   grated
5 eggs

1 lb Monterrey Jack cheese,
   grated
3½ c milk
½ c flour
1 tsp salt

Dry the well drained peppers on paper toweling. Place on bottom of 7½ × 13 baking dish and cover with cheeses. Beat eggs, add flour, milk and salt. Pour over cheese. Bake at 350° for 50 minutes or until custard sets and top is golden brown. Serve from baking dish. When entertaining, make this ahead and reheat at 350° for 30 minutes. It won't rise quite as high, but the guests won't know the difference. Serves 8.

Quick Curry Soup

1 tart apple	1 c cream
1 small onion	salt and pepper
4 c consomme	curry powder

Chop apple and onion. Simmer with consomme for 20 minutes. Strain, add cream. Season with salt, pepper and a little curry. Serves 6.

Crab Bisque

This soup makes a quick Sunday supper with bran muffins and a tossed green salad. We use this soup for entertaining, too. Serve from a soup tureen in small demitasse cups. It gives some substance to a buffet cocktail party. When doubling or making any large amount, increase your liquid substantially and approximate your crab, then season to taste. When I make 5 times this recipe, I use 4 lbs of crabmeat. Serves 5.

1 lb of crabmeat (lump or pieces)	¼ tsp curry powder
	shake of Beau Monde
1 can tomato soup	shake of Mei Yen
1 can green pea soup	3 tbsp sherry
3 c milk	salt and pepper to taste
¼ tsp worcestershire sauce	
¼ tsp Tabasco	

Bambe's Oyster Stew

1 gallon oysters	1 tsp worcestershire
1 lb butter	1 tsp Tabasco
4 tsp salt	1 gallon milk
1 tsp celery salt	1 quart cream (regular)
1 tsp paprika	

Heat together in a pot, the first 7 ingredients until the edges of the oysters curl. Heat 1 gallon milk and 1 quart of regular cream in another pot until boiling point. Mix together. Makes 2 gallons.

Cucumber Sandwiches

1 cucumber, peeled
oil and vinegar dressing
½ onion, sliced

thin sliced white bread
salt
pepper

Slice cucumber paper thin and marinate in oil and vinegar dressing with sliced onion for at least 30 minutes. Cut crust from thin sliced white bread. Put mayonnaise lightly on 1 side of bread. Take thin slices of cucumber out of marinade and place on mayonnaised side of bread. Sprinkle with salt and pepper and make sandwich. Cut any way you wish.

Open Faced Cheese Sandwich

3 slices bacon
mayonnaise
American cheese

white bread
2 slices of peeled tomato

Slightly grill 3 slices of bacon. Put mayonnaise on piece of white bread. Place slice of American cheese on top of mayonnaise. Add 2 slices of peeled tomato. Run under broiler until cheese is melted. Add lightly grilled bacon and return to broiler until cheese is bubbly. Be careful bacon does not burn.

Avocado and Cucumber Salad

1 avocado, chopped in
    small cubes
2 cucumbers, peeled and
    sliced thin

oil and vinegar dressing
lemon juice
Boston lettuce

Squeeze lemon juice over avocado. Combine avocado with sliced cucumber. Pour oil and vinegar over this mixture. Place on Boston lettuce. Serve chilled. Serves 4.

Avocado Bacon Salad

1 avocado, chopped in
  small cubes
5 slices bacon, crisp
3 tbsp mayonnaise

2 tbsp ketchup
1 tbsp worcestershire
  sauce
salt and pepper to taste

Crumble bacon over avocado. Combine mayonnaise, ketchup, worcestershire, salt, and pepper. Mix avocado and bacon with sauce. Serve in champagne glass or on top of lettuce leaf. Serves 2.

Crispy Cole Slaw

½ head cabbage, shredded thin
¾ c mayonnaise

3–4 tbsp white vinegar
fresh cracked pepper

Shred cabbage early and place in the icebox with ice cubes on top. Mix mayonnaise (homemade is best, but if you are in a hurry, use Hellman's with 1 tablespoon lemon juice) with the white vinegar and fresh cracked pepper. At the last minute, remove ice cubes from cabbage and mix dressing with cabbage. Serves 5.

Potato Salad

5 white potatoes, chopped in
  small pieces
1 onion, chopped fine
5 Sweet Gherkins pickles,
  chopped fine
2–3 stalks celery, chopped fine
1 large tsp mustard

2 large tbsp mayonnaise
salt
pepper
cayenne
spike
paprika

Boil peeled potatoes in heavily salted water until tender. Drain and dry potatoes well. While hot, mix all ingredients together. Add more mayonnaise if not thoroughly moist. Season to taste. If you want to prepare this early for a weekend, do not add the onions until ready to serve. Spike is a health food seasoning which we find good on many foods. Serves 6–8.

Tomato Mince with Curry Mayonnaise

2–3 large peeled ripe tomatoes
1 cucumber, peeled
½ green pepper
½ small onion
white pepper

1 small can tomato juice
(5½ oz)
3 tbsp oil and vinegar
salad dressing
curry mayonnaise

Finely chop into a bowl, the tomatoes, cucumber, green pepper and onion. Add tomato juice, white pepper and salad dressing. Put in icebox to chill. This should have a crunchy texture. Serve in cold bowls with a teaspoon of curry mayonnaise on top. To make curry mayonnaise, add 1 teaspoon lemon juice and ¼ teaspoon curry powder to 3 large tablespoons of bought mayonnaise. Serves 4.

Artichokes with Curry Mayonnaise

2 artichokes
1 pod garlic, crushed
1 stalk of celery plus leaves
1 onion, cubed
1 tbsp oil

pepper corns
juice of 1 lemon
½ c Hellman's mayonnaise
½ tsp curry

Wash artichokes several times. Pour juice of ½ lemon over them. Boil covered for 35–40 minutes until tender in pan with crushed garlic, celery, onion, oil and pepper corns. In ½ cup of Hellman's mayonnaise, put juice of ½ lemon and ½ teaspoon curry powder and mix together. Serve this sauce with the artichokes. Serves 4.

Marinated Tomatoes

fresh tomatoes, sliced ½ c red wine vinegar
½ c safflower oil 2 tbsp Chef Howard's salt

Peel and slice tomatoes (thick slices). Combine vinegar and salt (Chef Howard's) and stir well. Slowly beat in oil. Pour over tomatoes and refrigerate overnight.

Mildred's Oil and Vinegar Dressing

2 tsp mustard, dry 1 c olive oil or safflower oil
¾ c sugar 3 tbsp water
1 tsp salt 1 tbsp onion juice
1 tbsp paprika 2 garlic cloves
1 c wine vinegar

Let salt and peeled garlic cloves stand together in bottle an hour or more before mixing. Add the remaining ingredients and shake well. The type of vinegar you purchase is important. Try making this with Spice Islands red wine tarragon and garlic or try a special wine vinegar of your choice.

Mayonnaise in Blender

1 egg, room temperature cayenne pepper
½ tsp salt 1 c Wesson oil
½ tsp dry mustard 2 tbsp lemon juice, added last
½ tsp sugar

Mix the egg, salt, mustard, sugar and cayenne pepper in the blender quickly. Slowly drip the Wesson oil (I use corn oil also) while the blender is on high speed. Add the lemon juice at the end slowly. This helps keep it from separating. If the mayonnaise does curdle, pour most of it into another container. Add an egg to a small amount of the curdled mayonnaise in the blender. At high speed, slowly add the remaining curdled mayonnaise and it will go back together.

Blender Hollandaise

This hollandaise keeps in the icebox. I fix it about once every two weeks and have it to spruce up our vegetables during the week. When you begin cooking dinner, take the hollandaise out of the icebox and put it near the stove. Stir it once or twice in the container. It will be room temperature by dinner and warm enough to put on your vegetables.

2 sticks butter
4 egg yolks
2 tbsp lemon juice

pinch of cayenne
¼ tsp salt

In small saucepan heat butter just to bubbling. Meanwhile, put egg yolks, lemon juice, salt and cayenne into electric blender. Cover container and turn blender on high speed. Immediately remove cover and add hot butter in steady stream. To keep, store in refrigerator. Yields 1¼ cups. If the sauce doesn't thicken, add the lemon juice after the butter.

French-Fried Shrimp

2 lbs jumbo shrimp

Prepare the batter immediately before frying the shrimp while the oil is heating.

1 c flour
½ c water

1 tsp baking soda
salt and pepper

The batter must be thick. If yours is runny, add more flour. Or, if it is too pasty, add a little water. Dip shrimp in batter and brown in hot fat about 5 minutes. Serves 6.

Sauce:

1 part catsup
1 part mayonnaise
Lea & Perrins

Tabasco
salt
pepper

Mix together mayonnaise and catsup, and season with Lea & Perrins, Tabasco, salt and pepper.

Italian Barbecued Shrimp

This is good as an hors d'oeuvre or as a main dish served with Risotto.

2 lb raw shrimp
½ c olive oil
1 tsp oregano
2 finely minced garlic cloves

2 tbsp lemon juice
salt
fresh cracked pepper

Peel and devein shrimp. Place shrimp in flat dish and pour marinade of oil, oregano, garlic and lemon juice over them. Season with salt and fresh ground pepper. Allow to stand for 3 or 4 hours. Skewer shrimp and broil over medium coals. Brush with marinade several times during the broiling. Serves 5–6.

Shrimp Newburg

This is a closely guarded Galveston recipe.

1 c cooked shrimp
1 large peeled tomato
2 tbsp butter
2 tbsp flour
2 tsp chopped parsley
½ clove garlic, peeled

¼ c heavy cream
4 tbsp sherry
   (Pedro Dominique Oloroso)
1 tbsp worcestershire sauce
1 dash of Angostura bitters

Melt butter and add garlic. Cook until garlic is golden brown. Remove garlic. Add parsley and tomato and cook together 5 minutes. Sprinkle flour over this and mix. Cook 2 minutes longer. Add cream and mix. Add sherry, worcestershire and bitters. Cook 5 minutes more. Add shrimp, salt and pepper. Serves 2. This is exactly how this recipe was given to me, but I have found when I double or make larger quantities that instead of sprinkling flour over the tomatoes, I make a roux of the flour and the garlic butter in the beginning, then add the parsley and tomatoes. Unless tomatoes are in season, I use canned tomatoes.

Shrimp Creole

Quick and easy and keeps well. It takes about 5 minutes to put together and simmers for 45 minutes to 1 hour in heavy iron skillet.

1 lb cooked shrimp
   (approximately 60)
1 c onion, chopped
1 green pepper, chopped
1 can tomato soup (10½ oz)
1 can tomato sauce (15 oz)
1 can water

lump of butter
worcestershire sauce
Tabasco sauce
juice of 1 lemon
creole seasoning
salt to taste
pepper to taste

Saute onion and pepper in butter and cook until amber color, but not crisp. Add soup, tomato sauce, seasoning and water. 15 minutes before dinner, add shrimp.

Crab Newburg

2 c picked crabmeat
½ pint cream
1 cup sherry (Pedro
    Dominique Oloroso)
2 tbsp butter

3 egg yolks
salt
paprika
cayenne

Melt butter in a saucepan and add cream. Bring to a boil and add the crabmeat. When the cream has again reached the boiling point, put the saucepan over a double boiler and add well beaten yolks to which the sherry has been added. Season to taste with salt, paprika and cayenne and allow to thicken for a minute, stirring from the bottom of the pan continuously. Serve with a stack of hot buttered toast allowing each person to help himself first to the toast and then to the newburg. Serves 5.

Nannie's Deviled Crab

1 lb lump crabmeat,
    picked clean
2 tbsp flour
4 tbsp butter
1 c milk
3 tbsp worcestershire sauce

3 tbsp catsup (heaping)
dash Tabasco
2 hard boiled eggs
salt
pepper
cracker crumbs

Make a cream sauce of the butter, flour and milk and add the worcestershire sauce, catsup and Tabasco. Add the picked lump crab. Season with salt, pepper and chopped egg. Our boys don't like the egg, so we leave it out. Put in baking dish and bake 30 minutes with cracker crumbs on top. When I am in a hurry, I just serve from the stove and skip baking the crab in the oven. Serves 5.

Salmon Croquettes

2 cans salmon
juice of 2 lemons
small onion, grated
1 tbsp worcestershire sauce
Tabasco, several shakes
salt
pepper
bread crumbs

3 tbsp flour
5 tbsp butter or margarine
1 c milk
2 egg yolks
¼ c milk
2 eggs
2 tbsp cooking oil

Bone salmon and season with lemon juice, grated onion, worcestershire, Tabasco, salt and pepper. Set aside. Make cream sauce with 5 tablespoons of butter, 3 tablespoons of flour and 1 cup milk. Add the 2 egg yolks, beaten with ¼ cup of milk. Take off stove when the sauce begins to boil. Let cool for 5 minutes. Fold in the seasoned salmon. Put in bowl and when cool, refrigerate for at least 1 hour. To make into croquettes, dip into 2 eggs beaten with 2 tablespoons of oil, roll in flour, then bread crumbs. Do twice if you have time. This insures a good crispy croquette. Fry croquettes in hot grease for 5 minutes on each side or until light brown. Serves 6.

Curried Shrimp

1 ½ lb raw shrimp
¼ tsp curry powder
¼ c parsley, chopped
1 stick butter

coarse cracked pepper
¼ c safflower oil
salt

Clean and devein shrimp, chop parsley and set aside. Saute the shrimp in oil and ½ stick of butter over moderate heat, about 2½ minutes on each side. Shake and turn shrimp often. Add ½ teaspoon salt and ¼ teaspoon black pepper. Place shrimp on plate to the side and wipe out skillet. Add remaining ½ stick of butter and shrimp. Cook, shaking pan, until butter begins to foam. Sprinkle curry powder and parsley over shrimp. Continue to shake pan vigorously for ½ minute. Serves 4.

Chicken Tetrazine

3 fryers
1 12 oz package spaghetti
chicken stock
salt
Lawry's seasoned salt
1 onion, sliced
1 bay leaf

3 cans cream of chicken soup
1½ lb fresh mushrooms, sliced
garlic powder
pepper
rosemary
2 stalks celery with leaves
Parmesan cheese

Cover fryers with water in a pan on top of the stove. Add onion, celery stalks, bay leaf, salt and pepper and cook in covered pan for 25 minutes. Remove from heat and leave covered for approximately one hour. Save the stock. Remove and skin chicken and cut meat into large bite sized pieces. Boil spaghetti in chicken stock, adding more water if necessary. When spaghetti is tender remove from stock and place in a large pan. Save stock. Mix spaghetti, cream of chicken soup, chicken pieces, sliced fresh mushrooms and seasonings together. Add chicken stock to obtain consistency you desire. Place in two large pyrex casseroles, 13½ × 8¾ in. Top with Parmesan cheese. Bake in 350° oven for twenty minutes or until bubbly. Serves 18.

Cream Chicken

1 boiled hen, cut in
   1" pieces
2 tbsp flour
2 tbsp butter
garlic salt
Accent

1½ c milk (use ½ chicken
   broth if you have it)
onion salt
Tabasco
sherry
dry mustard

Make a cream sauce and add seasonings to taste. Finish by adding salt and fresh cracked pepper. Put cut up chicken in sauce and serve over rice. To boil your hen, put hen in large pot with 3–4 cups of water (about ⅓ of pot). Add 2 stalks of celery with leaves, 1 green onion with leaf or regular sliced onion, 2 cloves of garlic, salt and pepper and cook covered about 2 hours or until wing moves easily. Serves 6.

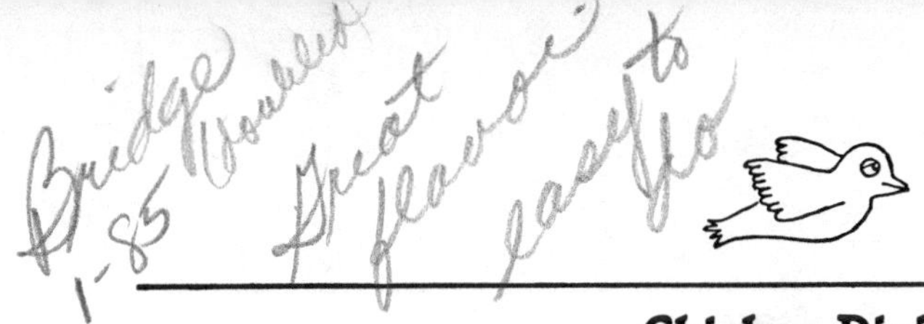

Chicken Divine

This is a dish you must think about ahead of time because the chicken goes in the refrigerator overnight.

6 boneless chicken breasts
1 c sour cream
2 tbsp lemon juice
1 tsp paprika
2 tsp celery salt

1 clove garlic, crushed
2 tsp salt
¼ tsp pepper
1 c bread crumbs
½ c butter, melted

Combine sour cream, lemon juice, paprika, celery salt, garlic, salt and pepper. Coat chicken well with mixture and refrigerate overnight, *uncovered*. Next day, roll chicken in bread crumbs and arrange in shallow baking pan. Spoon half of the butter over chicken. Bake at 350° for 40 minutes. Spoon remaining butter over chicken and bake 15 minutes longer. Serves 6.

Willie's Doves

salt
pepper
flour (self rising)

oil
doves

Clean your doves thoroughly. Dry. Salt, pepper and flour. Brown in skillet or Dutch oven with enough oil to cover ½ of the doves. Remove doves and set aside. Pour off half of the oil and add 2 tablespoons flour to the remainder. Brown flour well. Add water to make gravy. Return doves to skillet and simmer for half an hour. Two doves to a person.

Turkey

There is a warm happy feeling when your turkey turns out golden brown and juicy on the inside. If you follow these steps, you will have just that.

1. Be sure the turkey is perfectly clean the morning before you cook it. Remove all spongy portions along ribs and back bone, rinsing in cold water.

2. Using paper towels, pat the inside and outside of your turkey dry. Rub lightly inside with salt. Wrap in waxed paper and place in refrigerator.

3. Make Turkey Filling (see recipe following) and stuff turkey when the filling is cold—preferably the night before you go to bed. Don't over-stuff. Allow for swelling. Skewer neck and body skin over cavities—this is important!

4. Before baking cover lightly with turkey paste (see recipe following) and place on rack breast side up and begin roasting.

5. Allow approximately 25 minutes per pound for an 8 pound turkey, 20 minutes to the pound for a 12 pound turkey and 15 minutes per pound for a 20 pound turkey. Bake in 300° oven.

6.

Pounds	Minutes/Pound	Hours
7	25	3
12	19	3¾
18	17	5
22	15	5½

These are approximate figures

7. Put turkey in oven and bake. Do not add any water. Do not cover with any lid. Do not salt outside of bird. Do not baste.

Turkey Paste:

4 tbsp butter   2 tbsp lemon juice
5 tbsp flour   shake of cayenne pepper

Cream these ingredients together until you have a smooth paste. Rub

breast and wings and all parts well with this paste. It will bake and keep the bird moist. *Do not put on too thickly.*

Turkey Stuffing:

¾–1¼ c chicken or turkey stock
2 c cornbread
6 c day-old whole wheat bread
2 eggs, slightly beaten
¾ c melted butter
½ tsp each: sage, thyme,
   marjoram

1 tsp salt
1 unpeeled apple, diced
⅓ c finely minced onion
½ c finely minced celery
   (inner stalks with leaves)
handful of unbroken pecan
   halves

1. Make stock early in the week. This is very important for delicious turkey stuffing but if emergency arises, buy Swanson's clear chicken broth.

2. Make cornbread. I use Pioneer mix, but use your own favorite recipe.

3. Crumble cornbread and whole wheat bread into small cubes. Leave crusts on bread. Don't toast it, but let it dry slightly in oven.

4. Beat eggs foamy and stir in melted butter and seasonings.

5. Use large mixing bowl or roaster to combine breads, diced apple, onion, celery and pecans.

6. Add egg and seasoning mixture. Stir well.

7. Begin adding stock and test carefully after you've added about ¾ cup. Mix with hands. When dressing holds together and barely separates as you lift it with a fork, you've added the right amount of stock.

Rock Cornish Game Hens

Men will eat a whole game hen; women will eat a half. Clean game hens well, removing all spongy portions along ribs and backbone, rinsing in cold water. With paper towels, pat dry. Season early with seasoning salt and pepper and regular salt and pepper. When ready to bake, rinse some seasoning off and cover birds with soft butter and sprinkle with salt and pepper. Bake in preheated 350° oven for 1 hour. Serve with gravy.

Gravy for Game Hens:

giblets
onion, 1 medium, sliced thick
celery, 2 inside stalks
    with leaves
flour

2 chicken bouillon cubes
Kitchen Bouquet, several drops
drippings of game hens
sherry

Boil giblets, onion, and celery in 2½ cups of water. Bring to a rolling boil and then simmer for about an hour or until giblets are tender. Add salt and pepper and strain. Meanwhile, in another pot, boil 2 cups of water with 2 chicken bouillon cubes. Combine the 2 stocks and add flour paste (flour mixed with water). Finish by adding drippings from hens, Kitchen Bouquet for color, and 2 jiggers of sherry.

Turkey or Chicken Stock

1 chicken neck, gizzard,
    heart, etc.
2 stalks celery with leaves
1 carrot
1 onion, chopped

1 tsp salt
1 bay leaf
pepper corns
6 c water

Put the above ingredients in a large pot and bring to a boil. Reduce heat to simmer. Put a lid on and simmer as long as you can, up to 5 hours. Strain.

Marilyn's Chicken Hernandez

2 whole fryers, cut in pieces
2 red potatoes, peeled and sliced
2 apples, red (Delicious), peeled
1 orange for juice
3 small boxes raisins
1 12 oz package slivered almonds
2 whole jalapenos, seeded
  and chopped

1 onion, sliced
2 tomatoes, minced in blender
2 cloves, crushed
cinnamon
oregano
garlic, crushed
juice of jalapeno
flour

Lightly season chicken pieces with salt, pepper, *touch* of cinnamon, oregano, fresh crushed garlic, and cloves. In work bowl, pour juice of 1 orange over chicken and sprinkle flour over chicken. Remove chicken but save marinade. Lightly brown chicken in small amount of Crisco. Add sliced onion, blended tomato, jalapenos, and remaining marinade. Cook 10 minutes. Add potatoes and apple and simmer, covered, on low flame until tender. This may be done the day before. 20 minutes before dinner is ready to be served, place in large casserole; sprinkle raisins, almonds, and small amount of jalapeno juice over this and heat in 350° oven. Serves 8.

Lemon Barbecued Steak

1 tsp grated lemon peel
⅔ c lemon juice
⅓ c vegetable oil
1½ tsp salt

⅛ tsp pepper
1 tsp worcestershire sauce
1 tsp prepared mustard
2 green onion tops, sliced

Trim fat edges of meat and place in a shallow dish. Combine ingredients and pour over steak. Let stand 3 hours at room temperature or 6 hours in refrigerator, turning several times. Remove from marinade and blot to remove excess moisture. Grill over hot coals, brushing occasionally with marinade. Lemon juice tenderizes an economical cut of meat.

Spareribs

3½ lb spareribs   salt
1 clove garlic, minced   Accent
cracked pepper

Sprinkle meat with salt, pepper, Accent and minced garlic. Place in pan; cover with foil. Bake in 350° oven for 30 minutes. Remove foil, pour off juices and coat with barbecue sauce. (See recipe following.) Bake for 1 more hour in 350° oven. Baste several times with sauce. Spareribs can be cooked any time during the day and warmed before dinner. Serves 5.

Rib Roast

rib roast (5–7 lb)   cracked pepper
lemon pepper   salt

Take roast out of refrigerator 2–3 hours before ready to cook. Put lemon pepper, cracked pepper and salt on roast. Bake uncovered in preheated 500° oven in mid-afternoon for 30 minutes. Turn off and *never* open oven door. Roast will be rare when dinner is ready. This works for any 5–7 lb roast. Serves 6.

Beef Tender

Nothing is more disappointing than messing up a beef tender. I think they should be medium rare to rare and this is how we cook one. Take the meat out of the icebox early to get it to room temperature. Season your meat well with:

seasoning salt   worcestershire sauce
lemon pepper   garlic powder
seasoning pepper   salt
Guy's Seasoning   fresh cracked pepper

Bake, uncovered at 500° for 10 minutes to seal the juices. Cook 35 minutes more at 350°. This is for a 4½ lb tender. Cook larger tenders approximately 1 hour.

Beef Fondue

Our family thinks this is great and we all have fun fixing it.

1½ lb, 1" pieces of beef tender　　*mushroom sauce*
½ quart oil　　*Bernaise sauce*

Heat oil in fondue pot on the stove until hot. Bring to the table and place over sterno burner. Put meat on fondue skewers and place in hot oil at the table. In about 1½ minutes meat is ready to dip in mushroom or Bernaise sauce. Serves 5.

Em's Flank Steak

1 large flank steak　　*Lawry's meat marinade*
　(2–2½ lb)

This is an inexpensive cut of meat which makes a family favorite meal. For 7 people, buy 1 large flank steak (2½ lb). Marinate the flank steak in Lawry's meat marinade for 15 minutes. Broil marinated flank steak for 5 minutes on each side. Serve this flank steak with hot buttered flour tortillas, guacamole and fresh asparagus. Serve the plates with thin slices of flank steak and fresh asparagus. Place a bowl of guacamole and plate of hot tortillas on the table. Spread the guacamole on the tortillas and put a thin slice of flank steak on top of this and roll up. To slice flank steak, cut very thin at an angle instead of straight down. Serves 6.

Steak Teriyaki

4 beef fillets, about 5 oz each
½ c soy sauce
¼ c vermouth
½ tsp sugar
1 clove garlic

Trim all fat off steaks. Cut in thin slices. Dip in sauce marinade of above ingredients. Fry in hot skillet. Turn only once. Turning makes meat tough. This same marinade is also excellent for chicken. Buy chicken breasts. Remove skin. Cut in thin narrow strips and cook the same way. Serves 5.

Pepper Steak

2 lb 1" wide strips of ¼" thin [too wide]
round steak OR tenderized
3 tbsp Mazola oil
1 clove garlic, crushed
½ green pepper, chopped
1 can tomatoes 14½ oz
bunch green onions
1 medium onion, sliced
¼ tsp ginger
¼ tsp sugar
¼ c water
¼ c soy sauce
salt and pepper to taste

Brown meat in Mazola. Remove from the skillet when brown. Put salt, pepper, garlic, ginger, sugar, soy sauce, can of tomatoes, green pepper and water in skillet. Mix together. Return meat to the skillet. Cook on low heat, covered, for 1½ hours. If watery, add flour paste (1 tablespoon of flour in ½ cup of water) to the mixture. [corn starch] Serve over rice. This takes about 20 minutes preparation time before it's ready for the 1½ hours of simmering. Serves 6.

Beef Stroganoff

2 lb sirloin, cut in cubes
6 tbsp butter or margarine
1 lb fresh sliced mushrooms
1 pint sour cream
1 tbsp flour

1 tsp prepared mustard
½ tsp salt
1 tbsp caraway seeds
⅛ tsp pepper
2 c consomme

Saute meat in 3 tablespoons of margarine. Saute 1 lb sliced mushrooms in ½ pint of sour cream. Add to the meat. Melt 3 tablespoons of butter and add flour. Stir until bubbly. Add 1 teaspoon of prepared mustard, ½ teaspoon salt, ⅛ teaspoon pepper, 1 tablespoon caraway seed and 2 cups consomme. Mix the meat and mushrooms with the consomme. Simmer for an hour to an hour and a half—until meat is tender. Add rest of sour cream just before serving. Serves 6.

Willie's Stew

This is the best stew and makes a good meal. Serve with rolls and salad and you have a delicious meal.

2 lb lean stew meat
1 can tomatoes
1 onion
bay leaf
1 potato (diced)

1 pkg frozen mixed
   vegetables
salt
fresh cracked pepper
1 clove garlic

Season stew meat with salt and pepper. Cover bottom of large pot with shortening and brown garlic clove. (Put toothpick in clove.) Take garlic clove out and brown meat in garlic shortening. Add 1 large onion cut in pieces, 1 can of tomatoes, bay leaf and 2½ cups of water. Cook covered for about 3 hours. 10 minutes before serving, add frozen mixed vegetables and potato. Add thickening last—flour and water mixed together in thin paste. Serves 6.

Trennie's Meat Loaf

2 lb ground beef
2 plus tbsp worcestershire sauce
2 eggs, beaten
10 saltine crackers
1 onion, chopped
½ green pepper, chopped

4 tbsp chili sauce
2 tbsp tomato sauce
1 clove garlic, minced
1 slice bread, soaked in water
  and squeezed
salt, pepper, celery salt, paprika

Put meat and seasonings except tomato sauce in bowl. Mix well together. Form into loaf and cook in 350° oven for 1 hour. After 30 minutes, put about 2 tablespoons of tomato sauce on top. Serves 6.

Swiss Meat Balls

1 lb ground round
1 can celery soup
⅔ c bread crumbs
1 egg, beaten

chopped parsley
1 onion, chopped
1 tbsp worcestershire sauce
salt, cracked pepper

Mix chopped parsley, onion, salt, pepper and worcestershire sauce with meat. Add ¼ cup of celery soup, bread crumbs and egg to mixture. Mix well and roll in small balls the size of a walnut. Brown balls on all sides in skillet with 1 tablespoon oil. Pour in ½ cup of water and the remainder of the can of celery soup. Cut heat down and simmer 30 minutes. Add more water if needed for gravy. Serves 6.

Veal Piccata

The veal has to be sauteed at the last minute but you can have the lemon, parsley and flour ready early. Begin to saute the veal 15 minutes before you are ready to eat.

1½ lb <u>thin</u> sliced baby veal
salt
cracked pepper
all-purpose flour
lump of butter
3 tbsp water

3 tbsp lemon juice
parsley
6 lemon slices
consomme
1 garlic pod, crushed

Salt and pepper veal and dust with flour. Brown meat on both sides in butter. Do not crowd the skillet. Place the browned pieces on warm platter. Make gravy from drippings by adding lemon juice, water, garlic and consomme. Pour gravy over veal. Decorate with slice of lemon and parsley. Do not leave browned veal in gravy to simmer. The veal must be cooked just a few minutes. Serves 6.

Variation: Add parmesan cheese to the flour and white wine to the gravy.

Leg of Lamb

2½ tbsp soy sauce
1 tbsp worcestershire sauce
juice of ½ lemon
1 garlic clove, slivered
seasoning salt, 3 large shakes

salt
cracked pepper
oil
5–8 lb leg of lamb

Cut slits in lamb and insert garlic slivers. Marinate lamb overnight or, if you forget, the same day will do. Marinate in a mixture of the soy sauce, worcestershire sauce, lemon juice and seasoning salt. Cook this size lamb 2½ hours. Cook in preheated 500° oven for 30 minutes and then turn oven to 375° and cook 20 minutes to a pound. Keep ¼–½ cup of water in the pan throughout baking. Serves 6.

Daddy's Barbecue Sauce for Steaks

1 part soy sauce
1 part catsup

1 part vermouth
1 part butter

Sometimes I add a little more catsup. Mix together and heat for 5–10 minutes. This is excellent on steaks.

Barbecue Sauce for Chicken, Ribs or Brisket

1 onion, chopped
1 stick butter
½ 14 oz bottle catsup
½ c worcestershire sauce
1 tsp dry mustard
½ 12 oz bottle chili sauce
¼ c sugar

½ c wine vinegar
2 cloves garlic, crushed
1 tsp chili powder
½ c red wine
½ lemon, grated rind and juice
1 tsp salt

Saute onion in butter. Add remaining ingredients and cook over medium heat about 15 minutes.

Green Beans

1 lb fresh Kentucky
   Wonder beans
1 slice onion

salt to taste
pepper to taste
butter to taste

French style the green beans by destringing each side with a knife and then cutting down the middle. When finished, put the beans in a bowl with ice cubes on top. This makes any fresh vegetable nice and crunchy. Steam the green beans in a little water with the onion and butter on top until tender. This takes about 35 minutes. Test with a fork and do not let them cook too long. Drain beans and season with salt and pepper. Serves 6.

Alfred's Squash Casserole

1 lb fresh yellow squash
1 white onion (chopped in pieces)
1 large tbsp Mazola
dill

1 pt sour cream
Pepperidge Farm herb seasoning
*   bread crumbs*

Cook squash, onion and Mazola in skillet with *NO* water for five minutes. Place squash in a greased casserole. Mix with sour cream, sprinkle heavily with dill and put Pepperidge Farm herb seasoning bread crumbs on top. Bake in a 350° oven until bubbly (approximately 25 minutes). Serves 5.

Green Bean Casserole

3 tbsp flour
2 tbsp butter
1½ c milk, hot
1 c sharp cheddar cheese
onion juice, 1 tsp

1 tbsp worcestershire sauce
2 boxes frozen French style
*   green beans*
salt and pepper

Make a cream sauce with the flour, butter and milk. Add the grated cheese. Season with onion juice, salt, pepper and worcestershire. Pour over slightly cooked French style green beans. Bake in casserole in 350° oven until bubbly. Serves 8.

Carmen's Green Beans

These are delicious, easy to prepare ahead of time and good for a special family dinner or for entertaining.

2 cans of <u>whole</u> Blue Lake green beans
½ c catsup
¼ c sweet pickle juice

¼ c water
½ c pear juice
½ c pineapple juice
5 slices bacon

Wrap 8 beans with ½ slice of bacon. Repeat until all of the beans are wrapped. Mix sauce of the above ingredients. Place beans in shallow casserole and cover with the sauce. Bake uncovered at 400° for 30 minutes. Add water to keep beans from burning if sauce evaporates. Serves 6.

Green Bean Bake

1 can Campbell's cream of mushroom soup
1 can French fried onions (3½ oz size)

1 tsp soy sauce
3 c cooked French style beans
salt and pepper

In 1 quart casserole, stir 1 can of cream of mushroom soup and 1 teaspoon of soy sauce until smooth. Mix in ½ can (3½ oz size) French fried onion, 3 cups cooked French style beans, dash of salt and pepper. Bake in moderate oven (350°) for 20 minutes. Top with remaining onions. Bake 5 minutes more. Serves 6.

Baked Tomatoes

pulp scooped out of 4 tomatoes
Pepperidge Farm Dressing mix (all purpose)

½ c chopped celery
½ c chopped green onions

Saute celery and green onion. Add pulp of tomatoes. Cook for 5 minutes and add Pepperidge Farm Dressing mix until the thickness of dressing. Fill tomato and bake in 300° oven for 20 minutes.

Mae's Squash Souffle

2½ lb squash (yellow)
2 raw eggs
1 onion, grated
2 c thick white sauce

½ lb New York State cheese,
   grated
salt and pepper to taste
bread crumbs

Cook sliced squash until tender, drain and mash into fine pulp. Add grated onion, beaten raw eggs, grated cheese and white sauce. Put in casserole, top with bread crumbs and bake at 375° until bread crumbs brown. To make thick white sauce, I use 3 tablespoons of butter and 3 tablespoons of flour and 1 cup of hot milk. Serves 8.

Tony's Hot Broccoli Casserole

6 packages chopped frozen
   broccoli
2 large onions, chopped
1 stick butter
4 c cream of mushroom soup
3 packages garlic cheese

1 large can of mushrooms
   (Monarch button)
2 tsp Accent
1 c bread crumbs
1 c chopped blanched almonds

Saute chopped onions in butter. Mix in thawed frozen chopped broccoli. Add mushroom soup, garlic cheese, button mushrooms and ¾ cup of blanched almonds. Season with salt, pepper and Accent and top with bread crumbs and remaining ¼ cup of almonds. Bake uncovered 1 hour in 350° oven. Serves 16.

Broccoli Casserole

1 package chopped broccoli
2 c cooked rice
  (¾ c uncooked)
1 8 oz jar Cheese Whiz

1 can cream of chicken soup,
  undiluted
1 can sliced water chestnuts
bread crumbs

Cook and drain the broccoli and combine with other ingredients. Sprinkle top with bread crumbs and bake till hot. Serves 6.

Eggplant and Squash Casserole

2 lb zucchini squash, sliced
1 large eggplant, peeled
  and sliced
1 egg

12 oz Philadelphia cream cheese
1 small can chopped Ashley's
  chili peppers

Boil squash and eggplant until soft. Drain. Combine and mash in mixing bowl with cheese, egg and chopped chilies. Bake 30 minutes in 350° oven in buttered casserole. Serves 9.

Sauteed Apples

3 large Delicious apples
½ c granulated sugar
1 tbsp lemon juice

3 large tbsp butter
¼ tsp cinnamon

Peel and core apples, then cut in half and slice very thin. Melt butter over low heat in large skillet. Add sliced apples, sugar, lemon juice and cinnamon, and cook over medium heat until soft. Serves 5.

Baked Apples

1 tbsp brown sugar
1 tbsp hot water
pinch of cinnamon

squeeze of lemon juice
grated lemon rind
butter

This recipe is per apple. Core apples and put mixture of brown sugar, water, cinnamon, and lemon juice in the center of each apple. Squeeze lemon juice over apples. Grate lemon rind over apples. Place apples in pan with ½ cup of hot water. Dot each apple with butter and cover pan with foil. Bake about 1 hour in 375° oven.

Spinach Bake

2 packages frozen
chopped spinach
3½ oz package cream cheese
1 c condensed cream of
mushroom soup

dash worcestershire sauce
salt and cracked pepper
1 can (3½ oz) French fried
onion rings, crushed

Cook spinach until just done. Add cream cheese, soup, worcestershire sauce, salt and pepper. Stir until cheese is melted. Spoon into casserole and top with crushed onion rings and bake at 350° for 45 minutes. Serves 6–10.

Spinach Casserole A Bambe

4 packages frozen chopped
spinach
2 c sour cream
1 package onion soup mix

1 c buttered bread crumbs
salt to taste
pepper to taste

Cook spinach until just done and drain well. Stir in sour cream, onion soup mix, salt and pepper. Pour into ungreased casserole and top with buttered crumbs. Bake covered at 350° for 45 minutes. Serves 9.

New Potatoes

new potatoes
melted butter
dash of Tabasco

chopped parsley or
chopped chives

Peel new potatoes and boil in salted water in covered pan until tender. Test with fork so it goes smoothly in potato, but the potato is not mushy. Drain and dry them well. Pour melted butter and chopped parsley or melted butter and chopped chives and a dash of tabasco over potatoes. Serve hot. Prepare 2 potatoes per person unless you have a large man and prepare 3 for him!

Maria's New Potatoes

new potatoes
salt

pepper
butter

Boil new potatoes with skin for 10 minutes in salted water. This can be done any time during the day. Forty-five minutes to an hour before dinner, put the new potatoes with skins in a pan in 350° oven. Cover with salt, pepper and butter. Turn, be sure the potatoes are coated with more salt, pepper and butter. When skins are crispy, potatoes are ready. These will keep well in the oven if entertaining or dinner is delayed. 12 medium new potatoes serves 6.

Potato Crisp

These potatoes are especially good with steak.

4 white potatoes, thin sliced
(do not peel)
4 tbsp butter, melted

salt
white pepper
Parmesan cheese

Put thin sliced potatoes in pan of boiling water. Turn fire off and cover for 30 minutes. Place drained slices of potatoes on cookie sheet or shallow pan in rows slightly overlapping. Cover potatoes with melted butter. Sprinkle salt, white pepper and Parmesan cheese over the buttered potatoes. Run under broiler for 15 minutes or until browned. Watch carefully, do not burn. Serves 6.

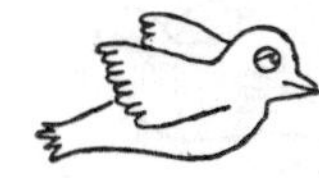

Risotto With Mushrooms

This takes a little longer than rice, but start chopping and you can put it to-gether in 10 minutes.

1 c rice
½ onion, chopped
1 can chicken broth (13 oz)
12 fresh mushroms, sliced

½ c white wine
2 tbsp Parmesan cheese
lump of butter

Melt butter and saute onions for about 5 minutes, until onion is soft. Add mushrooms and wine. Cook until wine is evaporated. Add rice and cook until well coated with butter. Add broth and bring to a boil. Cover tightly. Reduce heat to low and cook for 20 minutes without peeking. When ready to serve, toss rice with Parmesan cheese and another lump of but-ter. Serves 5.

Fettucini

Everything for dinner must be ready before you prepare this. You won't find these noodles in every store. I buy mine at an Italian specialty shop. They are worth having on hand because you can make this a meal all by itself.

1 lb fettuce noodles
½ pint cream or Half & Half
¾ c of grated cheddar cheese
large lump of butter

Parmesan cheese
  (several shakes)
salt
pepper

Cook fettuce noodles as directed on package. Put in colander and rinse well with cold water. Return fettuce to same pot minus the water. At a low temperature, add the cream, cheese and butter. Coat thoroughly. Add salt, pepper and Parmesan cheese. Toss a little more and serve at once. Serves 6.

Lasagna Casserole

2 lb ground beef
1 #2½ can tomatoes
1 8 oz can tomato sauce
½ box lasagna noodles
½ lb mozzarella cheese,
    sliced thin
½ lb ricotta cheese

2 tsp seasoned salt
½ c grated Parmesan cheese
2 cloves garlic, crushed
½ tsp pepper
1 package Lawry's spaghetti
    sauce mix

Brown meat with seasoned salt in a skillet. Add crushed garlic and pepper; simmer slowly, uncovered until the meat appears brown and well cooked. Stir in tomatoes, tomato sauce, and spaghetti sauce mix. Cover and simmer 15 minutes. Meanwhile, cook lasagna in salted boiling water until tender; drain and rinse. Into a baking dish, pour ⅓ of the sauce; cover with strips of lasagna; then slices of mozzarella and spoonfuls of ricotta. Repeat layers, ending with meat sauce and top with Parmesan cheese. Bake at 350° until bubbly—about 25 minutes. Serves 8.

Cheese Delight

5 slices bread, cut in cubes
¾ lb sharp cheddar cheese,
    grated
4 eggs, beaten
2 c milk

1 tsp dry mustard
1 tsp salt
dash of cayenne pepper
dash of worcestershire sauce
dash of basil

Alternate layers of bread and cheese in greased casserole. Mix milk, dry mustard, salt, pepper, basil and worcestershire sauce; add to eggs. Mix and pour over cheese and bread. Let stand overnight. Bake 45 minutes at 350° or until straw comes out clean. Serves 6.

Annie's Ice Box Rolls
Sweet or Dinner Rolls

These are the most delicious rolls anyone has ever tasted. They take time and patience, but devote a day to making bread and have fun trying this recipe. Annie is famous for her rolls and my old friend. She gave me permission to put this recipe in our book.

1 c shortening	*2 yeast cakes*
1 c sugar	*1 c cold water*
1 tbsp salt	*2 beaten eggs*
1 c boiling water	*6 c flour*

Mix shortening, sugar and salt well. Add 1 cup boiling water, mix together and let cool. In another bowl, mix 2 yeast cakes and 1 cup of cold water. Add 2 beaten eggs. Now add 6 cups of flour. Mix the second mixture into the bowl with the shortening. Put dough in greased bowl and let rise for 4 hours in icebox. For best results, keep the dough in icebox overnight.

For dinner rolls: roll out ¼–½" thick. Cut in rounds with small biscuit cutter or small glass. Dip both sides of roll in melted butter and fold over. Place in greased pan. Let rise until double in size. Bake in 350° oven for 17–20 minutes or until brown.

For sweet rolls: roll dough as thin as possible; spread dough with melted butter, cinnamon, and sugar. Sprinkle with raisins and pecans, if desired. Roll up. Cut in slices, about ½" thick. Place slices in greased pan or in muffin pans. Let rise until double in size. Bake as directed. When cold, top with a powdered sugar mixed with milk and 1 teaspoon of vanilla.

Orange Buttered Rolls

1 box powdered sugar   juice of 1 orange
1 stick of butter, softened   grated rind of orange

Mix all together until smooth. Cook rolls and cool slightly. Put orange butter on top.

Spoon Bread

This takes 15 minutes to put together and 30 minutes to cook. Everyone loves it and I get extra credit for a special dish. It is very simple. Men particularly like it.

2 c milk   3 eggs, separated
½ c white cornmeal   ½ stick butter
1 tsp salt   ½ tsp baking powder

Scald milk, add the cornmeal and cook constantly, stirring until thick. Add the salt and baking powder. Remove from fire and add butter. Let cool 5 minutes. Add slightly beaten egg yolks. Beat egg whites until peaks form. Fold into the batter. Pour into warm, buttered casserole and bake in a 375° oven for 25–30 minutes. Serves 6.

Soft Gingerbread

1 c butter   1–2 tsp soda
1 c sugar   2 c dark Karo syrup
3 c flour   3 eggs, beaten
2 tsp ginger   1 c buttermilk
1 tsp cinnamon

Cream butter and sugar. Sift dry ingredients together. Add syrup and eggs to creamed mixture and then dry ingredients and buttermilk alternately. Place in approximately 13″ × 9″ greased pan. Bake at 350° for 20–30 minutes. Serves 12.

Greek Oranges

6 juice oranges
2 oranges for juice only

½ jar Black Currant Jelly (12 oz)
rind of 2 oranges

Peel oranges and reserve rind of 2. When peeling, be sure to cut deep enough so as not to leave any white fiber. Grate the reserved rind. Mix juice of 2 oranges, with grated rind and jelly. Cook slowly until dissolved. Place the whole peeled oranges in a flat pyrex dish and pour hot juice over them. Baste frequently, serve cold. This is a nice party dessert.

Em's Chocolate Dessert

Make this ahead of time and put whipped cream over it just before serving. There are many ways to prepare this. You may use pieces of angel food cake or substitute lady fingers in a lovely glass bowl or molded as a cake.

2 packages German Sweet
*   chocolate*
2 tbsp hot water
4 tbsp powdered sugar
4 eggs, separated

1 pint whipping cream, whipped
*   (reserve some for topping)*
small bought angel food cake or
*   2 packages of lady fingers*

You will need 3 bowls—one small bowl for yolks and 2 medium size bowls for whites and whipping cream. Put asbestos pad on the burner and melt the chocolate with the hot water directly over the fire or melt in double boiler. This pad saves a pot. Add the sugar. This mixture sometimes looks lumpy. Don't worry. Cool a few minutes. Use electric hand beater to add the 4 slightly beaten egg yolks. Now the mixture should be smooth. Fold in the previously beaten egg whites. Fold in the ½ pint of whipped whipping cream. Put the pieces of cake or lady fingers in glass bowl or mold. Pour chocolate mixture over. Repeat layers and put in the icebox. Serve with whipped cream on top. Serves 8.

Bambe's Hello Dollies

1 stick of margarine
1 c crushed graham cracker
  crumbs
1 package (6 oz) semi-
  sweet chocolate chips

1 c chopped pecans or walnuts
1 c Angel Flake coconut
1 c Eagle Brand sweetened
  condensed milk

Melt margarine in a medium size pyrex dish. Add graham cracker crumbs and press into a very thin layer. Over crumbs, sprinkle layer of coconuts, then chocolate chips, nuts and milk. Bake in 350° oven for 30 minutes. Cool before cutting into small squares. Serves 6.

Bambe's Chocolate Fudge Pudding

1 c sifted flour
2 tsp baking powder
1 tsp salt
⅔ c granulated sugar
½ c milk
2 tbsp melted shortening
  (margarine)

6 tbsp cocoa (divided into
  2 tbsp and 4 tbsp)
1 tsp vanilla
½ c chopped pecans
1 c brown sugar, packed

Sift flour, baking powder, salt, granulated sugar and 2 tablespoons cocoa. Add milk, shortening and vanilla. Mix only until smooth. Add pecans. Put in greased shallow 1 quart baking dish. Mix brown sugar and remaining 4 tablespoons cocoa. Sprinkle over mixture in baking dish. Pour 1½ cups of boiling water over the mixture. Bake in moderate oven at 350° for 40 minutes. Serve warm or cold with whipped cream or ice cream. Serves 8.

Meringue Shells

6 egg whites, room temperature
1½ tsp lemon juice
2 c sugar

salt
⅛ tsp cream of tartar

Preheat oven to 400°. Beat egg whites with electric beater until soft peaks form. Add cream of tartar; add lemon juice and sugar gradually, beating constantly until very stiff. Drop on ungreased brown paper on cookie sheet. Hollow out center with back of spoon. Place in oven; turn oven off. Do not open oven door for at least 5 hours. Yield: 12.

Trifle
Mrs. Kavanaugh

lady fingers
red currant jelly
pale dry sherry

boiled custard
meringue

Split lady fingers; line 9 × 13 pyrex dish. Cover bottom of dish with lady fingers, split side up. Blend jelly and sherry to pouring consistency. Cover lady fingers generously. Top with lady fingers, split side down. Sprinkle generously with sherry. Let age for at least 24 hours. Cover with custard; top with meringue. Bake in 250° oven till meringue is lightly browned. Yield: 20 servings.

Old Fashioned Boiled Custard
Mrs. Kavanaugh

1 gallon milk
12 eggs
pinch of salt

3⅓ c sugar
yellow food coloring
dash of nutmeg

Heat milk in double boiler till hot but not boiling. Blend eggs; add salt and sugar. Cream together on low speed of electric mixer. Add 2 cups hot milk to egg-sugar mixture; return to double boiler with remaining hot milk, stirring with wire whip. When custard coats spoon, remove from heat; add food coloring and strain into crock or stainless container, stirring occasionally till it cools. Serve cold with whipped cream and a dash of nutmeg. Yield: 16 servings.

Nannie's Chocolate Sauce

1½ c sugar
1 c milk
2 squares bitter chocolate

2 tbsp butter
1 tsp vanilla
¼ tsp salt

Melt chocolate (I put the pan on top of the asbestos pad on the burner). Add milk, sugar, salt to the melted chocolate over low heat. Stir until all is dissolved and back to a dark chocolate mixture. Let the sauce come to a low boil and boil for 5 minutes. Take off the stove and add the butter and vanilla. When cool, store in a jar in the refrigerator.

Quick Chocolate Chip Ice Cream

1 quart vanilla ice cream

12 Oreo cookies

Let ice cream become soft. Put Oreo cookies in blender a few at a time until all are thoroughly minced. Mix with soft ice cream. This is a good quick dessert that children like. Serves 6.

Raspberry Ice

½ c sugar
2 c cold water

6 boxes frozen raspberries
juice of 1 lemon

Combine all ingredients in a blender and mix well. Put in ice cream freezer and freeze. Use the same day because ice becomes very hard when left in the freezer. Serves 16.

White Coconut Cake

This is a delicious cake and if I can make it, so can you. I can't tell you how excited I was when I made this and it was good. Be sure to remember to have eggs and butter at room temperature before beginning.

½ c butter
1½ c sugar
3 c sifted cake flour
3 tsp baking powder
½ tsp salt

1 c milk
1 tsp vanilla
¼ tsp almond extract
4 egg whites

1. Get each ingredient out and put next to mixing bowl.

2. In mixing bowl, cream butter until smooth and then cream the butter and sugar together.

3. Sift flour with baking powder and salt and add 3 tablespoons of it to the butter and sugar mixture. Beat well, as this keeps butter and sugar from separating.

4. Then, add the remaining flour, alternately with the liquid, beating after each addition. Add about ½ cup flour each time and about ¼ of the milk each time. Add vanilla and almond extract.

5. Beat the egg whites until stiff but not dry. They should still slip in the bowl as you tilt it, and be moist. Carefully fold into batter.

6. Turn batter into 2 (8") round cake pans lined with wax paper.

7. Bake in moderately hot oven (375°) for from 25–30 minutes. Test with toothpick. When it comes out clean it is ready.

8. Turn out onto wire cake rack. When cool, ice with fluffy white icing (see index). Coat with grated coconut.

Carol's Pound Cake

This is a very easy, delicious pound cake. The only thing to remember is to take the eggs and butter out early to get to room temperature.

1¼ c butter
2¼ c sugar
7 eggs

2½ c flour, sifted 3 times
2½ tsp vanilla

Heat oven to 350°. Grease and flour bundt pan. Cream the butter and sugar together. Add the unbeaten eggs, one at a time. Add the sifted flour slowly. Add the vanilla and bake in preheated oven for 1 hour or until straw comes out clean.

Roseline's Cheese Cake

3 8 oz packages cream cheese
4 eggs
1 c sugar
1 tsp vanilla
1 pint sour cream
5 tbsp sugar

1 tsp vanilla
1 can prepared pie filling,
    cherry, blueberry, etc.
lemon wafers
1 stick butter

Crust is made by combining 1½ cups lemon wafer crumbs with the stick of melted butter and pat around sides and bottom of a spring form pan. Combine the first 4 ingredients in mixer and beat for 30 minutes. Bake at 375° (20 minutes—soft; 25 minutes—very good). Remove from oven and cool 10 minutes. Combine next 3 ingredients—sour cream, sugar and vanilla and pour over cheese cake and bake 6 minutes at 475°. Let cool and top with pie filling if you like. Refrigerate overnight before serving.

Creme Brulee

2 c whipping cream
4 egg yolks
2½ tbsp granulated sugar

1" vanilla bean
¼ c sifted brown sugar

Heat cream with split vanilla bean until scalded. Beat egg yolks, adding granulated sugar gradually. Remove cream from heat, extract bean and pour slowly, beating constantly into egg mixture. Pour into a 1½ quart casserole. Place in pan of hot water and bake uncovered at 325° about an hour until custard is set. Remove from oven and sprinkle brown sugar over top. Place under broiler for a couple of minutes until sugar is melted and glassy looking. Chill. Serves 6.

Sugar Cookies

1 stick of butter
1 egg
1 c sugar

1 c self rising, sifted flour
5 tsp vanilla

I always double this recipe when I make it. Sometimes I double the vanilla and sometimes I use only 5 teaspoons. Try it both ways. Be sure to take butter and eggs out early to get to room temperature. Cream butter and sugar. Add egg, flour and vanilla. Drop from teaspoon onto greased cookie sheet. Bake 7–10 minutes in a 350° oven.

Mrs. Kavanaugh's Texas Toffees

½ lb butter
1 c sugar
pinch of salt
1 egg, separated

2 c all-purpose flour
1 tbsp cinnamon
almost 1 lb chopped pecans

Cream butter, sugar and salt. Add egg yolk and beat. Sift flour with cinnamon and add to mixture. Pat onto a buttered 13 × 17 cookie sheet or 2 small sheets. Cover with slightly beaten egg white, sprinkle generously with chopped nuts, and bake in a 250° oven 1½–2 hours until very firm to touch. Cut and loosen while hot. Makes 4½ dozen bars. Freezes well.

Pecan Squares

2 c dark brown sugar
1 c butter
2 c flour

2 eggs, beaten well
1 c coarsely chopped pecans

Cream together 1 cup dark brown sugar and 1 cup butter. Add and mix well, one beaten egg. Work in gradually 2 cups flour. Spread mixture in thin layer on greased baking sheet about 11 × 16. Brush on the other beaten egg. Sprinkle with ½ cup dark brown sugar and then 1 cup coarsely chopped pecans. Don't spare the pecans. You may need 2 cups. Cover with ½ cup dark brown sugar. Bake at 350° for 20–25 minutes. This is very similar to Texas Toffees, but not as crisp.

Waverly Cookies

1 c butter (or oleo)
1 c packed brown sugar
1 6 oz package chocolate chips
1 c chopped nuts (pecans
or almonds)

9 sections of waverly wafers
(⅓ package)

Grease a 9 × 13 pyrex dish with crisco. Line bottom of pan with crackers. Sprinkle chips on top. Melt butter and sugar. Boil 3 minutes. (Stir constantly.) Add nuts. Pour over crackers and bake 10 minutes in 350° oven. Cut when cool. (Makes 50 or more small cookies if cut in 1″ squares.)

Pecan Pralines

2 c sugar
1 c buttermilk
1 level tsp soda
1 stick margarine

2 tsp vanilla
2 tsp bourbon
2 c large pecan halves

Cook sugar, milk, soda and margarine until soft ball stage, between 230° and 240° on the candy thermometer. Take off heat and add vanilla, bourbon and pecan halves. Drop with teaspoon on cookie sheets. If candy runs then you haven't cooked it long enough. Put back in pan and cook longer. Remember to make candy on a dry day. The weather affects candy.

Fudge

2 tbsp butter
2 c granulated sugar
¾ c cream

salt, a few grains
2 squares Bakers chocolate
1 tsp vanilla extract

Melt chocolate in a 4 quart saucepan over asbestos pad on stove. Add sugar and mix. Add ¾ cup of cream. Stir back and forth until completely dissolved. Do not boil. Now increase heat and bring to a boil. Boil briskly without stirring. Touch bottom of pan occasionally with wooden spoon to make sure candy isn't sticking. Test with candy thermometer. When thermometer reads 233°, test in glass of water to see if chocolate makes soft ball. Take pan off stove and let cool a few minutes. Add butter and vanilla. Stir, stir, stir until fudge has dull color and texture. Spread on greased platter. When it sets well, dip knife into hot water and cut in squares.

Neimans

Punch

2 large cans pineapple juice
2 large cans (12 oz) frozen
  orange juice
2 large cans frozen lime juice
2 large cans frozen lemon juice

4 quarts ginger ale
2 quarts white soda
1 box frozen strawberries
1 c sugar

Mix juices together, without adding any water. Add ginger ale and soda. Serve with partially thawed strawberries floating on top. (May also float fresh mint on top.) Serves 100.

Irish Coffee

1 c coffee
1 jigger Irish whiskey

2 tsp sugar
whipped cream

Mix whiskey and sugar with coffee. Float whipped cream on top.

Buddy's Bloody Marys

1 fifth vodka
1 large can tomato juice
1 large can V-8 juice
1 small bottle Lea & Perrins
½ bottle Pickapepper

1 bottle lemon juice or fresh
  lime juice
1½ tbsp salt
pepper to taste
tabasco to taste

Mix all ingredients. Serve with a celery stick in each glass, if desired. Drink heartily for this does not keep well.

Cheese Straws

1 c grated sharp cheese
1 c flour
salt

cayenne pepper
2 tbsp butter

Sift dry ingredients. Add butter and water a little at a time as needed to make dough the right consistency to roll out. Roll; then cut in narrow strips. Bake in 450° oven.

Vegetable Soup Dip

1 pint sour cream

1 packet Knorr's
vegetable soup mix

Combine above ingredients. Refrigerate. Serve with Fritos.

Toasted Cereal

1 package Cheerios
1 package Rice Chex
1 package pretzels
1 lb pecans or 2 cans mixed nuts
  peanuts
1 lb margarine

1 bud garlic, crushed
3 tbsp chili powder
2 tbsp worcestershire sauce
2 tsp Lawry's seasoned salt
1 tsp Tabasco
2 tsp salt

Mix last 7 ingredients. Pour over cereal and nuts, and stir. Bake 1½ hours in 250° oven, stirring every 20 minutes.

Pickled Shrimp

2 lb boiled shrimp
2 c sliced onions
7 or 8 bay leaves
¾ c white vinegar

2½ tbsp celery salt
1½ tsp salt
2½ tbsp capers with juice
1½ c olive oil or salad oil

Alternate shrimp, onion, and bay leaves. Mix sauce and pour over shrimp mixture. Chill at least 24 hours before serving. This will keep for one week. It is also good added to lettuce and tomatoes and served as a salad.

Curried Cheese on Muffins

2 c grated cheese
½ c finely chopped shallots
½ c finely chopped ripe olives
½ c mayonnaise

½ tsp salt
½ tsp (scant) of curry powder
English muffins

Mix all ingredients except muffins. Spread on the muffins and place under the broiler until bubbly. Serves 4 or 5, allowing two muffins per person.

Emily's Easy Tacos

1½ lb hamburger meat
1 package Lawry's taco
   seasoning
1 small can tomato sauce

chopped tomatoes
chopped lettuce
grated sharp cheddar cheese
taco shells

Brown hamburger meat in a skillet. Season with salt, pepper, and taco seasoning. Add tomato sauce and a can full of water. Simmer covered for about 15 or 20 minutes, until meat is fairly dry. When ready to serve, fill taco shells with meat, cheese, lettuce and tomatoes. Guacamole, sour cream, and/or refried beans are good added to these.

Shelley's Mexican Rice

1 c rice
1 cooking spoon of Crisco
1 can tomatoes
½ can Rotel Tomatoes
1½ tsp chili powder
2 tbsp salt

Cook rice over high flame in Crisco until white. Add chili powder while cooking. Pour in tomatoes, Rotel tomatoes, salt, and one tomato can of water. Simmer for one hour or until all of the liquid is absorbed.

Tamale Pie

¾ c Wesson oil
2 medium onions
1 clove garlic
2 lb ground meat
4 tbsp chili powder
1 #2 can tomatoes
1 #2 can cream style corn
1 c cornmeal
¾ c milk
3 eggs

Brown meat and onions in Wesson oil. Add 4 tablespoons chili powder, tomatoes, and corn. Then add cornmeal that has been soaked in milk, 3 well beaten eggs, and salt. Bake in 350° preheated oven about 45 minutes. Serves 6–8.

Watercress Soup

2 cans cream of potato soup
1 can cream of onion soup
2½ c milk
1 bunch cut watercress
½ tsp pepper
cayenne pepper
½ c cream

Mix all ingredients except cream and bring to a boil; then simmer for 5 minutes. Puree in blender. Add ½ cup of cream and chill. Serves 6–8.

Seafood Gumbo

Almeta Scott has cooked for many Houston families. I feel fortunate that she has shared with us some of her famous recipes, of which gumbo is #1. Vera Harris (Bebe), the Bruce's family cook for many years, made her gumbo a little different—but with much the same results. Try it both ways!

Almeta's Gumbo:

bacon grease or other grease
2 tbsp flour
1 lb okra
1 large can tomatoes
1 tomato can of water
1 c chopped celery
1 c chopped onion

¼ c chopped bell pepper
salt and pepper to taste
1 tsp gumbo file
1 can white crab
1 can dark crab
1 lb cleaned shrimp
  (1½ lb uncleaned)

Add 2 tablespoons flour to grease in a large pot. Brown this very well. Add onions, celery, and bell pepper. Stir while cooking a few minutes. Add tomatoes, water, okra, salt and pepper. Cook slowly one hour or until the vegetables are well done. Add shrimp and crab plus gumbo file. I often add a few shakes of Tabasco. Serve over rice. Serves 8.

Variation: Substitute goose or duck for the seafood. Boil until tender. Skin and tear into bite size pieces. Substitute broth for water.

Bebe's Gumbo:

Bebe sautes 2 onions, 1 green pepper, and 1 pod of garlic in the grease from four slices of bacon. Then she adds a pound of okra and a large can of tomatoes, salt and pepper and gumbo file and cooks 1½–2 hours slowly. She adds crabmeat and crumbled bacon at the end.

Cheese Soup

½ c margarine
2 c chopped onions
2 c chopped celery
2 c chopped carrots
½ c flour
¼ c cornstarch
1 quart milk

pinch of soda
3 cans Swansons chicken broth
1 lb grated American or Velveeta cheese
½ c chopped fresh parsley
salt
pepper

Saute onions, salt, and pepper in melted margarine in pot you are making soup in. Mix cornstarch and flour. Add to milk. Add this to onions. Add chicken broth. Add celery and carrots and cook until done. Remove vegetables; put in blender. Return pureed vegetables to soup. Add cheese and soda. Add parsley just before serving. Reheat soup over very low heat.

Cabbage Slaw

8 c shredded cabbage
2 c seedless grapes

1 c toasted almonds

Dressing:

¾ c mayonnaise
2 tbsp vinegar
1 tsp sugar

2 tsp prepared mustard
1 tsp salt

Toss cabbage, grapes, and toasted almonds with dressing that has already been mixed. Serves 8.

Orange Gelatin Salad

2 packages orange Jello
½ c boiling water
1 small can frozen orange juice

1 large can crushed pineapple
3 cans Mandarin oranges, drained

Mix ingredients. Refrigerate until set. Serves 8.

Strawberry Molded Salad

1 large package strawberry Jello
2 c boiling water
1 small can crushed pineapple

1 package frozen strawberries
2 mashed bananas
sour cream

Mix all ingredients except sour cream. Put half of Jello mixture in a 9 × 12 pyrex dish. Refrigerate this until set. Spread this with a layer of sour cream. Top with remaining half of Jello mixture and refrigerate.

Avocado Mold

½ c chopped Rotel tomatoes
1 envelope unflavored gelatin
   (I add a little more)
2 medium avocados
1 tbsp plus one tsp lemon juice
½ c minced onion

½ tsp crushed sweet basil
½ tsp Worcestershire
½ c sour cream
½ c mayonnaise
salt and pepper to taste

Soften gelatin in a little juice from tomatoes. Add to heated tomatoes and stir until dissolved. Cool. Mash avocados with lemon juice in medium-sized bowl. Add gelatin and remaining ingredients. Pour into lightly greased one quart mold. Refrigerate until firm. Unmold and serve with bacon flavored crackers. Pimento strips are a decorative addition. Serves 8 but the recipe may be easily doubled.

Tomato Aspic

1½ c tomato juice
1 package Knox gelatin
½ c cold water
onion

salt and pepper
1 tsp horseradish (I use 2)
lemon juice (1 large or 2 small)

Simmer all ingredients except gelatin for a few minutes. Then add gelatin and strain. Pour in mold and refrigerate. Serves 4.

Marinated Vegetables

small fresh yellow squash
can of small string beans
canned artichoke hearts
canned hearts of palm

fresh cauliflower
fresh carrots
fresh broccoli
cherry tomatoes

The vegetables above are just suggestions—use all or some, or add one of your own. Cook the fresh vegetables (except for the tomatoes) in salted water until *barely* tender. Pour La Martinique French dressing (or your favorite dressing) over the hot vegetables plus the canned ones and refrigerate. For a party Almeta adds a layer of chopped green onions and makes her own dressing:

Almeta's French Dressing:

1 c lemon juice
1 tsp salt
1½ c olive oil

1 tsp pepper
3—4 pods of garlic

Tuna Pineapple Tossed Salad

romaine lettuce or 1 package
  spinach
1 small package walnuts
small can of crushed pineapple,
  drained

can of water-packed tuna,
  drained
package Ranch Style Dressing,
  mixed as directed

Wash lettuce or spinach and tear into bite-sized pieces. Toast walnuts under broiler. Toss all ingredients together and add just enough Ranch Style Dressing to coat. Serves 4 amply.

Green Goddess Dressing

1 small clove crushed garlic
3 tbsp anchovy paste
3 tbsp shallots
⅓ c chopped parsley

1 tbsp lemon juice
3 tbsp tarragon vinegar
1 c mayonnaise
½ c sour cream

Blend all ingredients except mayonnaise and sour cream. Then, add mayonnaise and sour cream.

Oil Dressing

½ clove garlic, crushed
¼ tsp prepared mustard
1 tsp salt
pepper

¼ tsp worcestershire sauce
1½ tbsp vinegar
4 tbsp salad oil

Mix all ingredients together.

Crabmeat Casserole

1 green pepper, diced
2 whole pimentos, diced
1 tbsp hot mustard
1 tbsp salt
½ tsp pepper

2 lightly beaten eggs
1 c homemade mayonnaise
1 tsp Accent
3 lb lump crab

Mix hot mustard, salt, pepper, eggs, mayonnaise, and Accent. Add green pepper and pimentos. Add crab and toss lightly. Sprinkle with paprika. Bake in 350° oven for 25–30 minutes. Serve either hot or cold. Serves 8–10.

Stuffed Crab

2 cans crab	*worcestershire sauce (shake)*
¼ lb melted butter	*juice of 2 lemons*
2 heaping tbsp flour	*2 egg yolks*
2½ c milk	*1 jigger sherry (optional)*
1 medium onion	*saltine crackers*
salt	*butter*
garlic salt	

Saute onion in butter. Add flour and milk. Add seasonings. Pour a little of mixture over egg yolks; then add the remainder. Add sherry if desired. Pour over crab. Place in shells and top with crushed saltine crackers. Dot with butter. Bake in 350° oven for 25–30 minutes. Serves 6 to 8.

Cold Crab

1 can lump crabmeat	*homemade mayonnaise*
1 jar capers	

Toss ingredients lightly. This is good served on crackers or melba toast, or as a salad with lettuce and tomatoes. Serves 4.

Baked Oysters

2 quarts oysters	*1 tbsp worcestershire sauce*
½ c finely chopped shallots	*2 tbsp lemon juice*
salt and pepper	*½ c melted butter or margarine*
Tabasco	*2 c fine cracker crumbs*
paprika	*¾ c Half & Half*

Place a layer of oysters in bottom of a greased shallow 2 quart baking dish. Sprinkle with ½ of parsley, shallots, seasonings, lemon juice, butter and crumbs. Make second layer of the same. Sprinkle with paprika. Just before baking, pour Half & Half into spaces. Bake at 350° about 30 minutes, until hot and bubbly. Serves 8.

Oysters Erminie

1 quart oysters, semi-defrosted
6 green onions
1 white onion
4 stalks celery
butter

1 package Pepperidge Farm
   Herb Dressing mix
salt and pepper
1 clove garlic
parsley

Chop oysters fine while semi-defrosted. Brown green onions, white onion, and celery in butter. Add most of the package of Pepperidge Farm Herb Dressing mix, plus a little water if necessary. Add salt, pepper and garlic. Place in shells and sprinkle chopped parsley on top. Bake in 350° oven about 30 minutes. Serves 8.

Tom Kelly's Snapper

Really good

snapper or white fish filets
1 large onion
1 or 2 tomatoes, sliced
⅔ jar pimento
fresh mushrooms, sliced

⅓ c white wine
5 to 6 tbsp soy sauce
salt & pepper
bread crumbs

Place thinly sliced onions in bottom of casserole. Add pimento. Rub fish filets with tabasco and place on top of onions and pimento. Cover with fresh mushrooms and sliced tomatoes. Add wine, soy sauce, salt and pepper. Top with bread crumbs and bake in 350° oven for 30 minutes.

Tuna and Chip Casserole

1 can tuna
1 can mushroom soup

¼ cup Pet milk
potato chips

Combine tuna, soup, and milk. Place in a casserole and top with crushed potato chips. Bake 20–25 minutes at 350°. Serves 4.

Tuna Casserole

1 can tuna
1 can mushroom soup
¼ c water
1 c cashews
1 c chopped celery

¼ c chopped onions
¼ c chopped green pepper
salt and pepper
1 tsp worcestershire
1 can noodles, toasted

Combine ingredients and top with toasted noodles. Cook in 350° oven 30–40 minutes. Serves 4 to 6.

Simmered Chicken

fryer
salt

onion or ginger slices,
if desired

When a recipe calls for diced chicken pieces, use fryers, because the meat is more tender than hens. Cover 1 or more fryers with water on top of the stove. Add salt and onion or ginger slices, if desired. Cook covered for 25 minutes on a gas stove, 15 minutes on an electric stove. Remove from heat, but leave covered for at least 1 hour. Skim the chicken stock and freeze it (in ice trays if desired) for use in other recipes.

Chicken and Green Noodle Casserole

4 lb hen (or equivalent in fryers)
1 stick margarine
1 c chopped green pepper
1 c chopped onion
½ lb sharp cheese (plus extra
    for top, if desired)

1 c chopped celery
6 oz jar of stuffed olives
6 oz can of mushroom pieces
1 package of spinach noodles
4 c chicken stock
1 can mushroom soup

Boil chicken in enough water to make 4 cups of stock. Save the stock. Bone and chop the chicken. Saute pepper, celery and onion in margarine. Stir in cheese, olives, mushrooms, and chicken. Boil noodles in the chicken stock until almost all of the stock is absorbed. Add the can of mushroom soup to the noodles. Mix the noodles with the chicken mixture. Sprinkle extra cheese on top, if desired, and bake in a 300° oven for 45 minutes. Serves 10 to 12.

Chicken and Chip

2 c cut chicken
2 c celery
½ c toasted almonds
½ tsp Accent
½ tsp salt

2 tsp grated onion
1 c mayonnaise
2 tbsp lemon juice
½ c grated American cheese
1 c crushed potato chips

Combine all ingredients except cheese and chips. Pile lightly into casserole. Sprinkle with cheese and chips. Bake in hot oven (450°) for 10–20 minutes.

Chicken Spaghetti

3 packages spaghetti (1 lb)
3 large hens
1 large can mushrooms
1 lb sharp cheese
garlic
5 or 6 large onions

1 ½ large stalks celery
1 bell pepper
3 c tomatoes
1 lb butter
parsley
4 slices bacon

Chop bacon fine and brown. Add a lump of butter. Brown onions and garlic. Add bell pepper, parsley and tomatoes. Simmer with 4 cups chicken stock for 3 hours. Season with Tabasco, celery salt, salt and pepper. Add celery, mushrooms and pieces of cooked chicken, plus more butter. Simmer 1 hour. Boil spaghetti. Add to sauce with grated cheese. Serves 25. This recipe may easily be cut into thirds.

Almeta's Liver and Onions

4 slices of calves liver
2 onions, sliced thin

salt and pepper
flour

Salt and pepper liver slices. Flour lightly and brown in cooking oil real fast. Remove from skillet and pour off oil. Put liver back in skillet and cook about 2 minutes uncovered. Put top on skillet and steam until tender.

Pot Roast

1 arm, chuck, or other kind of
  pot roast
1 ½ c red wine

1 package Lipton Onion
  Soup mix
1 can mushroom soup

Pour soups and wine over meat. Cover and cook in 250° oven for 5–6 hours.

Smoked Shoulder Clod

whole shoulder clod

Guy's Seasoning

Have butcher prepare whole shoulder clod. Rub it generously with Guy's Seasoning. Smoke slowly on a pit at opposite end from fire for 14–16 hours. Add more coals and hickory smoke chips as needed. One shoulder clod will serve about 20 people as a main course, or a crowd at a cocktail party.

Variation: Prepare brisket in same manner. Smoke 5 or 6 hours.

Laurie's Scrambled Hamburger

hamburger meat
catsup

worcestershire sauce
salt and pepper

Crumble hamburger meat into a skillet over medium flame. Pour catsup over meat. Season with worcestershire sauce, salt and pepper. Stir and let sizzle until completely cooked. Serve on a bun.

Variation: Add a package of Sloppy Joe seasoning mix.

Betty's Zutoni

1½ lb ground round
2 cans tomato soup
  (may use 3)
1 can tomato sauce
1 large can cream style corn
1 large onion
2 cans mushrooms

1 lb grated New York state
  sharp cheese
1 large package spaghetti,
  broken and cooked
2 cloves garlic
1 green pepper
olive oil

Cook meat in mushroom juice. Fry chopped onion, garlic, and green pepper in olive oil. Add soup, corn, tomato sauce, mushrooms, and ½ of grated cheese. Cook 5–10 minutes. Add meat and spaghetti and put in a casserole with the other half of the grated cheese on top. Heat thoroughly in a 350° oven before serving. Serves 10 to 12.

Beef and Rice Casserole

1½ lb ground beef
½ c celery
½ c onion

½ c bell pepper
½ stick margarine

Brown above ingredients in margarine.

Add:

1 can mushroom soup
1 can chicken noodle soup
salt

pepper
1 tbsp worcestershire
1 c raw rice

Place in casserole. Top with: ½ cup grated cheese and bread crumbs. Bake in 300° oven for 1½ hours. Serves 10 to 12.

Veal Cutlets Italienne

veal cutlets
green pepper
mushrooms
onions

red wine
salt and pepper
butter
mozzarella cheese

Salt and pepper cutlets, and brown in butter in a skillet. Place in a casserole. Brown enough chopped onions, green pepper and mushrooms to top each cutlet generously. Pour red wine over this and top with mozzarella cheese. Bake covered in foil in a 350° oven for about 1 hour and 15 minutes, checking occasionally to be sure that more wine or water is not needed.

Crown Pork Roast

Crown pork roast cut to serve
  desired number of people
3 tbsp lemon juice
3 tbsp salad oil
1 clove crushed garlic

1 tbsp salt
1 tsp pepper
½ tsp poultry seasoning
3 tbsp flour

Preheat oven to 325°. Mix all ingredients together and pour half over the roast. Roast uncovered without the rack for 2 hours. Pour rest of mix over the roast with the pan drippings. Roast for one more hour.

To stuff: Add Stove Top Stuffing for Pork after the first two hours; baste with drippings and cook for the last hour.

Pork Chop Casserole

4–6 medium thick pork chops
1 c rice
1 tomato
1 bell pepper

1 onion
1 can consomme
salt and pepper

Sprinkle pork chops with salt and pepper. Brown on both sides in skillet Sprinkle rice in bottom of casserole. Arrange pork chops on top. On top of each pork chop, place a slice of onion, bell pepper, and tomato. Pour consomme over all. Bake in 350° oven about 1½ hours, until pork chops are tender and rice has absorbed all the moisture.

Broiled Ham Steak

center cut ham slices,
  ¼–½" thick

3 tbsp brown sugar
5 tbsp mustard

Place ham slices under the broiler for 5–8 minutes, depending on thickness. Turn and spread with brown sugar and mustard which has been mixed together. Place back under the broiler for 5–8 minutes more.

Bar-b-qued Leg of Lamb

leg of lamb, butterflied
¾ c salad oil
⅓ c lemon juice
¼ c dry sherry
2 tbsp grated onion

1 tsp salt
3 drops Tabasco
¼ tsp powdered oregano
¼ tsp crushed thyme

Mix all ingredients and pour over lamb. Marinate 8 hours or overnight. Bar-b-que directly over coals 20 to 25 minutes per side, or brown each side directly over coals and smoke covered away from the direct coals for about 45 minutes. This is delicious served with jalapeno mint jelly. Serves 6 to 8.

Broiled Tomatoes

tomatoes
oregano
Parmesan cheese
garlic salt

salt
pepper
bread crumbs soaked in
   olive oil

Select firm tomatoes and cut in half. Sprinkle each half with other ingredients. Place under broiler until bubbly.

Tomato Casserole

tomatoes, sliced
sour cream
Parmesan cheese

1 can French fried onions
salt
pepper

Alternate layers of tomatoes (which have been salted and peppered), sour cream, and Parmesan cheese. Top with French fried onions and bake in 350° oven until bubbly—about 35 minutes.

Onions and Almonds

12 small boiling onions
1 c diced cooked celery
4 tbsp butter
3 tbsp flour
1 tsp salt
⅛ tsp pepper

1 c milk
½ c light cream
½ c blanched almonds
paprika
Parmesan cheese
sharp cheddar cheese, grated

Wash and peel onions. Cook them in boiling salted water until tender. Drain. Prepare celery the same way. Make a cream sauce by melting butter in a saucepan, adding flour, salt and pepper. Cook over low heat until bubbly. Add milk and cream and cook until thick. Layer the onions, celery and almonds in a buttered casserole. Cover with cream sauce. Sprinkle with paprika and top with grated cheeses. Bake in 350° oven until bubbly and brown. Serves 6 to 8.

Mother's Squash

3–4 lb yellow squash
1 medium onion, minced
2 bay leaves
6 sprigs parsley
½ tsp thyme
6 tbsp butter
3 tbsp all-purpose flour
dash salt

1 tsp seasoned salt
dash worcestershire
1⅓ c grated Swiss cheese
3 eggs
cayenne pepper
buttered bread crumbs
nutmeg

Cut squash in ⅓" slices. Place in a large saucepan with onion, bay leaves, parsley and thyme. Cover with well salted water and bring to a boil. Cook slowly until squash is barely tender. Drain. Remove parsley and bay leaves. Mash squash and add butter, seasoned salt, dash of nutmeg and worcestershire. Sprinkle in flour. Add 3 beaten eggs. Stir in 1 cup of the cheese and cayenne pepper. Pour in a buttered casserole. Mix remaining cheese with buttered bread crumbs. Sprinkle on top. Bake at 350° for 35 minutes. Serves 10.

Stir Fried Squash

1 chopped onion
4 or 5 large squash
3 tbsp margarine

1 tbsp bacon grease
salt
pepper

Cook onion in 4 tablespoons bacon grease. Add sliced squash and stir a few minutes. Cover and cook over low heat, stirring often until tender. You may need to add a little water while cooking.

Acorn Squash

small acorn squashes
butter

brown sugar

Split squash. Bake open side down for 25–30 minutes in 350° oven. Turn up and rub entire open part of squash with butter and brown sugar. Bake 30 more minutes.

Stuffed Yellow Squash

squash
salt
pepper
minced green onion
grated onion to taste

crumbled crisp bacon
  (about 2 pieces)
2 tbsp melted butter
buttered bread crumbs

Boil squash in salted water for 10–15 minutes. Scoop out squash at stem end, leaving ¼″ shell. Mash and season with salt, pepper, minced green onion, and grated onion to taste. Add bacon and 2 tablespoons melted butter. Fill shells and sprinkle with buttered bread crumbs. Bake about 20 minutes in 350° oven.

Kentucky Wonder Beans

fresh Kentucky Wonder beans
bacon

salt and pepper

String beans and snap in half. Bring salted water (with a piece of bacon in it) to a boil. Add beans; bring back to a boil, then simmer covered for 10 minutes. Turn off heat and leave covered for a few minutes. (You may cook pieces of onion with the beans, if desired.)

Wini's Mushroom "Souffle"

¾ lb chopped mushrooms
1 large onion, chopped
2 eggs, beaten
⅔ c Half & Half

⅔ c milk
⅔ c bread crumbs
1 tsp salt
pepper

Preheat oven to 350°. Butter casserole or souffle dish. Brown onions and mushrooms in butter. Add rest of ingredients. Pour into casserole and bake about 50 minutes until the top is golden brown. Serves 4 to 6.

Stuffed Potatoes

baking potatoes
milk
butter
salt

pepper
sharp cheddar cheese
sour cream or bacon bits,
    if desired

Bake potatoes in 400° oven for about 1 hour. Split potatoes lengthwise and scoop potato from peeling. Add butter, salt, pepper and heated milk until mixture is a good consistency to restuff in potato shells. (Sour cream and bacon bits may be added with other ingredients, if desired.) Top with grated cheese. Just before serving, place in 350° oven for about 20 minutes—until hot and the cheese is melted.

Almeta's Biscuits

5 c flour
2 c shortening
½ c milk

3 tsp baking powder
2 tsp salt

Mix together 4 cups flour, 1½ cups Crisco, salt and baking powder. Mix well. Add milk and mix well again. Melt ½ cup shortening. Let cool. Roll the dough with a rolling pin; fold it over and roll it again. Cut the dough into the size biscuit you like, dip in shortening, and bake on a cookie sheet in a 400° oven until brown.

Jalapeno Cornbread

1 c cornmeal
½ tsp baking powder
¾ tsp salt
1 c buttermilk
2 beaten eggs
½ c melted butter

1 medium onion, chopped
1 17 oz can yellow cream
    style corn
1 c grated sharp cheese
1 chopped jalapeno

Preheat oven to 350°. Mix all ingredients except cheese and jalapeno, and pour half in a hot greased 9 × 9 pan. Spread with cheese and jalapeno mixture. Pour rest of cornmeal mixture on top. Cook for 45 minutes and cool before serving. Serves 8.

Fried Corn Pones

2 c cornmeal
½ c flour
2 tsp salt

2 c boiling water
cooking oil

Mix cornmeal, flour, and salt with enough of the hot water to make a stiff moldable dough. Run your hands under cold water and form cakes about 3 × 1 × 1. This will make 10–12 of these. Fry in oil until brown.

Gingerbread

2 eggs, beaten until light
1 c sugar
1 c molasses
1 heaping ½ c butter and
   shortening mixed

2 tsp ginger
1 tsp cinnamon
2 c flour
1 c sour milk or boiling water
1 tsp soda

Add sugar, molasses, butter, ginger, and cinnamon to the beaten eggs. Mix soda into the flour and add to the mixture. Then add sour milk or water. Bake about 1 hour in a 350° oven. Serve with lemon sauce.

Lemon Sauce:

2 tbsp flour
2 c boiling water
1 c sugar

juice and grated rind
   of 2 lemons

Mix sugar and flour. Add boiling water. Cook in double boiler until thick. Remove from heat and add lemon and lemon rind.

Banana Pudding

¾ c sugar
½ c flour
¼ tsp salt
2 c milk

2 eggs, separated
1 tsp vanilla
vanilla wafers
bananas

Blend ½ c sugar, flour, and salt together in top of double boiler. Add ½ cup milk; then add remaining milk. Cook over boiling water, stirring frequently until thick. Cook 15 minutes covered. Add egg yolks. Cook 2 minutes. Remove from heat and add vanilla. Line dish with vanilla wafers. Arrange layers of bananas and custard. Beat egg whites stiff with ¼ cup of sugar. Spread over custard. Bake 20 minutes at 325°. Serves 6.

Bread Pudding

1 c bread crumbs
  (without crusts)
2 tbsp sugar
1 tbsp melted butter

⅓ c milk
1 egg yolk
juice and rind of a quarter
  of a lemon

Put bread crumbs into a baking dish. Mix 1 tablespoon sugar and 1 tablespoon melted butter. Add ⅔ cup of milk. Heat this and pour it over the bread crumbs. Keep this hot. Beat together the yolk of 1 egg, 1 tablespoon sugar, lemon juice and rind, a pinch of salt, and ⅓ cup of cold milk. Pour this over the bread also, and bake the pudding for a few minutes in a hot oven. Top with meringue or serve with custard sauce. Serves 6 to 8.

Meringue:

Beat several egg whites until stiff. Add ⅓ cup sugar, and ½ teaspoon lemon juice. Spread this over the pudding and set it in the oven for a few minutes to brown.

Custard Sauce:

See index for recipe for Floating Island.

Chocolate Pudding

4 tbsp flour
1 c sugar
3 tbsp Hershey's cocoa
    (powdered)

3 eggs
2 c milk
2 tsp vanilla
hunk of butter

Mix all ingredients except butter and vanilla. Cook in double boiler, stirring constantly, until mixture thickens. Add vanilla and butter, and beat until smooth. Serves 6.

Baked Custard

8 egg yolks (10 if baked
    in 1 dish)
⅓ c + 1 tbsp sugar
¼ tsp salt

1 quart hot milk
1 tsp vanilla
½ tsp lemon juice
nutmeg (if desired)

Beat egg yolks, sugar, and salt. Add hot milk, vanilla and lemon. Rub 9 × 12 casserole lightly with butter, or use individual custard cups. Place casserole or cups in water and bake in 350° oven until firm—about 45 minutes. Nutmeg may be sprinkled on top of custard before baking, if desired. Serves 8.

Boiled Custard

3 egg yolks, beaten
¼ c sugar
2 c milk

1 tsp vanilla
⅛ tsp salt

Mix egg yolks, sugar and milk. Cook in top of double boiler, stirring constantly, until thick. Add salt and vanilla. Cool and refrigerate. Serves 3 to 4. May be easily doubled or tripled.

Floating Island

1 quart milk
4 eggs
4 tsp sugar

2 tbsp cornstarch
½ tsp salt
1 tsp vanilla

Heat milk in a double boiler. Beat egg yolks until light. Add sugar, cornstarch which has been mixed in a little cold water, and salt. Add this gradually to the hot milk, stirring well. Cook for 5 minutes. Add vanilla. Beat egg whites until stiff, adding a little bit of sugar. Heap mounds of meringue on top of custard, and run under the broiler quickly to brown them, if desired. Serves 8.

Almeta's Lemon Mousse

1 c sugar
½ c water
8 egg yolks
1 ½ pints whipping cream

1 c lemon juice
2 envelopes plain gelatin dissolved in a little cold water

Mix sugar, water and egg yolks in double boiler. Cook until it begins to thicken. Add gelatin and keep cooking until this is well mixed. Add lemon juice and cook 1 minute more. Let cool. Whip cream and fold it into lemon mixture. Pour into a tube cake pan well-greased with butter and put in icebox until firm. To unmold, run knife around edges. Do not put in hot water. This is delicious served with cracked lemon drops on it, or topped with strawberries or raspberries. Serves 10 to 12.

Lemon Pudding

¼ c flour
1 c sugar
¼ tsp salt
¼ c lemon juice

1 ½ tsp grated lemon rind
2 eggs
1 c milk

Sift flour, sugar and salt. Stir in rind. Beat egg yolks until light and add milk. Add to flour mixture. Fold in stiffly beaten egg whites. Pour in shallow buttered baking dish. Set in pan of hot water. Bake 35—45 minutes in moderate oven. Serves 4 to 6.

Lemon Bisque

1 13 oz can Carnation milk
1 package lemon Jello
1¼ c boiling water
2½ c vanilla wafer crumbs

⅓ c honey
⅛ tsp salt
3 tbsp lemon juice
  (plus grated rind)

Dissolve Jello in water. Add honey, lemon juice and rind. When slightly thick, whip can of milk and fold in. Line pyrex casserole with vanilla wafer crumbs, saving some for the top. Then add Jello mixture and sprinkle with remaining crumbs. Refrigerate. Serves 12.

Almeta's Apricot Souffle

2 c stewed apricots, pureed
  in blender
1 c flour
½ tsp salt
1 c sugar

1 c milk
1 tsp baking powder
6 egg yolks
6 egg whites

Mix flour, sugar, baking powder, and salt. Add milk. Then add lightly beaten egg yolks. Mix in apricots and butter that has been melted. Beat egg whites until stiff enough to form peaks. Fold these into the apricot mixture. Place in souffle dish and bake in 350° oven for about 1 hour. This is delicious served hot, topped with Cerise Sauce (see following recipe). Serves 8.

Cerise Sauce

1½ c powdered sugar
pinch of salt
yolks of 2 eggs and 1
  unbeaten white

2 tbsp butter
1 tsp vanilla or juice of
  maraschino cherries to taste

Cream butter, sugar, salt and eggs. When quite smooth, add vanilla or cherry juice. This is also good with a touch of bourbon for flavoring, and it may be frozen.

Meringues

4 egg whites
½ tsp cream of tartar

¼ tsp salt
1 c sugar

Beat egg whites until foamy. Add cream of tartar and salt. Add sugar, 2 tablespoons at a time, while beating. Bake in greased pyrex plate at 275° for 50 minutes. Or make individual size meringues on wax paper. This may be topped with ice cream, fruits or custards.

Peach Ice Cream

2 eggs
1½ c sugar
2 c milk

1 pint cream
1 pint whipping cream
12 peaches, peeled and sliced

Make a custard of eggs, milk and ½ cup of sugar. Stir while cooking, until thickened. Sugar fruit with about a cup of sugar. You may vary the amount according to the sweetness of the fruit. Add to the custard along with the cream. Place in an ice cream freezer and freeze. Serves 10 to 12.

Strawberry Ice Cream

Make the ice cream the same as above, except use strawberries and 1 cup pureed apricots (optional).

Lemon Ice

1 c lemon juice
4 c water
2 c sugar

whites of 2 eggs,
    beaten stiff

Mix lemon juice, sugar and water. Freeze partially. Then add stiffly beaten egg whites. Freeze again until ready to serve.

Ice Cream Balls

Form balls of vanilla, peppermint or other ice cream. Roll in chopped pecans (that have been browned under the broiler). Serve topped with Fudge Sauce (see recipe following). Hershey's Fudge Sauce is good if you are in a hurry.

Variation: Roll vanilla ice cream in coconut and top with crème de menthe.

Fudge Sauce

½ c butter
2¼ c powdered sugar
⅔ c evaporated milk

6 squares Baker's unsweetened chocolate
cream

Mix butter and powdered sugar in top of double boiler. Add ¾ cup evaporated milk and chocolate. Cook over hot water 30 minutes. Do not stir. Remove from heat and beat. Add cream to make it thinner, if desired.

Marshmallow Sauce

1 c water
½ c sugar

⅓ lb marshmallows,
cut in quarters

Cook water and sugar for 1 minute. Add marshmallows and stir well. Cook in top of double boiler until the desired consistency. This is good on chocolate ice cream with nuts on top.

Angel Food Cake

1½ c egg whites
1½ c sugar
1 c sifted flour
1 tsp cream of tartar

½ tsp salt
1 tsp vanilla
½ tsp almond extract

Beat egg whites until foamy. Add salt and cream of tartar. Beat until it makes 2 peaks. Add sugar gradually; then add vanilla and almond extract. Fold in ½ of the flour, then the rest. Bake in floured tube pan, in 325° oven for 40 minutes. Turn upside down to cool. Serves 12.

Chocolate Angel Food Cake

Use above recipe except substitute ⅓ cup cocoa and ⅔ cup flour for 1 cup flour in the white angel food cake recipe. This is also good with ½ cup well chopped nuts sprinkled in the batter.

Angel Cake Filling

¼ c cold water
1 envelope gelatin
¾ c sherry

1 c whipping cream
½ c sugar

Dissolve gelatin in water. Heat sherry to boiling. Add gelatin. Let cool. Whip cream. Add sugar and fold in gelatin mixture. Let congeal and spread between angel food cake layers.

Pound Cake

½ lb margarine
2 c sifted flour
1⅔ c sugar

1 tsp vanilla
5 eggs
¼ tsp salt

Cream butter and sugar. Add eggs, one at a time. Sift in flour and salt. Just before adding batter, run cold water in a tube pan and invert the pan to dry. Then add batter and bake in a 325° oven for about one hour.

Walter's Favorite Lemon Pound Cake

1 package yellow cake mix
1 package instant lemon pudding
¾ c Wesson oil mixed with
* ¾ c water*
4 eggs at room temperature

2½ c powdered sugar
juice of 1 orange or 1 c of
* orange juice*
juice of 1 lemon plus
* grated rind*

Combine 2 dry mixes at low speed adding 1 egg and ¼ cup liquid alternately. When blended, beat at high speed for 4 minutes. Pour in greased and floured tube pan with wax paper on bottom. Bake on low rack in 375° oven for 45–50 minutes. Mix 2½ cups of powdered sugar, orange juice, lemon juice and rind. Loosen sides of cake while hot. Pour juice mixture over cake. Let soak at least 24 hours.

Bernice's Broiled Cake

⅛ lb butter
½ c milk
2 eggs

1 c sugar
1 c flour
1 tsp baking powder

Combine butter and milk. Bring to a boil. Mix eggs, sugar, flour and baking powder. Add butter and milk mixture. Bake in greased pan about 15–20 minutes.

Topping:

⅛ lb butter
6 tbsp brown sugar (heaping)

2 tbsp cream
pecan halves

Melt above ingredients on stove. Add pecan halves. Spread on top of cake and run under broiler until bubbly and brown.

Almeta's Apple Cake

2 c flour
2 c sugar
1 tbsp cinnamon
2 tsp soda
1⅓ c salad oil

4 eggs
3 c chopped apples
1 c stewed apricots
1 c white raisins
1 c nuts

Heat oven to 350°. Grease a tube pan or 2 small loaf pans. Sift dry ingredients together. Add oil. Add eggs, one at a time, and beat. Stir in apples, apricots, raisins, and nuts. Bake for 1 hour and 20 minutes (or slightly less in loaf pans).

Mrs. Brazelton's Lemon Jelly Icing

juice and rind of 2 lemons
1 c sugar
2 eggs, beaten separately

2 tbsp flour
1 tbsp melted butter

Mix sugar and yolks of eggs. Add whites; then add lemon juice and rind. Into this mixture, pour 1 cup boiling water. Add 2 tablespoons flour that has been stirred into ½ cup cold water. Beat in 1 tablespoon melted butter.

Upside Down Cake

⅓ c butter
1 c sugar
2 eggs, well beaten
½ c milk
1¾ c flour

½ tsp salt
½ tsp vanilla
2 tsp baking powder
canned pineapple slices
cherries

Grease pan and make design of pineapple and cherries. Cream butter. Add ½ sugar and beat. Add remaining sugar to eggs. Combine with butter and sugar. Mix and sift dry ingredients and add alternately with milk to first mixture. Add vanilla. Turn into pan with design and bake 35 minutes at 350°.

Almeta's Plum Cobbler

2 lbs plums, seeded and
  cut in fourths
1 c sugar
½ stick butter

½ tsp nutmeg
½ tsp cinnamon
1 tsp vanilla

Line a deep pyrex bowl with crust. Put plums, sugar, butter, spices and vanilla in it. Put crust on top. Bake in 350° oven until brown.

Topping:

Philadelphia cream cheese

cream

Soften cream cheese with cream until desired consistency.

Plum Cobbler Crust:

2 c flour
1 c shortening
1 tsp baking powder

¼ tsp salt
⅓ c ice water

Mix dry ingredients; then add ice water. Divide dough in half to roll out. Mold one piece in bottom of pyrex bowl; add filling and then add top crust. Crimp edges of top crust and pierce holes in it with a fork.

Deep Dish Apple Pie

5 or 6 apples, peeled
  and sliced
3 tbsp sugar

3 tbsp water
cinnamon
nutmeg

Sprinkle apples with sugar, water, cinnamon and nutmeg.

Topping:

½ stick butter ¾ c flour
½ c brown sugar

Mix above ingredients. Press together in hands and place on top of apples. Bake 40 minutes in 325° oven. Serve topped with whipped cream or ice cream.

Fudge Pie

½ c butter 1 tsp vanilla
1 c sugar 1 ½ squares Baker's chocolate,
2 eggs, unbeaten   melted
¼ c sifted flour

Cream butter; add sugar. Beat until creamy. Add eggs and beat. Fold in flour. Add vanilla and chocolate. Pour into greased pyrex pie plate. Bake 25 minutes in 300° oven. Serve topped with ice cream.

Graham Cracker Pie

1 c graham cracker crumbs ½ tsp vanilla
1 c sugar 3 egg yolks (lightly beaten)
½ tsp baking powder 3 egg whites (beaten stiff)
½ c chopped nuts

Combine all ingredients but egg whites. Fold these in last. Bake in greased pie plate at 375° for 25–30 minutes. Serve with whipped cream.

Lemon Angel Pie

4 egg whites   *¼ tsp cream of tartar*
¾ c sugar

Beat egg whites until frothy. Add cream of tartar. Beat, while adding sugar gradually, until stiff. Spread in a 9" pie plate and bake at 300° for 1 hour. Cool.

Lemon Filling:

Mix: *6 egg yolks*   Add: *3 tbsp orange juice*
      ¾ c sugar   *3 tbsp lemon juice*
      ½ tsp salt   *1 tsp orange rind*
                                             1 tsp lemon rind

Cover and cook over hot water until thick. Cool and spread over meringue.

Topping:

whipping cream   *toasted almonds*
sugar

Whip cream with a little sugar (and vanilla if desired). Place on top of pie right before serving. Sprinkle with toasted almonds.

Ice Cream Pie

chocolate wafers   *ice cream*
butter

Make crust of crushed chocolate wafers and enough butter to hold them together. Press in pie plate. Bake in 350° oven for 10 minutes. Cool. Fill with ice cream soft enough to spread. Freeze.

Brownies

½ c shortening
2 eggs
2 tsp vanilla
2 tsp milk
1 tsp baking powder

1 c sugar
1 c flour
½ c cocoa
1 c nuts

Combine ingredients. Bake 15–20 minutes at 350°.

Icing:

1 cup sugar
2 tbsp cocoa
½ c milk

salt
a hunk of butter
1 tsp vanilla

Cook sugar, cocoa, milk and salt to soft boil stage. Add butter and vanilla. Spread.

Fruit Cake Cookies

1 c brown sugar
½ c butter
4 beaten eggs
3 tbsp milk
3 c flour
1 tsp cinnamon
allspice
nutmeg

½ package seedless raisins
1½ lb pecans
½ lb red pineapple
½ lb green pineapple
½ lb candied cherries
1 jigger whiskey
3 scant tsp soda

Chop fruit. Mix with other ingredients. Bake 15–20 minutes in 300° oven. Sprinkle brandy over the cookies and place in tightly covered can or jar.

Chocolate Cookies

1 package chocolate dots
⅔ c condensed milk
1 tsp vanilla

½ tsp salt
1 c chopped pecans

Melt chocolate dots and condensed milk in double boiler. Add other ingredients. Drop by spoonfuls on greased cookie sheet. Bake 10 minutes in 350° oven.

Drop Sugar Cookies

1 c butter
1 c sugar
2 eggs
2 c flour

1 tsp salt
1 tsp vanilla
pecan halves

Mix all ingredients except pecan halves. Drop by teaspoonfuls on greased cookie sheet. Press a pecan half into each mound of dough. Bake in 350° oven about 7 minutes, until edges are brown.

Oatmeal Cookies

¾ c shortening
1 c sugar
2 eggs
1 c flour
1 tsp cinnamon

a little soda dissolved in
   2 tbsp water
1 tsp nutmeg
2 c oatmeal
1 cup chopped nuts

Preheat oven to 350°. Cream sugar and shortening. Add beaten eggs. Then add flour, water, oatmeal, spices and nuts. Drop dough by teaspoonfuls on a greased cookie sheet. Sprinkle with sugar, and bake at 350° until they begin to brown.

Pecan Squares

4 eggs
2 c brown sugar
6 tbsp flour (heaping)

½ tsp baking powder
2 c pecans
1 tsp vanilla

Combine all ingredients. Line shallow pan with greased wax paper: then pour in mixture. Cook pecan squares at 350° for 20 minutes. Remove from pan at once. Cool and ice.

Icing:

½ c butter
3 c powdered sugar

1 tsp vanilla
2 tbsp milk or cream

Cream butter and sugar. Add cream and vanilla. Spread on cooled pecan squares.

Sugared Walnuts

½ lb walnuts
1 ½ c sugar

1 tsp grated orange rind
½ c orange juice

Cook sugar and juice to soft ball stage. Simmer and beat in orange peel. When mixture gets cloudy, pour in nuts. Remove nuts and cool on wax paper.

Party Scrambled Eggs

1 dozen eggs
1 heaping c cream style
  cottage cheese

2 tbsp butter
optional: bacon bits, sausage
  bits, cheese

Mix ingredients together and scramble in butter in a skillet. Then put eggs in a greased pyrex dish and keep in warmer at 150° until ready to serve. Serves 8 to 10.

Kirk's Egg Omelette

1 or 2 eggs
grated Mozzarella or
* other cheese*

salt and pepper
optional: bacon bits, or ham

Beat eggs; then pour in a small skillet. Sprinkle the cheese on one side of the eggs. Add bacon bits or ham and let it sit. Then flip the uncovered side of the eggs over the covered side. Let it cook until slightly brown.

BUD
RN

Willie's Low Calorie Tea

Bring 4 quarts of water to a boil. Add 3 regular Lipton's tea bags. Steep for 5 minutes. While hot, add 7 packages of Sweet & Low and juice of 3 lemons and 3 limes. You may add 2 cups cold water if you choose. Serve over crushed ice with garnish of fresh mint, fresh pineapple spear and fresh slices of lemon. Makes 1 large pitcher.

Barbie's Sangria

1 fifth Paisano red wine
8 oz simple syrup
6 oz fresh lemon juice

6 oz pineapple juice
6 oz Maraschino liqueur
2 oz Orange Curaco liqueur

Stir all together. Let refrigerate for several hours. When you are ready to serve, add fresh slices of fruit in season—strawberries, pineapple, lemon, lime, orange or peaches. You may freeze this and it is delicious. You may also let thaw and serve as a slush in parfait glasses. Serves 6.

PTA Punch

5 half-gallons of lime
  sherbert

20 quarts of gingerale

Put one ½ gallon sherbert in punch bowl and break into large chunks. Pour gingerale over it and stir. This makes a divine, refreshing punch and it's so easy. You can also use orange sherbert. Serve in small, clear plastic cups. As you dip out a cup, try to get some ice cream along with the ale. As the sherbert is used, add another ½ gallon and more gingerale.

Brandy Freeze

1 half-gallon Bluebell Supreme
  French Vanilla Ice Cream

1 cup Brandy

Blend in blender until well mixed and creamy. Pour into stemmed glasses and place in freezer or serve immediately.

Rudy's Pink Squirrel

3 oz Creme de Noyaux
3 oz Creme de Cocoa

1 c vanilla ice cream

Mix in blender until very thick. Pour into frosted glass. Serves one.

Muppet

Put ¾ tequilla in a shot glass, fill with 7-up, cover, bang glass on table to fizz—drink down—instant joy!

Hot Spinach-Crab Dip

1 white onion, chopped
½ c butter
1 package frozen spinach,
*   cooked and drained*

1 lb crabmeat
¾ c grated Parmesan cheese
¼ c dry white wine

Saute onion in butter. Add spinach, crabmeat, cheese and wine. Heat until bubbly. Serve in hot chafing dish with sesame rounds or crackers.

Fried Oysters

Wash and drain fresh oysters on paper towels. Season each oyster with Lawry's seasoned salt and red pepper. Dip in batter of 1 beaten egg mixed with ½ cup water, then dip in cornmeal. Fry in Mazola oil for several minutes on each side or until golden brown. Drain on paper towels and place in 250° oven until ready to serve, but should be served immediately.

Red Chili Sauce for Oysters

½ stick butter
1 bottle Hunt's chili sauce
½ c Hunt's catsup

¼ c Lea & Perrins
*juice of 1 lemon plus put whole
    squeezed lemon in saucepan*

Put all ingredients into a saucepan and cook slowly for about 20 minutes. Remove lemon peel and serve hot with oysters.

Crabmeat Sharman

16 oz cream cheese
2 tbsp mayonnaise
4 tbsp grated onion
*1 tbsp cream style
    horseradish*

2 tbsp milk
13 oz crabmeat (fresh)
juice of 1 lemon
*Lea & Perrins worcestershire
    sauce*

Mix all ingredients together until smooth. Add a dash of Lea & Perrins worcestershire sauce and juice of lemon. Bake in 10 ounce buttered pie plate for 30 minutes at 350°. Cover with a sprinkle of paprika. Delicious! This dish makes a fabulous main dish or hot dip. Serve with sesame or rye Old London Melba rounds and toast. This and a good salad are quite a meal! Serves 6 or 20 as a dip.

Guacamole Salad

4 ripe avocados
¼ onion, grated
juice of 1 lemon
2 tbsp vinegar
3 dashes Tabasco sauce

*1 tsp Lawry's garlic salt or
    1 pod garlic, crushed*
seasoned salt to taste
pepper to taste

With mixer, whip peeled avocados to chunks. Add other ingredients and whip to smooth (to make this stretch or add consistency, add 1 (4 oz) package Philadelphia cream cheese). Put 1 or 2 seeds back into dip to keep it from turning black until you use it. Serves 6.

Chile Con Queso

2 lb box of Velveeta cheese
¼ c chopped onion
1 pod chopped garlic

2 tbsp butter
3 jalapeno peppers, chopped
1 can Rotel tomatoes and chiles

Melt cheese in a double boiler. Saute onion and garlic in butter. Add to cheese with tomatoes and peppers. If you have small pieces of other hard cheese, add to mixture for flavor. Monterrey Jack or cheddar are good.

Tacos

1 lb ground beef
1 onion, chopped fine
1 pod garlic, chopped fine
2 small jalapeno peppers,
    chopped
1 can Rotel tomatoes and chiles
    (or 1 large fresh tomato peeled
    and grated for pulp)

2 tsp cumin
1 tsp Lawry's seasoned pepper
1 package chalupa shells
1 package Lawry's taco
    seasoning mix (optional)
1 c grated cheddar cheese
1 c shredded lettuce
½ c chopped, fresh tomatoes

Mix beef, onion, garlic, pepper, tomatoes, seasoned pepper and cumin and cook until beef is done. Add Lawry's seasoned mix, if it is being used, when meat is almost done. Heat taco shells in oven and fill at the last minute with meat mixture. Add grated cheese and top with lettuce and tomatoes. Serves 4. A wonderful idea for a party is to put all ingredients out and let each person fix their own taco to their liking! Add sour cream to your list of condiments.

Mexican Beans

Soak overnight 1 lb of pinto beans. Put beans in large earthen pot with 10 cups of boiling water, 2 cups chopped onions, 3 cloves garlic (chopped), hunk of smoked bacon (about ¼ lb or little more) and 1 large tablespoon of ground cumin seed.

Simmer this together for about 4 hours or until beans are very tender and slightly mushy. If it is necessary to add more water to the beans, be sure and add boiling water (cold water darkens the beans).

When beans are done, add salt to suit taste and make a paste of 5–6 tablespoons of chili powder mixed with bean juice. Add this paste to the beans and stir well. Add ¼ lb butter or margarine and you are ready to eat!

Hattie's Mexican Rice

1 c rice
4 tbsp butter
1 onion, chopped fine
½ c celery, chopped fine
1 can Rotel tomatoes and chiles

½ bell pepper, chopped fine
salt to taste
pepper to taste
1 can whole tomatoes

Brown rice with 2 tablespoons butter in skillet. Set aside. Saute in 2 tablespoons butter: onion, celery, bell pepper, salt and pepper. When tender, add to browned rice. Pour 1 can whole tomatoes and 1 can Rotel over rice. Cover and cook slowly for 35–40 minutes on low heat until rice is tender. Serves 4.

Enchiladas

Mix:

1 lb ground meat
1 onion, chopped fine
1 pod garlic, chopped fine
   or crushed
2 jalapeno peppers,
   chopped fine

grated cheese
1 tsp Lawry's seasoned pepper
2 tsp cumin
1 package corn tortillas
   (10 or 12)
1 #2 can any good chili

Put soft tortillas into hot oil for 1 minute. Remove and drain. Put tortillas into bowl of picante sauce, turn on both sides and remove. Fill each tortilla with 2 or 3 tablespoons of meat which has been cooked with onion, garlic and seasonings until well done. Roll up and place side by side in a 3 quart casserole flat dish. When all are filled, cover with any good chili. Top with grated cheddar or rat cheese and chopped onion. Cook 30 minutes in a 350° oven, or until bubbly. Serves 6. You may also add refried beans and grated cheese to your meat mixture before rolling. This is also delicious!

Leftover Mexican Idea

If you have taco meat, enchiladas, chili con queso or beans left over—layer the ingredients you have and top with freshly grated cheddar cheese. Freeze and thaw for another great meal. Serve on toasted tortillas and top with guacamole salad. Makes a divine casserole.

Hot Tamale Pie

2¼ c evaporated milk
1½ c water
½ c yellow cornmeal
¾ tsp salt
1 lb ground beef
3 tbsp chopped onion

2 tsp salt
2 tsp chili powder
¼ tsp pepper
1 tsp cumin
½ c soft bread crumbs
½ tsp baking powder

Heat 1½ cups evaporated milk with water just until it boils. Stir in yellow cornmeal and ¾ teaspoon salt slowly so that milk continues to boil. Cook slowly for 5 minutes, stirring constantly. Put ground beef, onion, and 2

teaspoons salt, chili powder, pepper, cumin, bread crumbs and baking powder into a mixing bowl. Mix thoroughly with ¾ cup evaporated milk. Press into the bottom of a greased 2½ quart casserole dish. Leave space around the edges. Pour cornmeal mixture over the top, letting it run into the bottom in space left by meat mixture. Bake at 350° for 1 hour or until firm. Serve with guacamole and you may top with grated cheddar cheese if you wish. Serves 6.

Nachos Variations

Tortilla chips spread with refried beans and cheddar cheese with jalapeno pepper slice on top.

Tortilla chips with beans, finely chopped onions, grated cheese— topped after cooking with guacamole.

Tortilla chips with Velveeta only.

Burritos

1 package Jiminez flour tortillas
1 lb lean ground meat
1 large can Frito's bean dip or
 1 can refried beans
1 onion, chopped fine
1 package Lawry's taco
 seasoning mix

1 can Rotel tomatoes
1 clove garlic, crushed
1 tbsp cumin
1 c grated cheddar cheese

Cook ground meat with onions, tomatoes, garlic, taco seasoning mix and cumin. Cook until juice cooks out of the meat. Spread each tortilla with bean mixture. Place 1–2 tablespoons meat mixture in center of each. Place 1 tablespoon grated cheese on top. Roll tortilla tightly, being careful not to break. Fold ends under and place on teflon cookie sheet. Cover all with foil and cook 30 minutes in a 350° oven. Uncover and let get slightly brown or serve soft. You may cover with chili of your choice and grated cheese or chopped onions. We prefer guacamole on top. Sour cream would also be a treat!

Shelley's Sopapillas

1½ c flour
1 tsp baking powder
½ tsp salt

½ tbsp shortening
½ c water

Mix ingredients together, then roll flat on a lightly floured surface to a 10 × 12 rectangle. Cut into 3″ squares. Heat 3″ of cooking oil until hot. Drop 1 or more squares into hot oil, allow to puff, then turn to brown on the other side. Drain on paper towels. Roll in powdered sugar. Serve hot. This is Shelley's favorite breakfast. These ingredients are for small portions.

Navy Bean Soup with Franks

1 lb (2 c) small white navy
  dried beans
3 quarts cold water
3 medium potatoes, peeled,
  boiled and mashed
2 onions, chopped fine

6 ribs of celery, chopped fine
¼ c parsley, chopped fine
2 cloves garlic, crushed
1 lb ham, diced
salt and pepper to taste
franks

Soak beans in water overnight. Drain. Place beans in large Dutch oven and cover with clean water and cook slowly for about 1 hour or until beans are slightly tender. Drain. Add the 3 quarts of water, mashed potatoes, celery, parsley, onions, garlic and ham. Cook slowly for 2 hours, stirring every now and then. Reseason with salt and pepper and paprika. About 30 minutes before soup is done, cut your franks into small round slices about ¼″ thick and add to soup. Cook on until franks are done. Makes 2 quarts and freezes well.

Marian's Gumbo

To make good gumbo, a fine roux must be made. Into an *iron* skillet or dutch oven, put ¾ cup flour and ½ cup corn oil. Stir together and make a paste. Cook on low heat stirring very often until roux becomes chocolate brown. It should never burn, but must become very dark. Into your roux, add 4 cups of chicken stock and 4 cups of water; also add 1 or 2 cups of diced chicken (turkey can be used). To this add:

1 heaping tbsp of McCormick
   seafood seasoning
¾ c green pepper, chopped fine
¾ c onion, chopped fine
¾ c celery, chopped fine
2 bay leaves
2 pods of garlic, crushed

2 tbsp chopped parsley
1 tsp seasoned salt
1 tsp black pepper
2 tsp red pepper
1 tsp sugar
2 small cans of tomato sauce

Stir all together and add a few shakes of Tabasco sauce and Lea & Perrins worcestershire sauce. Simmer 2½ hours on low heat. For the last 30 minutes, add 1 package of frozen okra. Then add 1 can fresh crabmeat, 3 lbs of fresh, cleaned, deveined shrimp and 1 can of claw fingers. Simmer 15 minutes more with ½ cup chopped green onion tops. Serve on rice. Serves 10 generously.

Fresh Vegetable Soup

2 or 3 lb lean stew meat
1 large soup bone with lean meat
   surrounding it
2 packages chicken giblets
   (use left over giblets from fryer
   or baking chicken—freeze
   them for use in soup)
1 tbsp Vegesalt

2 pods fresh garlic
1 tbsp black pepper
2 bay leaves
1 tsp celery salt
2 large ribs finely chopped
   celery with several leaves
2 onions, finely chopped
¼ c chopped parsley

Cook first 8 ingredients for 6 hours on low heat. Just simmer. Remove chicken parts. Add last 3 ingredients. Cook another 2 hours. Add:

2 carrots, peeled and cut
   into thin slices
3 squash, cut into thin slices
4 ears of corn (cut off cob)
1 lb raw fresh Kentucky Wonder
   beans, snapped
1 lb fresh okra sliced into
   small pieces

1 package frozen small
   lima beans
1 large #2 can Hunts Whole
   Peeled Tomatoes
1 tbsp cracked pepper
3 tbsp Kikoman soy sauce
6 dashes Tabasco sauce

Cook another 2 hours. Let cool, skim off fat and freeze. Makes 6 quarts.

Here are some sandwiches my family loves!

Grilled Turkey Roma

Put mayonnaise on 2 pieces of bread. Fill with thin sliced turkey breast. (For cheese lovers, I sometimes add grated white or cheddar cheese to my filling. For pepper lovers, pepper generously. Green chives, chopped fine and crumbled bacon are also delicious added.) Close sandwich and butter both outer sides of the bread. Grill on griddle or in a skillet until golden brown.

Croque Monsieur

Put Dijon mustard (Grey Poupon is my favorite) on 2 pieces of white or rye bread. Fill with ham slices (and here you may add grated cheddar or white cheese to filling). Close and butter outer sides of bread and grill until golden brown.

Meat Loaf Sandwich Caliente

Slice meat loaf thin. On 2 pieces of white, or preferably Cookbook rye bread, put mayonnaise on 1 piece and mustard (French's or Grey Poupon) on the other. Add meat loaf and grated cheddar or Monterrey Jack cheese. Add chopped chives or thin sliced purple onion and small slices of jalapeno pepper. Close and feast! This may also be grilled.

Oven Dogs

Boil weiners in water until done (5 minutes). Place cooked weiner in hot dog bun and put chili, grated or chopped fine onions, and grated cheese in each hot dog. Place on a cookie sheet and put in a 350° oven until warm throughout and until cheese melts. A meal in itself. You may also put mayonnaise and mustard on your hot dog if you prefer, but it's not necessary.

Glenda's Tuna Delight

1 can tuna
juice of 1 lemon
Lawry's seasoned salt
* and/or pepper*

mayonnaise or salad dressing
* (Miracle Whip)*
cheddar or Mozzarella cheese

Mix tuna (drained and oil absorbed in paper towels) and the juice of 1 lemon. Add seasoned salt and/or pepper to taste, 2 tablespoons mayonnaise or salad dressing and mix. Spread mixture on slices of thin white bread or toasted rye. Top with grated cheese. Heat under broiler until cheese melts. Serve immediately.

Chubby's Pimento Cheese

4 oz Colby cheese, grated
4 oz sharp cheddar
½ c chopped green onions
1 large jar chopped pimentos

mayonnaise to desired
* consistency*
¼ c chopped purple onion
1 tsp Tabasco
dash worcestershire sauce

Combine all ingredients. Makes a wonderful sandwich plain or grilled. Try grilled on Cookbook rye bread. Good with sesame rounds or crackers.

Sukey's Pimento Cheese

1 lb grated cheese (Cracker
   Barrel or Longhorn)
1 large jar of chopped pimentos
1 tbsp sugar
1 tbsp mustard

big glop of Miracle Whip
   Salad Dressing
juice of ½ lemon
salt to taste
pepper to taste

Mix well and enjoy!

Chicken or Turkey Salad

2 c diced cooked chicken
   or turkey
½ c chopped green onions
½ c shredded cheddar cheese
¼ c celery chopped finely

salt and cracked pepper to taste,
   ½ tsp white pepper
3 tbsp chopped parsley
juice of 1 lemon

Mix ingredients together well. Add mayonnaise to desired consistency.
Men love this!

Cottage Cheese Flip

2 c cottage cheese
½ c diced tomato
¼ c diced cucumber
¼ c diced celery
2 tbsp chopped chives
2 tbsp vinegar

cracked pepper
seasoned pepper
1 tsp paprika for top
½ tsp cream style horseradish
few shakes Tabasco

Mix all ingredients, place in a quartered whole tomato pulled gently apart
to form a cup. Refrigerate until ready to serve. Serves 4.

Fresh Pineapple Lunch

Cut a fresh pineapple lengthwise and hollow out fresh center meat. Set aside. Put hollowed out halves into a baggie and put into refrigerator.

fresh pineapple meat
  cut into cubes
1 box fresh strawberries halved

1 grapefruit sectioned
  (you may use any fruits
  you choose)

Mix fruits together. When ready to serve, place fruit into pineapple halves. Garnish top of fruit with slices of Baby-eye Swiss cheese cut into thin strips. A beautiful and filling luncheon dish. Serves 2.

Artichoke Surprise

4 artichokes
1 tbsp lemon juice
2 tsp salt

2 tsp cracked pepper
1 onion cut in large pieces

Trim stem of each artichoke. Pull off leaves at the base. Cut off top third and spread each artichoke open. Dip out fuzzy center. Dispose of this. Place in a deep saucepan. Add water, lemon juice, onion, salt and pepper (you may also put in a few celery leaves for flavor) until artichoke is ½ submerged. Cover and bring to a boil and cook 40 minutes, or until a leaf pulls out easily. Remove and drain upside down on paper towel. Put in a bowl to fit snugly and pour ½ cup wine vinegar dressing over. Marinate overnight or for several hours.

Filling:

1 c diced cooked shrimp
½ c diced hearts of palm
½ c diced celery

½ c diced green onions
8 whole cooked shrimp

Mix all ingredients except whole shrimp. Remove artichokes from marinade and fill with mixture. Decorate with whole shrimp and chill.

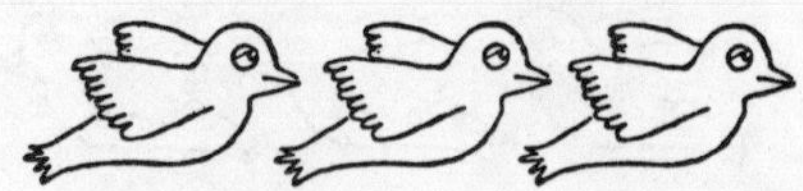

Seafood Salad

1 head of iceberg or
   Boston lettuce
green onions, chopped
Lawry's seasoned pepper

fresh tomatoes to suit (I prefer
   plum tomatoes)
Lawry's seasoning salt

Add: 1 cup fresh lump crabmeat or fresh cooked lobster meat and fresh,
cooked, chopped or whole shrimp.

Toss with a generous amount of oil and vinegar dressing with lemon juice. (I prefer La Martinique French dressing.) Serves 4. I prefer iceberg lettuce cut in chunks rather than torn. It gives a crunchy goodness to salads!

Spinach Salad

1 bunch fresh spinach
2 chopped green onions
4 sliced plum tomatoes

¼ c crumbled bacon
juice of 1 lemon

Season with Lawry's seasoned pepper and Lawry's garlic salt. Dress with La Martinique French dressing. Variations of this salad may include fresh mushrooms (chopped), crumbled Philadelphia cream cheese, grated cheddar or Monterrey Jack cheese. Chopped chicken or tuna also may be added for a luncheon main dish.

Greek Salad

fresh spinach
plum tomatoes
chopped green onions
Feta cheese, crumbled
4 avocados

garlic pod
seasoning salt
1 c of Berio olive oil
½ c Parmesan cheese
juice of 1 lemon

Combine salad ingredients. Squeeze lemon juice over all. Season with Lawry's seasoned salt and seasoned pepper, and a small amount of Lawry's garlic salt. Sprinkle Parmesam cheese over all. Add crushed garlic pod to oil and dribble over all. Toss and serve immediately.

Potato Salad

2 lb red potatoes
2 c mayonnaise
1 tbsp Dijon mustard
salt and pepper to taste

3 green onions chopped
¼ c red wine vinegar
2 tbsp lemon juice
cayenne pepper

Boil potatoes 30 minutes. Drain and cool. Peel and cut into chunks. Mix all other ingredients. Stir in potatoes. Refrigerate.

Boston Salad

2 heads Boston lettuce
3 green onions, chopped
chopped tomatoes
(if you prefer, but I prefer
not to in this salad)

2 avocados, chopped and mari-
nated in French dressing for
a few hours with the juice of
1 lemon

Toss with oil and vinegar dressing with 1 avocado mashed into the dressing, OR marinate chopped avocados, tomato and hearts of palm in dressing. A delightful addition to any salad! Serves 4.

Avocado Dressed Salad

1 3 oz package cream cheese,
softened
1 avocado, seeded, peeled
and mashed (½ c)
¼ tsp garlic powder
1 tbsp lemon juice

½ c mayonnaise or
salad dressing
milk
bibb or romaine lettuce
¼ c chives

In mixer bowl, combine cream cheese, mashed avocado, lemon juice, mayonnaise, and garlic powder. Beat until smooth. Stir in enough milk to make the dressing the proper consistency. In salad bowl, pour dressing over chilled, torn bibb and romaine lettuce and chives. Toss lightly to coat lettuce.

Vegetable Salad

3 zucchini squash, raw,
    thinly sliced
3 yellow squash, raw,
    thinly sliced
1 onion, thinly sliced and
    separated in rings

1 can artichoke hearts,
    drained
1 can hearts of palm, drained
    and sliced
1 can thin green beans,
    drained

Pour over all, La Martinique French dressing heated in a pan with ¼ cup cider vinegar added to it. Cover and refrigerate for 24 hours. Will keep for a week and get better every day.

Tomato Aspic

1 whole carrot
1 12 oz can V-8 juice
1 10 oz can Snappy Tom
1 tsp Tabasco
1 onion, chopped

1 lemon
1 rib celery, leaves too
1 package Knox unflavored
    gelatin

Cook above ingredients until vegetables are tender. Strain. Take 1 envelope unflavored Knox gelatin and dissolve in 1 cup of hot juice. Put it into other strained juice and add 1 teaspoon Tabasco sauce, ¼ teaspoon pepper, ¼ teaspoon cayenne pepper. Stir well and pour into a 9″ square pyrex or small, deep pyrex dish. Let chill for a little while in refrigerator. Take out and put chopped pimento olives, capers, cream cheese pieces or boiled shrimp pieces into the dish and stir. Chill until set (you may use 1 or 2 condiments or all, but I would not use olives and capers together).

Cabbage Surprise

shredded thin cabbage
tomatoes, chopped
thin, sliced onion

cracked pepper to taste
sliced cucumbers (marinated
    in dill and vinegar)

Dressing:

1 tbsp tarragon vinegar
1 tsp salt
¼ tsp sugar

½ c dairy sour cream
1 tsp minced onion
¼ c oil and vinegar dressing

Combine in a small bowl: vinegar, onion, salt and sugar. Fold in sour cream. Cover and chill. When ready to serve, toss salad mixture with oil and vinegar first, then add sour cream mixture and toss again.

Chopped Up Vegetable Salad

½ head of iceberg lettuce,
   chopped fine
¼ c purple onion, chopped fine
1 tomato, chopped fine

1 c celery hearts plus leaves,
   chopped fine
2 green shallots, chopped fine
   (stalks included)

Combine and toss with your favorite oil and vinegar dressing. Serves 4.

Shrimp Curry Willie

2 lb raw shrimp
1 stick butter (¼ lb)
2 tbsp cornstarch
1 tbsp curry powder
2 c milk

½ tsp salt
1 tsp paprika
½ tsp white pepper
juice of 1 lemon

Melt butter in skillet. Add cornstarch, paprika, and milk. Cook until it thickens. Add curry powder, white pepper, shrimp and lemon juice. Serve over rice. Serves 6.

Barbecued Pepper Shrimp

*50 medium size shrimp
  (unshelled and washed)*
OR
*30 jumbo shrimp (unshelled
  and washed)*
1 stick butter

2 tbsp salt
6 or 7 tbsp black pepper
2 tbsp soy sauce
*4 tbsp Lea & Perrins worcester-
  shire sauce*
juice of 2 lemons

Combine melted butter, salt, soy sauce, Lea & Perrins and lemon juice. Place shrimp in long, shallow baking dish or pan. Pour sauce over shrimp, then sprinkle black pepper over shrimp. Bake 20 minutes at 350° covered with aluminum foil; remove foil and bake 20 minutes more. Turn shrimp if desired and add more black pepper. Serve with a green salad and French bread. Messy, but good!

Beer Battered Fried Shrimp

24 medium to large shrimp
½ c flour
¾ c beer

2 tsp salt
*dash or red pepper OR ¼–½
  tsp black pepper*

Mix all ingredients together; add more beer if too thick, more flour if too thin (want the consistency that will adhere to shrimp). Wash and peel shrimp leaving tails on shrimp. Split shrimp to the tail and devein. Soak shrimp in milk for 1 hour. Dip shrimp in batter and fry in deep, hot fat. Eat immediately. Also, bell pepper rings and onion rings can be done in this batter. They are divine! Soak these in cold water before putting in batter to fry.

Deviled Crab

1 lb fresh crabmeat
1 onion, finely chopped
3 stalks celery, finely chopped
1 bell pepper, chopped finely
½ stick butter

2 pods garlic, crushed
1½ c cracker crumbs (fine)
2 tbsp parsley
2 tbsp Parmesan cheese
juice of 2 lemons

Saute: onion, celery, bell pepper, and garlic in a saucepan with butter. Simmer until tender (about 20 minutes). In a mixing bowl, put crabmeat and add cracker crumbs, parsley, and cheese. Mix and pour vegetables into crab mixture. Fold lightly together adding lemon juice. Fold again. Put into individual crab shells. Cook 15 minutes at 350° with a thin slice of lemon on each. Serves 8 and freezes well.

Trout La Marye
or
Trout Almondine

5 medium trout fillets
½ stick butter for frying fish
   (add more if necessary)
flour
salt
red pepper

1 lemon
1 package sliced almonds
½ stick butter for browning
   almonds
½ c Sauterne wine

Cover fillets with milk for about 20–30 minutes or longer. Heat ½ stick of butter in pan, do not burn. Remove fish from milk, flour and put into pan and fry to light golden brown. Do not over cook. Remove fish from pan and place on heated platter. Squeeze lemon and pour wine into pan and let cook for 3 or 4 minutes. Pour over fish, serve immediately.

Trout Almondine: Before frying fish, use another skillet and use ½ stick butter and brown lightly a package of slivered almonds. Remove from stove. After fish are cooked, pour almonds into frying pan. Pour Sauterne and squeeze lemon into pan. Cook 3 or 4 minutes and pour over fish. Serve immediately. Chopped parsley can also be added with the almonds for a wonderful taste addition.

Broiled Chicken

Salt and pepper both sides of chicken (split broilers) and rub with margarine and paprika. Broil in a 350° oven, meaty side down for 40 minutes. Turn over and cook 10 more minutes at 450°. Then pour ½ cup of vinegar or lemon juice over chicken and let it sit on 150° until ready to serve.

Chicken Picante

4 chicken breasts
⅓ c margarine
1 tbsp oil
4 shallots, chopped
1 pod garlic, crushed
parsley

2 lemons (juice)
Lawry's seasoned salt
paprika
pepper
flour

Remove bone from chicken breasts. Flatten with meat cleaver and cut into strips or smaller pieces. Season with Lawry's seasoned salt, paprika and pepper. Dust lightly with flour. Heat margarine and oil with chopped shallots and crushed garlic. Lightly saute chicken until golden brown, turn over and saute 3 minutes more. Remove chicken and add juice of lemons to sauce in skillet and boil 1 minute. Add chopped parsley and pour over chicken. Serve immediately. Serves 4.

Chubby's Barbecued Chicken Wings

24 chicken wings (or however many you wish)
2 sticks of butter
juice of 2 lemons
soy sauce

1 small bottle of Lea & Perrins worcestershire sauce
1 tsp salt
vinegar

Melt butter, lemon juice and Lea & Perrins for your sauce. Add soy sauce and vinegar. Make fire in round barbecue bucket with wadded-up newspaper. It will take several pieces of paper wadded tightly. Light fire and place chicken wings between a double-sided wire rack with a handle and clip that holds handle together. As you turn the wings from side to side, brush the sauce on each side as they cook. They will look almost burned, but they are so crispy and tasty. This is a "down South" way and so good!

To oven cook: Marinate all day in sauce. Place in shallow pan and broil *brown* at 500°. Turn and repeat. Reduce heat to 200° for 2 hours.

Chicken Wings with Rice

6 chicken wings
¼ c chopped celery
¼ c chopped bell pepper
1 onion, chopped fine

1 clove garlic, crushed
½ tsp black pepper
1 tsp salt
2 c water

Boil chicken wings with other ingredients until tender (about 30 minutes). When wings are almost done, add 1 cup of rice. Let rice cook until done. Serves 3.

Game Hens Pronto

6 Rock Cornish game hens
seasoned salt
seasoned pepper

lemon juice
parsley

Rub game hens inside and out with salt and pepper and lemon juice. Stuff with parsley. Cook breast side down for 50 minutes in a 500° oven. The last 10 minutes, turn them over to get the breast skin crunchy. Fast and delicious. You may pour 1 or 2 tablespoons of vinegar over birds after they are cooked and waiting to be served. Cover lightly if it will be awhile. Turn oven to 150° if they need to wait to be served. They will stay moist like this.

Wannie's Egg Noodles with Chicken

Boil a chicken until tender. Use the stock to cook noodles. Mix together:

2 eggs
2 tbsp milk

4 tbsp shortening or oil

Add enough flour to stiffen (about 2 cups). Salt and pepper to taste. Roll out on floured board. Cut into thin strips. Drop into boiling stock to which you have added ½ cup milk. Cook covered on medium heat about 20 minutes. Then add chunks of chicken to stock and noodles. Heat.

Dumplings for Chicken

1½ c flour
½ tsp salt
¼ c shortening

½ tsp baking powder
ice water

Sift all dry ingredients together, blend in shortening and add ice water and continue to blend until dough can be put on a board. Roll gently on floured board to pie crust thickness. Cut in strips or rounds and drop into boiling stock. Cook covered until done.

Chicken Willie

Stuff one whole fryer with 1 onion, 2 stalks of celery, salt and pepper. Cook until tender in 4 cups of water with giblets for flavor. Cool, debone and cut into chunks. Set aside.

Bring 4 cups of water and 1 teaspoon salt to a boil. Add 2 cups converted rice and cook for 15 minutes covered on high. Turn off, let set for 20 minutes. Cook 2 packages broccoli as directed on box and drain. Combine with rice.

In large bowl combine:

1½ c chopped onion
1½ c chopped celery
½ tsp white pepper
1 green fresh chili, chopped
4 slices jalapeno pepper
2 cans cream of mushroom soup
1 can cream of chicken soup

1¼ c sliced water chestnuts
few shakes Tabasco
1 c grated cheddar cheese
½ c grated cheddar cheese for
   topping chicken
rice and broccoli mixture

Put into 15″ × 10″ Pyrex. Cover with remaining cheese. Bake at 350° for 35–40 minutes. Serves 6 to 8.

Duck Delight

This recipe was completely originated by me and it removes all wild taste from birds.

1 stick butter
1 tbsp soy sauce OR Lea & Perrins
  worcestershire sauce
juice of 2 lemons

onion
apple
celery (leaves, too)

In a saucepan, melt first 3 ingredients. Stuff 6 ducks with slices of onion, apple and celery. Please put each bird in individual foil wrappers. Pour sauce on breast first, then turn bird over and baste again; leave breast down. Wrap tightly. Place in roaster on a rack. Cover and bake all afternoon (5–6 hours). Put a small amount of water in bottom of pan. Oven should be at 300°. Replace water if it cooks out. Juice will begin to flow from birds. About 1 hour before serving, open foil and turn breast side up. Remove lid and let birds get a crust on top. Serve with wild rice or rice pilaf. Gravy can be made from liquid in pan.

Willie's Dressing

Cook seasoned chicken or hen in 1½ quarts of water with celery leaves and chopped onions until tender. Remove hen. Let stock cool.

Make 1 9" pan of cornbread.

1 onion chopped fine
4 ribs of celery, chopped fine
1 garlic pod, crushed

1 fresh chili pepper, chopped fine
2 tsp salt
1 tbsp Lawry's seasoned pepper

Cook vegetables and seasonings in pan in ½ cup water until tender (about 20 minutes). Put cornbread, broken up and crumbled, in a mixing bowl with 4 slices white bread. Crumble breads together. Add 1½ cups of chicken broth (if you do not want to make fresh stock, you may use 2 cans of Campbell's chicken broth). Pour contents of pan into mixture. Mix well with a rotary beater. Add ¼ cup Mazola oil and 1 teaspoon cayenne pepper. Oil casserole dish, pour dressing into dish and bake at 350° for 45 minutes. Excellent stuffed in bird also.

Nanny's Meat Sauce for Spaghetti

2 lb ground round
4 tbsp Wesson Oil
1 c chopped onions (fine)
2 cloves of garlic (minced)
1½ tsp salt

1 tbsp ground oregano
½ tsp pepper
1 medium can of whole tomatoes
   (chopped fine)
1 medium can of tomato sauce

Brown the meat in the Wesson Oil. Add the next 2 ingredients and cook about 5 minutes, stirring often. Add the next 3 ingredients and stir. Now, add the tomatoes and the tomato sauce plus 2 cans of water. Bring all to a full boil. Turn heat immediately to simmer. Cover and cook slowly for 30 minutes. Stir occasionally. Cook thin spaghetti as directed on package. Before cooking, however, break spaghetti into small (about 2″) pieces. Drain and add to sauce.

Parker's Pound of Ground

This is my eleven year old son's recipe. All children seem to love it. He created it himself and cooks it often for his friends.

1 lb ground meat
Lawry's taco mix, small
   packet

Lawry's seasoned salt
Lea & Perrins worcestershire
   sauce

Put meat in skillet and sprinkle with seasoned salt, and seasoned pepper and a little "lean" Perrins. Let it cook awhile and add the packet of taco seasoning. Let it cook in the juice for awhile, then serve. Be sure to use Lawry's seasonings.

Meat Loaf

1 lb ground meat
1 whole onion, chopped fine
2½ slices white bread
1 8 oz can tomato sauce

½ tsp garlic salt
1 tsp fresh ground pepper
2 tbsp Parmesan cheese
⅓ c cheddar cheese, grated

Break meat into small pieces in a bowl. Take the 2½ slices of bread and run under faucet, soaking and then squeeze dry. Work into meat; add spices, grated cheese and ⅓ can of tomato sauce, reserving the rest for later. Form loaf. Put 1 can of water around loaf and cook fast at 375° for 30 minutes. Pour rest of tomato sauce over meat and cook slowly for 30 minutes more. Cover and let sit until ready to serve. Put cheddar cheese over top also, if you prefer.

Meatloaf Noodle Surprise

Prepare meatloaf as you desire. Onto a bed of cooked noodles, which have been drained and tossed with melted butter and green onions, place 2 tablespoons of cream cheese-sour cream mixture (you may omit the cream cheese if desired). Place a slice of meatloaf on top of this and top again with grated cheddar cheese. Spinach salad is delicious with this, as are small young peas.

Shish-ke-bob

1 c Mazola margarine
½ c lemon juice
½ c red wine
1 tsp Tabasco

1 tsp dry mustard
½ tsp thyme
2 bay leaves
2 tsp salt

Marinate beef cubes of your choice for 24 hours in the above mixture. Put on skewer with pearl onions, bell pepper slices and meat. Cook over coals on barbecue pit until done, turning often. This is also a good marinade for beef fondue.

Ginny's English Stew

2 lb stew meat
4 tbsp vegetable oil
1 tbsp minced onion (dried
    or fresh)
¼ c flour
3 c beef broth (MBT prime broth
    is very good)
¼ tsp thyme

1 tsp fine herbs (Spice Islands)
1 bay leaf
½ green pepper, cut into strips
¼ tsp pepper
½ tsp salt
1 tsp parsley
½ c Sauterne wine, or to taste

Season the stew meat with salt, pepper, Lawry's seasoned salt and garlic salt to taste. In Dutch oven or large stew pot, add oil and onion and brown with meat. Add flour and continue to brown over medium heat. Then add beef broth and bring to a boil. Cut heat back to simmer and add remaining seasonings. Cover and continue to simmer for 2 hours or longer until meat is very tender. After 1½ hours, if you like, add:

3 large carrots
4 potatoes, cut into thirds
small onions

fresh Kentucky Wonder beans,
    destringed

Cook until all vegetables are tender.

Beef Tender Supreme

1 beef tender: put into a long, shallow pan and marinate all day with:

½ c Berio olive oil OR Buttery
    Flavored Wesson Oil
1 tbsp paprika
Lawry's seasoned salt

4 tbsp Lea & Perrins
    worcestershire sauce
Lawry's seasoned pepper

Rub all of these ingredients into meat and pour ½ cup vinegar over all. Turn many times during the day and baste often. Cook at 450° for 1 hour, or put on smoker (*not* over coals) for 1½–2 hours in shallow pan.

Marinated Venison

Venison back strap steaks
1 c Wesson Oil
Lawry's seasoned salt
* and pepper*

Lawry's garlic salt
½ c vinegar
¼ c Lea & Perrins

Marinate steaks for at least 6 or 8 hours. Cook on charcoal broiler as you would any steak. No wild taste to this deer meat! Venison is always good if not cooked too done.

Barbequed Leg of Lamb

Cook 3 or 4 pound leg of lamb seasoned with seasoned salt and seasoned pepper, and paprika at 300° for 3 hours. You may stuff leg with fresh garlic slivers if you prefer—I do.

Sauce:

1 can Campbell's Tomato Soup
juice of 2 lemons

4 tbsp Hickory Smoked
* worcestershire sauce*

Combine and pour over lamb. Cook one more hour at 250°.

Lamb Shanks

5 or 6 lamb shanks
Lawry's seasoned salt

Lawry's seasoned pepper
soy sauce

Season each lamb shank, stuff with garlic, and cover with soy sauce. Wrap all in foil. Cook in a 200° oven for 2½ hours (very slowly). Serve with curried rice and small LeSueur peas. Serves 4.

Sauerkraut & Franks

4 beef knockwurst
1 #2 can of sauerkraut
2 tbsp chopped onion

1 tsp caraway seed
1 tsp cracked pepper

Drain sauerkraut. Add onion and seeds and saute in teflon skillet for 5 minutes. Add frankfurters and cover. Simmer for 30 minutes on low heat. Serves 4.

Pork Oriental

1 lb lean, boneless pork shoulder,
  cut into strips
2 tbsp cornstarch
2 tbsp soy sauce
⅛ tsp garlic powder
4 tbsp salad oil
¾ c whole, blanched almonds
1 c chicken broth

1 large onion, sliced thin
1 8 oz can water chestnuts,
  drained and sliced
1 6 oz package frozen snow peas,
  thawed
½ tsp Beau Monde seasoning
3 c of hot, cooked rice

In a bowl, combine pork shoulder strips and marinade of cornstarch, soy sauce and garlic powder. Let stand at room temperature for 20 minutes, stirring occasionally. Heat 1 tablespoon oil in a large skillet, add almonds and brown on medium heat, stirring constantly for about 2 minutes. Remove almonds and reserve. Heat remaining 3 tablespoons oil in the same skillet and add pork, marinade and onions. Fry, stirring constantly, over medium high heat for 5 minutes or until pork is done. Stir in almonds, water chestnuts, snow peas, chicken broth and the Beau Monde. Cook, stirring constantly until thickened. Serve over rice. Serves 4–6.

Oven Baked Pork Chops

6 pork chops
salt to taste

pepper to taste
cracker crumbs or flour

Flour both sides lightly or roll in fine cracker crumbs. Put in shallow pan with sides and place in oven to bake at 350° for 35 minutes or until golden brown.

Super Steak Sauce

Cover bottom of saucepan with vinegar. Add:

2 or 3 tbsp garlic salt, onion salt
  or crushed garlic

¼ stick margarine
½ c Lea & Perrins

Bring to a boil. Remove from heat and baste meat. Delicious!

Barbecue Sauce

½ c vinegar
1 c Wesson Oil or ½ lb of butter
1 bottle catsup
½ c water
2¼ c chili sauce (optional)
1 tsp salt
¼ tsp chili powder
3 tbsp worcestershire sauce

1 tbsp sugar
1 tbsp mustard
dash of cayenne pepper
dash of black pepper
dash of Tabasco or hot sauce
1 medium onion
1 clove garlic

Combine all ingredients and cook 30 minutes.

Soul Food

I love soul food! These are some of the recipes I have created myself and some I got from two wonderful cooks, Hattie Mae Porter and Willie Dean Harris. These are some recipes their families cooked when they were "down home" as children. They are *low calorie* and very delectable. If you love fresh vegetables, these are out of this world!

Cabbage & Field Peas

field peas (1 box)
small cabbage
1 sliced onion
juice of 1 lemon

2 tbsp margarine or butter
cracked pepper
1 c water, salted

Cook peas (frozen is fine) in salted water for 15 minutes. Shred cabbage and add to peas with the sliced onion laid on top of cabbage. Add margarine and let cook until peas and cabbage are crunchy (about 15 minutes longer). Squeeze the juice of 1 lemon and add cracked pepper to taste (I sometimes like to add a dash of vinegar in mine).

Black-Eyed Peas with Rice
(leftover idea)

bell pepper
2 slices bacon
¾ c chopped onions
¾ c chopped green onions

3 c cooked rice
1 tsp salt
1 large tomato, chopped
3 c cooked black-eyed peas

Fry bacon until crisp. Remove from grease and drain. Saute onions and a bell pepper in bacon drippings until tender. Stir in rice and salt. Heat thoroughly. Add tomatoes and bacon (crumbled). Toss together. Spoon rice mixture onto plates and top with peas. Serves 6.

Slang-Jang

1 package frozen or fresh black-
   eyed peas or field peas
1 c chopped fresh tomatoes
1 c chopped onions

1 c chopped bell pepper (fine)
1 hot fresh green chile
   chopped fine
cider vinegar

Cook peas as desired. Marinate vegetable mixture in cider vinegar. Season with Lawry's seasoned pepper. When peas are cooked, serve on plate, drained. Cover serving of peas with 1 or 2 tablespoons of salad mixture. Delicious!

Okra & Field Peas

field peas (1 box)
1 chopped onion
1 c of water
seasoned salt

seasoned pepper
fresh okra, (½ lb)
2 tbsp margarine
1 tbsp vinegar

Cook peas with chopped onion in 1 cup of water seasoned with seasoned salt and pepper. Cook 15 minutes. Cut fresh okra pods in half. Add okra, vinegar and margarine. Cook until okra is crunchy, about 15 minutes more. If you like your vegetables softer, cook a little longer.

Okra, Corn & Tomatoes

1 large can of tomatoes
2 lb okra (cut)
5 ears fresh corn, cut off the cob
1 clove garlic

1 large onion, chopped fine
1 bay leaf
salt to taste
pepper to taste

Place all ingredients in saucepan and cook on low heat until tender. So good!

Low Calorie Vegetable Snacks

Cucumber in Dill

Slice cucumbers thin and put in a dish. Cover with apple cider or white wine tarragon vinegar and add paprika and ½ teaspoon dill seed or seasoning. Cover and refrigerate. Thin sliced onion may be added to this.

Yellow Squash with Cloves

Cut squash into thin slices, about ¼" thick. Parboil 5 minutes. Drain. Marinate with cider vinegar and whole cloves and paprika.

Cauliflower Buds

Boil 1 cauliflower only a few minutes until it turns white and slightly tender. Drain and separate buds. Cover immediately with 1 cup cider vinegar, whole cloves and paprika and marinate in a covered dish for several days. Great for snacking between meals and wonderful added to salads.

Marinated Beets

Cook fresh beets until done. Drain. Slice in ¼" circles, put in a container and cover with vinegar and 2 tablespoons sugar. Cover and refrigerate as long as you wish. (I prefer no sugar, but some will consider this too sour, so sugar to taste. Sweet & Low may also be used.)

Fresh Cream Corn

5 ears of corn
salt to taste
pepper to taste
1 c of water

2 tbsp of flour or cornstarch
3 tbsp butter
1 tsp sugar

Cut corn off the cob and scrape milk from the ears. Place in skillet with all other ingredients and cook on medium heat until thick, about 30 minutes. Serves 4–6.

Stuffed Squash

6 or 8 yellow squash
2 tbsp margarine or butter
salt to taste

pepper to taste
½ onion, finely chopped
4 tbsp cracker crumbs

Cut both ends off of squash and slice in half. Parboil halves inside down 12–15 minutes in salted water. When tender, drain and remove pulp with spoon. Reserve. In a skillet, saute onions and parsley in margarine, salt and pepper to taste. Cook until tender. Add pulp and 3 tablespoons cracker crumbs and mash well. Put back into shells and sprinkle with cracker crumbs. Bake at 350° until brown. If you have leftover cornbread, use in place of cracker crumbs—delicious!

Hot German Cole Slaw

1 head red or white cabbage
2 tbsp finely chopped onion
¼ c cider vinegar

3 tbsp chopped parsley
2 tbsp vegetable salad oil
cracked pepper

Shred cabbage as fine as possible. Cover with boiling water for 5 minutes. Drain dry. Add rest of ingredients and toss lightly. Serve warm.

Ava's Marinated Carrots

2 lb carrots, sliced round
1 medium sweet onion
1 small sweet pepper
1 c water
1 c vinegar
1¼ c sugar

1 c oil
1 tsp prepared mustard
1 tsp worcestershire sauce
1 tsp salt
1 tsp pepper

Cook carrots & cool. Cut onion & green pepper into round slices. Mix with carrots. Mix remaining marinade ingredients & pour over vegetables. Place in sealed jar or covered container for 12 hours or more. Drain & serve. Will keep 2–3 weeks in refrigerator.

Brussel Sprouts

1 box frozen or 1 box fresh
   brussel sprouts
½ c water
4 slices jalapeno pepper

1 tbsp butter
salt and pepper to taste
1 tbsp vinegar
¼ c chopped onion

Cook 7 minutes or until crunchy. Do not overcook.

Eggplant Mozzarella

1½ lb eggplant, cut into ¼"
   thick slices
1 c dry bread crumbs

freshly grated Parmesan cheese
1–2 eggs, beaten
olive or vegetable oil

If desired, eggplant may be pared. Season each piece with Lawry's seasoned salt and Lawry's seasoned pepper. Mix bread crumbs with desired amount of Parmesan cheese. Dip eggplant slices into eggs, then coat with crumb mixture. Fry several slices at a time in mixture of half olive oil and half vegetable oil until lightly browned. Add oil as needed. Drain on paper towels. Place each slice on a cookie sheet and cover with 1 slice Mozzarella cheese. When ready to serve, sprinkle lightly with black pepper and put into oven at 350° and heat until cheese melts.

Eggplant Parmesan

Follow preceding recipe until you drain on paper towels. Then you need:

1 lb ground beef
salt and pepper to taste
garlic salt to taste
2 tbsp oregano

3 small cans tomato sauce
½ lb Mozzarella cheese, thinly
   sliced or grated

Preheat oven to 350°. Do eggplant as directed in previous recipe (Eggplant Mozzarella). Saute ground meat in a skillet until brown. Stir in seasonings and simmer sauce for 10 minutes. Alternate layers of eggplant, Parmesan cheese, sauce and Mozzarella in a 13 × 9 × 2 (or other large) baking dish. Bake, uncovered, in a preheated oven for 30 minutes or until sauce is bubbly and cheese is melted. Serves 4–6.

Chili Beans

1 can Ranch beans
1 can Wolf brand chili with beans
½ onion, chopped fine

1 tsp Lea & Perrins
2 tsp French's mustard
½ c grated sharp cheddar cheese

Mix all together except cheese. Cook 30 minutes at 300°. Top with grated cheese, cook until cheese has melted. Wonderful with barbecue beef or chicken or ham.

Rice Pilaf

1 can Campbell's Beef
   Consomme or Broth
½ c chopped onion
½ c chopped green bell pepper

3 tbsp butter or margarine
1 c rice
1 c water
paprika

Saute onion and pepper in ½ of butter. Braise rice in other ½ of butter with paprika. When rice turns light brown, pour into casserole and add broth, water and cooked onion mixture. Bake at 350° for 1 hour. The last 15 minutes of cooking, you may add 1 small can of drained tiny Leseur green peas. It makes a good accompaniment to lamb, beef or chicken. If you have a chicken dish, use chicken broth for consomme.

Au Gratin Potatoes

6 medium potatoes
1 ½ c cheddar cheese, grated
2 c milk
4 tbsp cornstarch
½ tsp salt

2 dashes Tabasco
¼ tsp white pepper
¼ tsp cayenne pepper
1 tsp paprika
½ stick margarine or butter

Peel and slice potatoes ¼" thick. Boil in 4 cups of salted water. Cook 6 minutes only. Drain. Put aside. Melt butter and add cornstarch until it bubbles. Add paprika, salt and white pepper. Gradually add milk and stir constantly until thick. Remove from stove and add your grated cheese. Add 2 dashes of Tabasco and cayenne pepper. Into oblong pyrex casserole, place drained, sliced potatoes evenly. Pour sauce on top. Cover with more grated cheese and cook at 350° for 20 minutes, or until it bubbles. Can be frozen. Serves 10 to 12.

Quick Oven Rice

1 c rice
2 c boiling water
1 stick Oleo

1 bouillon cube dissolved
into boiling water

Combine all. Place in covered dish and cook in oven at 350° for 45 minutes. Parsley chopped fine is delicious added to this.

Cheese Souffle
(for two)

2 tbsp of whipped margarine
3 tbsp cornstarch
1 c hot skim milk
¼ tsp white pepper

3 drops Tabasco
1 tsp prepared mustard
1 c grated cheddar cheese
3 eggs, separated

Melt margarine, add cornstarch and cook until bubbly. Add hot skim milk and seasonings. Bring to a boil, stirring constantly. Boil 1 minute—COUNT IT! (Keep stirring.) Remove and slightly cool. Add cheese and egg yolks which have been beaten until thick. Cool and fold in stiffly beaten egg whites. Pour into a small, slightly greased souffle dish. Bake at 300° until a knife inserted into center comes out clean. When you cook your souffle, place your souffle dish in shallow pan of water. Serve with chopped up vegetable salad.

Risotto Francesca

3 tbsp butter
1 c chopped leeks or onions
3 c chicken stock or broth
juice of ½ lemon

1 c Arborio Italian Rice
1 c grated Parmesan cheese
paprika

In 10″ skillet, melt butter. Add onion and lemon juice and saute until tender. Add rice and braise on medium heat for 3 minutes, stirring constantly. Add few shakes paprika. Add 2 c stock, stir and cover tightly for 15 minutes. Add remaining cup of stock and cook 5 minutes or until broth absorbs. Remove from heat, stir in cheese with 1 tablespoon butter. Serve immediately.

Willie's Sweet Potatoes

4 medium sweet potatoes
1 c sugar
1 tsp cinnamon
1 tsp vanilla

½ stick butter
¼ c sour cream
1 small can crushed pineapple

Peel and boil potatoes. Cook until tender and drain. Place potatoes in bowl and whip. Add all ingredients and mix. Put in casserole and top with marshmallows. Bake at 300° until bubbly and slightly brown.

Fried Garlic Bread

1 loaf French bread (I like
   San Francisco)
1 jar Lawry's Garlic Butter Spread
chopped parsley

1 stick margarine or butter
Lea & Perrins to taste
   (about ¼ c)

Slice bread about 1" thick. Melt other ingredients in iron skillet. Mix well and simmer a few minutes. Then dip each side of bread in mixture and place on a cookie sheet. Cover with foil until ready to serve. At the last minute, place, uncovered, in a 400–450° oven until brown on top. Flip over and brown on the other side. A real treat with gumbo or Italian dishes.

Annette's Cheesebread

2½ c margarine or butter
½ tsp poppy seed
1 tsp dry mustard
1 lb Kraft Swiss cheese slices, long
   (each slice quartered)

1 tsp oregano
1 tsp basil
1 loaf french bread
Parmesan cheese

Slice bread. Melt butter and add seasoning. Paint each side all through loaf with mixture. Place 2 slices of cheese between each slice of bread. Paint top with remaining butter. Sprinkle with Parmesan cheese. Wrap in heavy duty foil and bake for 30–40 minutes at 350°.

Banana Bread

2 tsp baking powder
¼ tsp soda
1 tsp salt
2 c flour
½ c shortening

⅔ c sugar
2 eggs
3 ripe bananas, mashed
1 tsp vanilla
1 tbsp lemon juice

Sift baking powder, soda, salt, and flour together. Set aside. Cream shortening and sugar and add eggs one at a time. Beat after each egg is added. Stir in bananas, lemon juice and vanilla. Add flour mixture slowly, beating thoroughly. Pour batter into greased loaf pan. Bake at 350° for 50 minutes. Makes 2 small loaves or 1 large loaf.

Hot Water Corn Pones

1 c of yellow or white cornmeal
½ tsp salt

¼ c flour
1 tsp sugar

Pour boiling water over all ingredients until good consistency to shape into pones. Fry in deep fat until golden brown. Drain on paper towels. Eat hot.

Maude's Ice Box Rolls

1 c sugar
3 packages yeast
4 c flour
½ c instant potatoes
2 eggs

1 tsp salt
½ c Crisco
⅔ c hot water
1 c lukewarm water

Dissolve yeast in lukewarm water. Dissolve Crisco in hot water and sugar then add salt and flour to sugar. Let hot water cool before adding yeast and water. Let rise about 30 minutes. Work out on a floured board and let rise again for about 30 minutes. Roll out and make in shape of Parker House or clover leaf rolls and brush with melted butter or Crisco. You can put the dough in the refrigerator covered and take out and use as needed. It will take longer for them to rise since they will be cold. When you take dough out, knead a bit before you roll them out.

Hattie's Bread

8–9 c all-purpose flour
1 c sugar
1 tsp salt
1½ c milk

3 packages active dry yeast
1 c butter or margarine
2 eggs

About 4½ hours before serving:

1. In large bowl, combine 2 cups flour, sugar, salt and yeast. In medium saucepan over low heat, heat milk, ½ cup water and butter or margarine until very warm (120° to 130° F). Butter or margarine does not need to melt.

2. With mixer at low speed, gradually pour liquid into dry ingredients. Increase speed to medium; beat 2 minutes, occasionally scraping bowl with rubber spatula. Beat in eggs and 2 cups flour; continue beating 2 minutes. With spoon, stir in enough additional flour (about 4½ cups) to make a soft dough.

3. Turn dough onto lightly floured surface and knead until smooth and elastic, about 10 minutes. Shape dough into ball and place in greased large bowl, turning over so that top of dough is greased. Cover with towel; let rise in warm place (80° to 85° F), away from draft, until doubled, about 1 hour.

4. Punch down dough. Turn dough onto lightly floured surface; cut dough into thirds or halves, as directed in recipe, cover with towel for 15 minutes. This makes cinnamon-nut bread, cinnamon rolls or any bread you need.

There is nothing to compare to the smell of homebaked bread in the oven especially on a cold wintry day. It makes the spirits soar to accomplish the feat of this endeavor! Eat it right out of the oven.

Biscuits

2 c sifted flour   3 tsp baking powder
⅓ c Crisco   ¾ c milk
1 tsp salt

Cut shortening into flour mixture until it looks like cornmeal. Add cold milk and stir until you form a soft dough ball. Turn onto a floured surface. Knead dough until dough hangs together well. Roll out and fold over and roll again. Cut with a biscuit cutter and bake on a greased cookie sheet or cake pan in a 425° oven for 12–15 minutes. Makes 16 biscuits.

Bananas Foster

4 bananas, sliced lengthwise   1 orange
⅓ c butter   1 ½ jiggers Cointreau or Triple Sec
⅓ c brown sugar   1 jigger Brandy
1 lemon   vanilla ice cream, already
1 orange   scooped and frozen in
⅛ tsp cinnamon   dishes in freezer

In skillet, melt butter and sugar until slightly bubbly. Add cinnamon, juice of orange and lemon. Stir until good and hot. Add Cointreau, then add bananas and stir gently only until bananas are hot. Then add Brandy and stir until bubbly to cook off the alcohol; *do not stir* if you light the Brandy with a match. Remove from fire and let cool few minutes. Pour over vanilla ice cream.

Easy Peach Ice Cream

4 c mashed fresh peaches   juice of 2 lemons
¼ c sugar

Mash peaches with sugar and lemon juice—set aside.

1½ c sugar
6 eggs
¼ tsp salt
1 can Pet Evaporated Milk
   (large size)

2½ pints whipping cream
2 tsp vanilla
2 tsp almond extract
milk to within 1″ of top of can
   (ice cream freezer)

Mix sugar, eggs, vanilla, small amount of evaporated milk; pour into can. Add other ingredients. Add almond extract last. Freeze. Remove dasher immediately and put back into freezer. Ice cream stays smooth and soft. Delicious!

Old Fashioned Ice Cream

6 eggs, beaten well
2 c sugar
2 c milk

2 tsp vanilla
3 tbsp cornstarch or flour
1½ pints whipping cream

Combine 2 cups milk, 1½ cups sugar and cornstarch and bring to a bare boil. Remove from heat and cool. Beat eggs well with ½ cup sugar. Pour milk mixture over eggs, mix well. Add whipping cream and vanilla. Freeze. Makes 2 quarts.

Hot Apricot Whip

1 c diced apricots
juice of 1 lemon
4 egg whites

sugar to taste (Sweet & Low
   may be used for low calorie)

Cover apricots with water. Add lemon juice and simmer until soft. Mash apricots. Sweeten to your taste. Fold into beaten stiff egg whites. Pile into a dish slightly buttered and bake at 350° for 30 minutes. If you would like it cold (and I love it) just simply fold into egg whites and refrigerate. Add 1 teaspoon vanilla. Prunes may also be substituted for apricots for delicious prune whip.

Orange Sorbet

¼ c sugar
1 c fresh peaches, mashed

1 c frozen or fresh orange juice
juice of 2 lemons

Mash peaches with sugar with a potato masher. Add orange juice and lemon juice. Put in ice trays until frozen around the edges. Remove from trays and put in mixing bowl and beat at medium speed until smooth. Put back into trays and freeze. Cut into slices. Delicious for dessert or salad. Wonderful for children's snacks!

Strawberry Ice

2 quarts fresh strawberries
1 c honey

3 tbsp lemon juice
1 c cold water

Pour honey over hulled and washed berries. Mash and let stand 30 minutes. Put in blender or force through a sieve. Add water and lemon juice. Freeze in trays.

Quick Orange Ice

1 can frozen orange juice

3 cans crushed ice

Put into blender frozen orange juice concentrate. Add 3 cans of crushed ice and whip. Put into ice tray. When a little frozen, take out of ice tray and put into a bowl and re-whip in blender. Refreeze and serve. This recipe was created for an ailing Mom by her ten year old son. It is a superb dessert, breakfast drink or pick-me-up when well or sick!

Leslie's Cheese Cake

1½ c Graham Cracker crumbs
3 tbsp butter
2 tbsp sugar
1 lb cream cheese
½ c sugar
½ tsp vanilla

Rind of 1 lemon
1 tbsp lemon juice
2 eggs, separated
1 c thick sour cream
1 tbsp sugar
½ tsp vanilla

Blend the crumbs with melted butter and 2 tablespoons sugar. Press into bottom and sides of 8" spring form pan. Place in 250° oven to set the crust. Cool. Warm the cream cheese to room temperature. Beat until soft. Blend the sugar and lemon juice, rind and vanilla. Drop in the egg yolks one at a time and beat well. Beat the egg whites until stiff and fold into mixture with a spatula. Pour over crumb base and bake for 45 minutes at 300°. Mix one tablespoon sugar and the vanilla into sour cream. Spread lightly over the top of cake and return it to oven for 10 minutes more.

Old Time Cake with Pineapple Glaze

½ c butter
1½ c sugar
1 c milk
2¾ c flour

½ tsp salt
3 tsp baking powder
4 egg whites
1 tsp vanilla

Blend shortening, sugar, salt and vanilla until fluffy. Sift together dry ingredients and add to creamed mixture alternately with milk. Add well beaten egg whites and divide equally into 2 layer cake pans and bake at 350° until done.

Pineapple Filling

2 tbsp cornstarch
½ c sugar

2 c crushed pineapple

Mix the cornstarch and the sugar. Add pineapple. Cook slowly until thickened. Put between layers and ice with Ginny's fluffy white icing or double filling recipe.

Fluffy White Boiled Icing

In double boiler top:

2 egg whites　　　　　　　　　*⅛ tsp salt (pinch)*
⅓ c white corn syrup　　　　　*1 tbsp hot water*
¾ c sugar　　　　　　　　　　*1 tsp vanilla or almond extract*
¼ tsp cream of tartar

Put ingredients over boiling water and beat immediately for about 4–5 minutes or until icing forms firm peaks. Remove pan from boiling water and add vanilla. Beat a few minutes more. Ice.

Hershey Chocolate Cake

Mix together and cream:

½ lb butter　　　　　　　　　*2 c sugar*

Add:

8 melted Hershey bars　　　　*1 c buttermilk*
4 eggs　　　　　　　　　　　*2½ c flour*
1 tsp soda　　　　　　　　　*3 tsp vanilla*

Bake in a 9″ × 12″ pan at 325° for 1 hour.

Gertie's Pound Cake

3 sticks of butter (softened)　*3 c flour*
3 c sugar　　　　　　　　　　*1 tbsp vanilla*
5 eggs　　　　　　　　　　　*1 c milk*

Cream your butter and sugar together well until fluffy. Add eggs, 1 at a time. Beat after each egg. Add milk and beat again. Add sifted flour, 1 cup

at a time until all is used and well blended. Add vanilla. (The secret of this cake is the beating!) Pour into a greased and floured tube or bundt pan. Cook 1 hour in a 350° oven or until done. Let cool for a little while before turning out of pan. Ice with confectioners sugar beaten with milk or lemon juice until desired consistency. Dribble over top and let harden.

Pecan Pie

1 c sugar
1 stick butter (¼ lb)
1 c light corn syrup
¼ tsp salt

3 eggs
1 c pecans
1 unbaked 9" pie shell

Cream sugar and butter together until smooth. Add syrup and salt, beat well. Beat in eggs, 1 at a time. Add chopped pecans. Pour into pastry-lined pie pan. Bake in 350° oven about 1 hour and 10 minutes, or until knife comes out clean when inserted in pie. Cool and serve plain or with whipped cream.

Julia's Soda Cracker Pie

16 crackers (crushed fine)
3 egg whites, beaten until frothy
    with
¼ tsp cream of tartar

1 tsp vanilla
1 c chopped pecans
1 c sugar

Add sugar gradually as you beat egg whites stiff. Fold in crackers and nuts and vanilla. Cook in buttered pie pan at 325° for 40 minutes. Cool. Top with ½ pint of beaten whipping cream combined with 1 package of thawed and drained frozen strawberries.

Fluffy Lemon Icebox Pie

1 can Eagle Brand Sweetened
   Condensed Milk
1¼ c graham cracker crumbs
1 tsp evaporated milk
¼ c sugar

⅓ c butter or margarine
3 eggs, separated
½ c fresh lemon juice
1 tbsp grated lemon rind

Beat egg yolks until fluffy. Add to condensed milk and slowly stir in lemon juice and rind. Fold in egg whites stiffly beaten. Pour into graham cracker crust. Refrigerate 2 or 3 hours. Sprinkle a few crumbs over pie.

Crust: Mix crumbs with 1 teaspoon of condensed milk, ¼ cup sugar, and butter until well blended. Press into bottom and sides of ungreased 9″ pie pan (preferably pyrex). Bake at 400° for 10 minutes. Let cool.

Apple Pie in Paper Bag

1 unbaked 9″ pastry shell
2½ lb good baking apples (Green
   Granny Smith's are good)
¾ c sugar (for filling)
½ tsp cinnamon
2 tbsp flour (for filling)

½ tsp apple pie spice
2 tbsp lemon juice
½ c sugar (for topping)
½ c flour (for topping)
1 stick butter or margarine (¼ lb)

Pare, core and quarter the apples and slice or cut into chunks, about 7½ cups of apples. Place into large bowl. Combine ¾ cup sugar, 2 tablespoons flour and spices; add to apples and mix well. Pour into pastry shell and sprinkle with lemon juice. Combine ½ cup sugar, ½ cup flour and butter. Work into crumbs with fingers. Sprinkle mixture over apples. Pie will be high. Slide pie into a *heavy* brown bag large enough to cover pie loosely. Fold end over and fasten with paper clips. Heat oven to 400°, bake pie for 1 hour and 15 minutes. Check to be sure bag does not get too hot; it shouldn't unless oven temperature is not adjusted properly. Remove pie from oven, slit bag open with scissors, take pie out and cool on a rack. Serve plain or with ice cream or cheese. This is delicious and juice will not be in your oven—"It's in the bag!"

Duncan-Crocker Brownies

*1 Duncan Hines Family Size
    Brownie Mix*
1 tbsp vanilla

*1 Betty Crocker Chocolate Fudge
    Frosting Mix*

Prepare your brownie mix as directed on package, but only cook for 25 minutes. Remove from oven and while hot, ice with frosting mix, prepared as directed on package. Add vanilla. Spread icing on warm brownies and it glazes and hardens. Delicious for people in a hurry. So easy to prepare and quite a treat, I've been told.

Chocolate Cookie Parker

*1 box Famous Nabisco
    Chocolate Wafers*
½ pint of whipping cream

1 tbsp sugar
1 tsp vanilla
1 jar Kraft Hot Fudge Sauce

Whip your cream, adding sugar and vanilla. Beat until it forms stiff peaks. Place 1 cookie on plate with 1 heaping tablespoon of cream. Press on another cookie, repeat cream, then cookie—top with cream again. Make stacks until all cookies and cream are used. Refrigerate. Heat fudge sauce when ready to serve. Cover each cookie tower with hot fudge sauce. Serve. Makes 10. Everyone loves this!

Mincemeat Cookies

1 c vegetable shortening
3 eggs, well beaten
4 c (approximately) enriched
*   flour*
1 c prepared mincemeat, or 1 box
2 c sugar

1 tsp salt
1 tsp baking soda
⅛ tsp ginger
1 tsp ground cloves
1 tsp nutmeg
½ tsp salt

Cream shortening and sugar. Add well beaten eggs along with enough flour to avoid curdling. Mix well and add mincemeat. Sift remaining flour with dry ingredients and add flour a little at a time until dough is the consistency of rolled dough. Drop by teaspoons onto a greased cookie sheet and bake at 375° for 12 minutes. Makes about 100 2″ cookies. You may add nuts, if desired, or chopped candied cherries. They are crisp when first baked, and become chewy in a tight container.

Chubby's Pralines

1 c milk
2 c sugar
½ tsp salt

1 tbsp vanilla
¼ stick butter
½–1 c pecans, chopped

Bring sugar and milk to a boil; boil on medium heat, stirring occasionally, until mixture forms a hard ball in a cup of cold water. Remove from heat and add salt, butter and vanilla and beat until it becomes white and creamy. Add pecans. When it looks thick enough to turn hard, pour out in spoonfuls on waxed paper. This was my father's old Louisiana praline recipe. It is the best candy you will ever eat!

Glenda's Spicy Butter Thins

⅔ c butterscotch chips
½ c butter
¾ c flour
¼ c sugar
1 tsp cinnamon

1 tsp coffee (instant)
1 tsp ginger
1 egg
½ c chopped pecans
⅓ c butterscotch chips

Preheat oven to 300°. Grease 15″ × 10″ pan. Melt butter and ⅔ cup chips over low heat. Add flour, sugar, cinnamon, coffee, ginger and egg. Mix well. Pour into greased pan. Sprinkle with pecans and ⅓ cup chips. Bake at 300° for 20 minutes.

Almond Lace Cookies

⅔ c blanched almonds,
    finely ground
½ c sugar

½ c butter or margarine
1 tbsp all-purpose flour
2 tbsp milk

About 1½ hours before serving or up to 1 week ahead:

Preheat oven to 350°. Grease large cookie sheet. Into 10″ skillet, measure all ingredients. Cook over low heat, stirring, until butter or margarine is melted and mixture is blended. Keep mixture very warm over very low heat. Drop 4 heaping teaspoonfuls, about 2 inches apart, onto cookie sheet. (Do not place more than 4 on cookie sheet, because after baking they must be shaped quickly before hardening.) Bake 5 minutes or until golden. Remove cookie sheet from oven and, with pancake turner, quickly loosen and turn cookies over, one by one, and roll around handle of wooden spoon. (If cookies get too hard to roll, reheat in oven a minute to soften.) Cool on wire racks. Repeat until all batter is used, greasing cookie sheet each time. Store in covered container. Makes about 2½ dozen.

FASHION

Bloody Marys
(1 gallon)

12 oz lemon juice
10 dashes of Lea & Perrins
1 fifth Vodka

5 pints of V-8 tomato juice or
   Snappy Tom
salt
pepper

Add all the ingredients and chill. To serve, pour over ice to which you have added 10–12 good dashes of Tabasco. Slices of lemon to garnish.

Orange Juice Delight

1 can frozen orange juice
3 cans of water

1 scoop of ice
1 tbsp of honey

Pour orange juice in blender and add water and 1 scoop of ice and honey. Blend for 1 minute or until all ice is crushed into fine pieces. Orange may be substituted with lemonade, limeade or any other frozen juice. Serves 6 to 8.

Vodka Cooler

1 jigger of Rose's lime
   juice
1 jigger of Vodka

fill remainder of glass with Fresca
   or Sprite
lime wedge

Fill glass with crushed ice. Squeeze ¼ lime over it, then add all ingredients and stir.

Welu's Special Manhattan Cocktail

1 oz Grenadine
4 oz Southern Comfort
4 oz straight bourbon (no blend)

8 oz Martini & Rossi Sweet
Vermouth

Add all ingredients. This will make 1 pint. If you double this recipe you will make 1 quart.

Artichokes with Caper Sauce

4 artichokes
salt

pepper
6 tbsp olive oil

Put enough water into a pan to cover half of the artichokes. Salt and pepper thoroughly and pour 6 tablespoons of olive oil into the water. Bring to a boil and boil for 30–35 minutes. Remove from pan and turn upside down on paper towel and drain at least 15 minutes. Cool.

Sauce:

1 c of Hellmann's mayonnaise
¼ c lemon juice

½ bottle capers, mashed
salt and pepper

Mix thoroughly and dip artichokes into sauce, Absolutely delicious!

Artichoke Pie

2 cans drained artichoke hearts
1 lb Swiss cheese
6 eggs, beaten well

salt
pepper

Line bottom of 9" × 12" pan with artichokes cut up. Grate 1 lb of Swiss cheese and beat 6 eggs well. Mix together and pour over artichokes. Salt and pepper. Bake at 350° for 30 minutes or until brown and bubbly. Cut into squares and serve. Serves 8 to 10.

Betty's Hot Artichoke Dip

3 (8½ oz) cans artichokes in
   water (drained)

2 c mayonnaise
1 c Parmesan cheese

Chop artichoke hearts. Add mayonnaise and cheese. Bake in oven heated at 350° until bubbly. Serve with melba toast rounds. Serves 20.

Avocado-Crab Dip

1 large avocado
1 tbsp lemon juice
1 tsp worcestershire sauce
1 (8 oz) package cream cheese
dash of hot sauce
1 tbsp grated onion

¼ tsp salt
pepper
1 can of lump crabmeat
   (fresh if possible)
¼ c dairy sour cream

In blender, or by hand mixer, combine avocado, lemon juice, onion and worcestershire sauce. Blend until smooth. Add cream cheese, sour cream, salt and blend until smooth. Stir in crabmeat, chill and serve on assorted crackers. Great for parties.

Chili Dip

1 (1 lb 8 oz) can of chili
   without beans
1 (2 lb) box of Velveeta cheese
2 jalapenos (chopped)

juice of jalapeno peppers
   (to taste)
garlic salt

Put chili in pan. Add cheese and cook until all is melted. Add peppers, juice and garlic salt. Serve in chafing dish. Good for a group.

Olive Cheese Balls

8 oz crock of cheese
½ c of soft butter
1 c of sifted all-purpose flour

½ tsp salt
1 tsp pepper
48 large stuffed olives

Blend cheese with butter. Stir in flour, salt, pepper and mix well. Wrap 1 teaspoon of mixture around each olive covering completely. Arrange on a baking sheet or a flat pan and freeze. After frozen, place the olives into a zip-lock bag. When ready to use, bake 15 minutes at 400° or just bake after being completed. Makes 4 dozen.

Sour Cream Stuffed Eggs

12 hard cooked eggs
1 3 oz package cream cheese,
softened
½ c sour cream

½ tsp dill weed
1 tbsp capers
10 bacon slices, diced and
cooked crisp

Shell eggs and cut into halves lengthwise, Remove egg yolk, place in bowl, mash with fork and set aside. Beat cream cheese until fluffy, blend in mashed egg yolks, sour cream, dill, capers and bacon. Generously fill egg whites with mixture and chill overnight.

Cream Cheese Hors d'Oeuvre

1 (8 oz) package cream cheese

Cover cream cheese with any one of these:

Pick-a-Pepper sauce
jalapeno jelly

Chutney and add chopped green
onions or chives

Serve on melba rounds. A great snack everyone enjoys! Serves 8 or more.

Jalapeno Pie

2 or 3 jalapeno peppers
  (chopped)

6 eggs, beaten well
1 lb sharp cheese, grated

Mix all ingredients and pour into ungreased pan, 8½" × 11" or smaller. Cook at 350° for 30 minutes. Cut and serve warm. Serves 6.

Sausage Rounds

1 (1 lb) round of Owen's
  Hot Sausage (uncooked)
1 tsp salt

1 (10 oz) package sharp cheddar
  cheese (grated)
3 c Bisquick

Mix all above ingredients together. Cut off sections of sausage mixture and roll into a ball, about the size of large olives. Bake 20 minutes at 350°. These may be frozen. When ready to serve, remove from freezer and heat 20 minutes at 350° before serving.

Super Summer Salad

1 lb 4 oz can of pineapple slices
1 package orange gelatin

cherries (Maraschino)
1 c of cottage cheese (drained)

Drain syrup from the can of pineapple slices and add enough water to make 1½ cups of liquid. Bring to boil and stir in 1 package of gelatin. Cool until almost syrupy. Arrange pineapple and cherries in an 8" cake pan and pour on ½ of gelatin mixture. Set aside rest of gelatin mixture and keep at room temperature. Chill this first layer until set. Combine remaining gelatin mixture with 1 cup of drained cottage cheese and pour over first layer. Let salad set and chill. To unmold, dip pan in warm water, cover with plate on open side. Invert and shake firmly. Serves 6.

Pat's Party Salad

12 tbsp of mayonnaise
juice of 2 lemons
2 small onions (chopped fine)
4 c of frozen peas (do not thaw)
salt and pepper

2 c of Swiss or cheddar cheese or
1 c of Swiss and 1 c of cheddar
(cut in strips)
4 c of romaine and head lettuce
16 slices of crisp crumbled bacon

The night before serving, combine mayonnaise, lemon juice, onion, frozen peas and cheese in a bowl. Stir well and add salt and pepper and cover and refrigerate. Before serving, add lettuce and bacon and toss well. Ready to serve. Serves 10 to 12.

Three Green Salad

1 head Iceberg lettuce
1 head Romaine lettuce
1 package fresh spinach

1 purple onion
1 box fresh mushrooms
salt and pepper

Tear lettuce and spinach into bite size pieces. Slice onion and fresh mushrooms thin. Put into large salad bowl and toss with oil and vinegar dressing. Serves 12–18.

Hot or Cold Chicken Salad

2 c diced chicken (4 breasts)
   (cooked)
2 c diced celery
½ c toasted slivered almonds
½ tsp salt

2 tsp lemon juice
2 tsp minced green peppers
1 c mayonnaise
½ c American cheese (grated)
½ c crumbled potato chips

Combine all ingredients except for cheese and chips. Pour into a greased 13″ × 9″ pan. Sprinkle with cheese and chips. Cook at 400° for 15 minutes. To serve cold, omit cheese and chips. Double all ingredients for a large casserole. Serves 10–12.

Taco Salad

2 c shredded lettuce
1 lb can (2 c) kidney beans
   (drained)
2 medium tomatoes (chopped
   and drained)
1 tbsp green chilies (chopped)
½ c sliced ripe olives
1 large avocado (mashed)
½ c dairy sour cream

2 tbsp Italian salad dressing
1 tsp grated onion
¼ tsp salt
¾ tsp chili powder
dash of pepper
½ c sharp cheddar cheese
   (grated)
½ c coarsely crushed corn chips

Combine lettuce, beans, tomatoes, chilies and sliced olives and chill. Combine avocado, sour cream, salad dressing and onion. Chill. Mix together, add salt and pepper. Toss lightly with dressing. Top with cheese and corn chips. Serves 4–6.

Fresh Fruit Salad

Take any four fruits of your choice. Cut each fruit into small pieces. Toss fruits thoroughly until they create their own juices.

Molded Raspberry Salad

1 box family size raspberry Jello
   (6 oz)
1½ c boiling water

1 package thawed frozen
   raspberries (10 oz)
1 can applesauce (#3 can)

Make Jello, cool. Add berries and applesauce. Put in refrigerator until molded. When ready to serve dip into hot water quickly to unmold. Serve with dressing of ½ cup of sour cream and ½ cup of Hellman's mayonnaise. Make this in a 2 quart mold.

Emily's Salad Dressing

½ c Hellman's mayonnaise
½ c sour cream

½ tsp Spice Islands Beau Monde pepper

Mix thoroughly and chill.

Tarragon Mayonnaise

¾ tsp of tarragon leaves
(crushed finely)

¾ tsp of onion powder
mayonnaise

Stir in tarragon leaves and onion powder to mayonnaise. Place into blender and mix thoroughly. Very good on fish and vegetables.

Tom's Salad Dressing

½ c vinegar
1 c sugar
2 tsp salt
2 tsp dry mustard

2 tbsp grated onion
2 tsp celery seed
2 c warm salad oil

Mix all above ingredients except salad oil in a bowl. Then add the warm salad oil slowly, beating at lowest speed until thick and creamy.

Tiki Boiled Crabs

In a large pot, big enough for 1 dozen crabs:

1 dozen crabs (alive)
1 box of crab boil

½ c salt
juice of 2 lemons

Bring water and all ingredients except crabs to a rolling boil. Place live crabs into the pot. After all the crabs have been placed into the pot, it should stop boiling. Bring water to another boil and cook crabs for another 15 minutes. Remove crabs and clean immediately. Eat with green sauce or red sauce (see Sauces).

Crab Salad

1 can lump crabmeat
2 slices of hearts of palm
4 green onions (chopped)

4 tomatoes (peeled and sliced)
1 head of lettuce

Place 2 large slices of tomatoes on each bed of lettuce. On top of tomatoes, put large handful of crabmeat. Place hearts of palm on side of lettuce and sprinkle all with green onions. Pour oil and vinegar dressing over salad.

Fried Fish Fingers

trout or redfish
French's mustard
Tabasco sauce

salt
pepper
cornmeal

Fillet fish. Take halves and cut into strips the lengths of fingers or smaller. Mix mustard, Tabasco sauce, salt and pepper in a large bowl. Soak fish in this mixture for at least 1 hour. Dip fingers in cornmeal and fry until golden brown. Serves 2 to 10. Depending on number of fish.

Ronnie's Fish Fillet

fillets of your choice
flour
½ stick butter

½ can sliced mushrooms
(drained)

Dust fish fillets in flour. Then shake off excess flour. Melt butter and add mushrooms. Lightly fry fillets 4 minutes on each side. Serve immediately, pouring sauce over fish. The above recipe is for 3 small fillets.

Stuffed Flounder

1 can lump crabmeat
6 tbsp Pepperidge Farm stuffing
½ stick butter

1 lemon
flounder

Have fresh flounder, small for a few and larger for more. Take sharp knife and make large cross across the top of the fish. Slide knife under cross and cut close to bones so there is a nice size pocket for the stuffing. Open each side by flapping over sections and fill with stuffing.

For stuffing: Saute crabmeat and stuffing in butter. Melt other half of stick of butter with the juice of the lemon. Then pour over flounder. Broil for 10 minutes or wait until white and flakey. Serves 6.

Tiki Boiled Shrimp

5 lb large or jumbo shrimp
salt

pepper
juice of 4 lemons

Fill a large pot with water, add ½ box of salt and pepper heavily. Add the juice from the 4 lemons and bring mixture to a rolling boil. When shrimp are added, the water should quit boiling. Bring water to another boil and cook for 7–10 minutes. Chill and serve.

Shrimp Salad

5 lb large shrimp
8–10 stalks of celery

pepper and salt
2 green onions (minced)

Fill large pot of water, add 1 bag of crab-shrimp boil and boil shrimp for 7 minutes. Drain. Cut shrimp into bite-size pieces. Chop celery very finely and add minced onions. Salt and pepper to your taste. Toss with green sauce until totally coated (see index).

Emily's Oven Broiled Shrimp

5 lb uncooked shrimp in shells
salt and pepper

1 ½ lb butter (not margarine)
French bread

Use a very large pan, large enough so shrimp do not cover one another. Melt butter in pan or pans. Put shrimp in melted butter and soak thoroughly on each side by turning over at least twice. Have broiler hot and generously salt and pepper until pepper is covering shrimp. Broil on 1 side for 7–10 minutes or until pink. Turn shrimp over and salt and pepper other side. Broil 7–10 minutes or until pink. When done, pour into large bowl for serving. Serve in individual bowls, giving each serving ample amount of butter for dipping French bread into. Also, give each person an extra plate for shrimp shells. It is fun to give each guest a bib because this dish can be a little messy, but sure good. Serves 5 to 8.

Seafood Casserole

2 slices of bread, soaked in ¾ c of
  water (set aside)
½–1 c of chopped celery
½–1 c of chopped bell pepper
½ c onion
1 lb lump crabmeat
1 lb cooked shrimp
½–1 c mayonnaise

1 small can of water chestnuts
1 egg (beaten well)
1 lb grated sharp cheese
1 dash Tabasco
2 tbsp of worcestershire sauce
1 c of crumbled potato chips
2 tbsp butter

Brown celery, pepper and onion in butter. Set aside to cool. Combine all ingredients and mix gently. Before baking top with crumbled potato chips. Bake at 350° in a 13″ × 9″ pan for 30–45 minutes. This casserole can be made the day before and refrigerated. Serves 8 to 10.

Tiki Island Seafood Casserole

2 10½ oz cans of condensed
  cream of shrimp soup
½ c of mayonnaise
1 small onion (grated)
¾ c of milk
3 lb raw shrimp (cooked
  and cleaned)
salt
pepper
seasoned salt
cayenne pepper

paprika
2 c fresh crabmeat
1 5 oz can of water chestnuts
  (drained and sliced)
1½ c diced celery
3 tbsp fresh parsley (minced)
1⅓ c uncooked white long-grain
  rice (cooked until dry and
  fluffy)
slivered almonds

Blend soup into mayonnaise in large bowl. Stir until smooth. Add onion, then milk. When mixture is well seasoned, combine all other ingredients except paprika and almonds. Check seafood and add a few drops of milk if mixture seems dry. Turn into large casserole dish. Make sure dish is buttered, then sprinkle with paprika and almonds. Bake uncovered at 350° for about 30 minutes or until hot and bubbly. You may freeze. Serves 10 to 12.

Jenkins Fried Oysters

*3 dozen oysters for a
   family of 6
cornmeal
2 eggs*

*½–1 c of milk
salt
pepper
flour*

Make batter by adding 2 eggs, ½–1 cup of milk. Dip oysters into batter, then into flour that has been seasoned with salt and pepper. Then dip into cornmeal and drop into hot grease. Cook for 1 minute or until golden.

Easy Oysters on the Half Shell

*24 oysters
10 slices of (very thin) Pepperidge
   Farm bread
3 green onions*

*parsley
1 lb of crabmeat (lump)
3 tbsp of butter (melted)
4 tbsp of Parmesan cheese*

Loosen oysters from shell. Chop bread and onions, tops of parsley. Mix together and add butter, crabmeat and cheese. Mix well. Place oysters on cookie sheet and bake at 350° until slightly curled. Remove from oven and cover with crabmeat mixture. Return to oven and brown until thoroughly heated. Serves 4 to 6.

Smoked Chicken

chicken halves
Lawry's seasoned salt
salt

pepper
garlic salt
hickory seasoning

Main secret to this recipe is season before freezing. Use white or dark meat chicken halves. Season with Lawry's seasoned salt, salt, pepper, garlic salt and hickory seasoning. Season each piece heavily. Put 2 halves in a zip-lock bag and freeze after seasoning. When ready to cook, chickens can be put on barbecue pit frozen or thawed. If frozen, cook 4–6 hours. If thawed, cook 3–4 hours. Never need to turn or baste. Use barbecue pit with cover that has air holes. Have coals hot. Stack coals on one side and put chickens on other side—not over coals. This recipe can be cooked for 2 or 20.

Oven Baked Chicken

1½ whole split broilers
garlic salt
salt

pepper
Lawry's seasoned salt
creole seasoning

Season chicken with garlic salt, pepper, salt, Lawry's seasoning salt and creole seasoning. Make sure you season thoroughly. Serves 6.

Sauce:

juice of 2 lemons
1 stick butter, melted

¾–1 c worcestershire sauce

Line pan with heavy duty foil, enough to cover chicken. Brown chicken in 400° oven on both sides. Lower oven to 350° and soak chicken thoroughly until all sauce is gone. Bake for 1½–2 hours. Serves 4 to 6.

Lois' Country Casserole

1 hen boned or a 5–6 lb chicken
1 dozen tortillas (broken up)
1 onion, chopped fine

2 c grated cheddar cheese
salt to taste
pepper to taste

Sauce:

1 can mushroom soup
1 can cream of chicken soup

1 can Rotel tomatoes
½ c broth from the chicken

Beat sauce well. Cook chicken until it falls off the bone. Then cut into bite size pieces. Grease casserole dish. Then layer accordingly. First, place chicken, tortillas, cheese, onion and sauce. Repeat until all ingredients are gone. Bake about 1 hour at 350°. Serves 10 to 12.

Chicken Breasts and Ham Casserole

4 chicken breast halves, skinned, boned
4 thin slices cooked ham
¼ c butter or margarine, melted
⅓ c fine dry bread crumbs
½ tsp salt
¼ tsp pepper

1 can cream of mushroom soup
2 tbsp sour cream
1 tsp wine (optional)
2 c hot cooked rice (cooked in chicken broth)
2 tbsp chopped parsley (optional)

Place chicken, cut side up, between wax paper or Saran Wrap. Beat each with flat side of meat mallet until thin, forming about a 4-inch square. Place a ham slice on each piece of chicken. Roll up as a jelly roll. Brush each roll well with butter, roll in a mixture of bread crumbs, salt and pepper. Place in a buttered, shallow, 2 quart baking pan and bake at 375° for 30 minutes. Combine soup, sour cream and wine. Heat thoroughly. Combine rice and parsley. Toss lightly. Top chicken with sauce, and serve with rice.

Italian Meat Sauce

1 lb ground chuck
1 stick butter
4 green onions
2 pieces garlic (chopped
   near fine)

½ bunch of parsley
4 stalks of celery
2 cans of mushrooms (stems
   and pieces)

Saute above in skillet until meat is done and vegetables limp. Set aside. In a large pot, place:

3 #2 cans Hunt's tomato sauce
3 cans of water
1 stick of butter

1 tsp of Italian seasoning
salt
pepper

Boil slowly for 2 hours. Add other cooked ingedients and simmer for about another hour. Serve hot.

Hamburger Noodle Bake

1½ lb hamburger meat
2 cans tomato sauce
1 onion (chopped)
1 8 oz package Philadelphia
   cream cheese

½ pint of sour cream
1 c of grated rat cheese
1 10 oz package noodles
salt and pepper

Brown ground meat and onion until done. Add tomato sauce and 1 can of water, salt and pepper and simmer for 20 minutes. Cook noodles as directed on package. Mix cream cheese and sour cream together making a soft consistency. Layer meat, noodles and sour cream mixture until all is gone. Top with grated cheese and bake for 30 minutes at 350°. Serves 8 generously.

Veal Chops

White veal chops ¾" thick

Squeeze lemon on each one. Sprinkle with salt, garlic salt, and pepper. Brown in olive oil and shallots. Turn and sprinkle with a mixture of Italian seasoning. Cook about 30 minutes over low heat covered. Cover top of each chop with a thin piece of Swiss cheese and run under broiler or return cover of pan and cook until cheese melts. You may also put some ragu on chops and then cheese and cook the same as above. This may also be done with the tenderized veal patties.

Barbecued Country Backbones

You should use about 8 ribs for a family of 6. Season ribs with:

Natural Season Salt	*salt*
garlic salt	*pepper*
Lawry's seasoned salt	

Line pan with foil and put ribs in pan and bake at 500° until brown, turning ribs twice. After brown, pour barbecue sauce over all. Soak ribs thoroughly and bake covered at 350° for 1 hour.

Beef Tender

5–6 lb beef tender	*Guy's seasoning salt*
pepper	

Season tender thoroughly with seasonings. Preheat oven to 450°. Put tender in oven for 45 minutes. Remove from oven, slice and serve immediately. Meat is medium on the outside and slightly pink on the inside. If you like your meat a little more well done, cook about 10–15 minutes longer. Serves 8.

Eye of Round Roast

*1 (4–5 lb) roast, seasoned
   heavily with Guy's seasoning*

This recipe is for the roast to be cooked outside on a gas grill. Cook on high heat until brown but watch carefully so it does not burn. Lower heat to medium and cook for 1 hour. Turn grill off and leave roast on grill for 1 more hour. Brown on outside but pink on inside. Absolutely delicious for sandwiches. Serves 8 to 10.

Chuck Roast Charcoaled

5–8 lb chuck roast   *1 medium size jar of mustard*
1 box of rock salt

Coat roast generously with mustard first and rock salt on both sides. Place roast on barbecue pit, away from coals. Cook for 3 hours. The larger the roast, the more mustard and rock salt should be used.

Smoked Brisket

1 can of beer   *1 quart of white vinegar*

Mix vinegar and beer to use for basting. Mop meat thoroughly with mixture. Let soak for 30 minutes to 1 hour. Coals should be white before placing brisket on pit. Make sure the brisket is not placed directly over coals while cooking. Baste brisket every 20 minutes with vinegar and beer mixture for 2 hours. Remove from pit, baste meat once more thoroughly before wrapping tightly in heavy duty aluminum foil. Return to pit and cook for two hours longer. After four hours of cooking, if you are not ready to eat, remove from pit, open foil slightly as meat will continue to cook in the air tight seal. Very tender and juicy. Serves 12 to 14.

Smoked Ham

1 Hormel Cure 81 ham

Cover whole ham with paste of brown sugar, mustard, and orange juice. Place coals on one side of pit. When coals are very hot, put ham on *opposite* side of pit (not over coals). Smoke 2 hours.

Hot Ham Sandwiches

Slice ham and wrap in foil. Reheat. Open foil and place slice of Swiss or Monterrey Jack cheese on each slice of ham. Remove from oven when melted, and place on Cookbook Rye bread with mustard, mayonnaise or dressing of your own choice.

Hot Dogs with Chili

12 hot dogs   *1 1 lb can of chili*

Place chili in a large pot, add hot dogs. Never add any water to mixture. Cook until hot. Spoon hot dogs and chili onto buns together, add cheese and onions if desired.

Pork and Sauerkraut Roll

1 lb ground pork   *½ tsp worcestershire sauce*
½ c fine dry bread crumbs   *1 (1 lb) can of sauerkraut*
1 slightly beaten egg   *(drained and cut)*
1 tsp salt   *5 slices of bacon*
¼ c chopped onion

Combine ground pork, bread crumbs, egg, salt, pepper and worcestershire sauce. Mix thoroughly. On foil, try to construct a 10 × 7 × 7 inch triangle with the mixture you just prepared. Then add sauerkraut and onion and spread evenly. Starting at point of triangle, roll up. Place loaf in shallow dish and arrange bacon slices on top. Bake in 350° oven for 40–45 minutes. Serves 6.

Center Cut Fried Pork Chops

I use 8 pork chops for a family of 6. Pork chops should be at least ½"
thick. Season well with:

Natural seasoning salt   *pepper*
garlic salt

Lightly flour moist chops on both sides. Fry in oil. Fry on 1 side until
brown, then turn over and brown opposite side also. Good supper for
families that are eating at different times!

Stuffed Pork Chops

6 1" pork chops   *salt*
2 c of stuffing   *pepper*
½ onion   *garlic salt (optional)*
1 stalk of celery

I prefer Pepperidge Farm stuffing, but any kind is fine. Saute onion and
celery in ½ stick of butter. Mix stuffing and all seasonings together. Have
your butcher cut pockets in each of your pork chops. Fill pockets with
stuffing. Anything which is leftover, place on top of pork chops. Cover
with foil and bake for 1½ hours at 350°. A great dinner for a family on the
move. Serves 6.

Barbecue Sauce

2 sticks of butter   *1 c worcestershire sauce*
1 large or 2 small onions   *½ c sugar*
2 14 oz bottles of catsup   *1 c vinegar*
2 cloves of garlic

Saute onion in butter. Add remaining ingredients and stir. Cook over
medium heat about 10 minutes. Makes ½–1 quart of sauce.

Tartar Sauce

1 c mayonnaise
¼ small onion (grated finely)
1 dill pickle (chopped finely)
juice of ½ lemon

cayenne pepper
salt
lemon pepper

Mix all ingredients thoroughly and chill.

Green Sauce

1 pint sour cream
1 jar Gerber's baby spinach
juice of 1 lemon

1 large tsp horseradish
½ grated small onion
salt and pepper

Mix all together thoroughly. Let stand for 3–4 hours. Especially good on crabmeat, shrimp or any fish.

Baked Beans

1 large onion (diced)
1½ tbsp worcestershire sauce
½ tsp Louisiana hot sauce
1 tsp garlic salt
2 heaping tbsp brown sugar

1½ tsp dry or regular mustard
1 tsp vinegar
2 15½ oz cans of pork & beans
bacon strips (as many as desired)

Cook onion, worcestershire sauce, hot sauce, garlic salt, mustard, brown sugar, and vinegar in a small amount of bacon drippings until onion is clear. Mix with beans in large baking dish. Sprinkle brown sugar. Bake 1 hour at 325°. Serves 8.

Fresh Mushrooms and Onions

1 lb of fresh mushrooms	*½ stick butter*
1 large onion (chopped)	*salt and pepper*

Saute onion, mushrooms, salt and pepper in covered skillet until tender. It should cook about 15–20 minutes. Very delicious on steak or roast. Serves 4.

Louise's Mustard Greens

2 bunches of greens	*2 stalks of celery*
3–4 slices of bacon	*salt and pepper*

Wash greens at least 5 times. Last wash before cooking, pour a lot of salt in water to bring back crispness. Fry bacon in pot. When done, add greens, celery, salt and pepper. Cook until tender.

Carrot Souffle

1 package fresh carrots	*½ tsp pepper*
2-3 eggs	*1 c grated cheddar cheese*
½ c crushed waverly	*(sharp or mild)*
crackers	*1 tbsp sugar*
1 c milk	*½ stick melted butter*
1½ tsp salt	

Mash cooked carrots and mix with remaining ingredients. Bake 45 minutes at 375°. Serves 6-8.

Fresh Spinach and Noodle Casserole

1 package fresh spinach	*1 c sour cream*
1 box noodles romanoff	*cheddar cheese*
1 small onion (chopped)	*1 tbsp butter*

Cook spinach and noodles separately. Drain. Mix together and add butter and onion. Mix sauce from box of noodles with sour cream. Add sauce to spinach and noodle mixture. Pour into buttered dish. Sprinkle cheddar cheese on top and bake for 30 minutes at 350°. Serves about 8 to 10.

Fresh Spinach Casserole

1 package fresh spinach
   (washed and chopped)
3 well beaten eggs
6 tbsp of flour
1 tsp of salt

2 c slim or creamed
   cottage cheese
2 c cheddar cheese (grated)
pepper to taste

Beat eggs and flour until smooth. Then mix the rest of the ingredients. Bake uncovered in a 2 quart casserole dish for 1 hour at 350°. Let stand a few minutes before serving. Serves 8 to 10.

Skillet Vegetables

2 medium yellow squash
2 medium green zucchini
2 tomatoes (peeled)
1 can mushrooms (drained)

1 stick butter
1 c grated cheese
salt
pepper

Cut squash, zucchini and tomatoes into slices. Place 1 layer of squash, salt and pepper and a few pats of butter in skillet. Layer remaining vegetables following same directions as above. Now, pour mushrooms over all and cook on medium heat. Cook about 30 minutes, but before completely being done, pour the grated cheese over top and cook. Serves 6 to 8.

Cooked Cabbage

1 whole cabbage
3 slices of bacon

salt & pepper to taste
2 tbsp butter

Fry bacon. Wash and chop cabbage and place in medium size pot over bacon and grease. Season and cook until tender, approximately 15–20 minutes. While the cabbage is cooking, add the butter. Makes great dinners as well as lunches! Serves 4.

Vegetable Quiche

Cover bottom of 9″ × 9″ buttered baking dish with chopped green onions. Add a layer of thin sliced tomatoes, chopped green chiles, sliced ripe olives, add a layer of sliced fresh mushrooms. Cover with grated Monterrey Jack cheese. Beat six eggs well, add one cup of Half & Half, pour over casserole. Bake at 350° for 45 minutes to 1 hour.

Baked Cheese Squash

1 lb of yellow summer squash	*salt and pepper*
1 lb of zucchini squash	*Lawry's seasoned salt*
1 c grated cheddar cheese	*sour cream or Half & Half*
1 large onion (chopped)	

Cook squash and zucchini together with onion in small amount of water, as squash makes its own water until tender. Add salt, pepper and Lawry's while cooking to your taste. When finished cooking, drain. Put layer of squash and then layer of cheese. Layer twice. Cover with sour cream or Half & Half. Bake at 350° until bubbly. Serves 8 to 10. Even kids love it!

Fried Zucchini

zucchini	*salt*
pancake mix	*pepper*

Slice large zucchini. Use Aunt Jemima pancake mix, Bisquick, or any other pancake mix of your choice, following pancake mixture on box. Dip zucchini into batter and fry until golden brown. Salt and pepper to your taste. Easy and delicious!

Mixed Vegetable Casserole

2 packages of frozen English peas
2 packages of frozen French
  style beans
1 c whipping cream

2 packages of green lima beans
1 pint of mayonnaise
Parmesan cheese

Cook each separately as directed on package. When done, drain and put all together in a large casserole dish. Then salt and pepper; do not add butter. Whip 1 cup of whipping cream and fold in 1 pint of mayonnaise (sometimes you will not need the whole pint, so add ¾ pint and add the rest if necessary.) Fold this into vegetables. Sprinkle a lot of Parmesan cheese on top. Place in oven for about 20–30 minutes until heated thoroughly and cheese is melted. Will serve 20–24.

Marinated Vegetables

2 bunches carrots, cut in strips
  and cooked slightly
1 lb asparagus cleaned and
  cooked slightly
2 lb green beans cooked slightly
2 17 oz cans of sliced beets,
  drained
2 tsp salt
1 bunch scallions

⅔ c vegetable cooking liquid
2 tbsp finely chopped
  green peppers
2 tbsp finely chopped pimento
1½ c corn oil
¾ c of vinegar
2 tbsp of sugar
¼ tsp of pepper

Arrange carrots, asparagus, beans and beets in a large, shallow dish. Combine cooking liquid, scallions, green pepper, pimento, corn oil, vinegar, sugar, salt, and pepper. Pour over vegetables. Cover and marinate in refrigerator for at least 3 hours, basting occasionally. Remove vegetables and arrange on large platter. Serves about 12.

Rice Au Gratin

¼ c butter
¼ c flour
1 tsp salt
⅛ tsp pepper

2 c milk
1½ c shredded American cheese
3 c hot cooked rice

Melt butter; stir in flour, salt, pepper and blend well. Add milk and cook, stirring constantly until smooth and thickened. Add ¼ cup of cheese and stir until cheese is melted. Alternate layer of rice and cheese sauce in a buttered 1 quart casserole dish. Top with remaining ¼ cup of cheese. Bake in a 350° oven for 20 minutes until lightly browned. Serves 6. Easy to double for a larger crowd.

Baked Potatoes with Guacamole Sauce

4 baking potatoes
1 avocado
2 tbsp sour cream
salt

pepper
4 slices bacon, crisply cooked
  and crumbled
1 tbsp chopped chives (optional)

Cook potatoes in 400° oven for 1 hour to 1½ hours. Mash avocado to creamy consistency. Mix sour cream in, salt and pepper. When potatoes are done, cut down center. Spoon in avocado mixture and sprinkle on crumbled bacon. Try pouring over boiled new potatoes.

Garlic Cheese Grits

1 c of grits
2 eggs
milk

½ stick butter
1 roll garlic cheese

Cook 1 cup of grits as directed on box. Remove from fire and add butter, garlic cheese and 2 eggs that have been put in a cup and beaten slightly. Also, add milk to make 1 cup. Add to grits and put in a greased 2 quart casserole dish. Cover with foil and bake 1 hour at 350°. Take off cover and place grated sharp cheese on top and return to oven for 10 minutes. Serves 8 to 10.

Aunt Fay's Macaroni and Cheese

*1 (12 oz) package of Skinner
  macaroni*
2½ lb rat cheese
1 can evaporated milk

1 stick of butter or margarine
salt
pepper

Boil macaroni until tender, according to directions on box. Drain and place layers of macaroni, cheese, several pats of butter and salt and pepper. Continue layers until all ingredients are gone. Pour milk over all ingredients until milk comes to top. Take hand and press casserole down until packed. Bake at 350° until brown. Serves 6 to 8.

Macaroni Salad

1 12 oz bag of shell noodles
1 8 oz pack of cheddar cheese
½ jar sweet pickles

salt
pepper
mayonnaise

Cook the macaroni according to the directions on package. Cool. Cut cheese into small squares and also do the same with the pickles. Then mix with the macaroni. Add mayonnaise until mixture is creamy enough to your satisfaction. You may add any other ingredients that you would think might add more flavor. Serves 8.

American Lasagne

1 lb ground beef
2 cloves garlic (minced)
1 tbsp hot fat
1 6 oz can tomato paste
1 1 lb 4 oz can tomatoes (2½ c)
1 tsp salt

¾ tsp pepper
½ tsp oregano
hot, boiled noodles
  (8 oz uncooked)
1 12 oz carton cottage cheese
8 oz Swiss cheese (1½ c, grated)

Brown beef and garlic in hot fat. Add tomato paste, tomatoes, and seasoning. Cover and simmer 20 minutes. Heat oven to 350°. In oblong baking dish, 11½" × 7½" × 1½", alternate layers of cooked noodles, Swiss cheese, cottage cheese and meat sauce. Bake 20–30 minutes. Serve with grated Parmesan cheese. Makes 6 to 8 servings.

Country Noodle Casserole

½ lb sliced bacon
1 large package of thin noodles
3 c cottage cheese
3 c sour cream
2 cloves garlic (crushed)
2 onions (minced)

2 tbsp of worcestershire sauce
1 dash of hot sauce
4 tsp of salt
3 tbsp of prepared horseradish
1 c of Parmesan cheese

Fry and crumble bacon into small pieces. Then cook noodles and drain. Mix all ingredients except cheese. Then add bacon and noodles. Bake in a 3 quart casserole dish at 350° for about 35–40 minutes. Be sure to cover and right before removing from oven, remove lid and add cheese, then return to oven and bake for 15 more minutes. Serves 8 to 10.

Cornbread Dressing
with Mushrooms and Waterchestnuts

2 tbsp chopped onion (or more)
1 c chopped celery

1 c mushrooms
(you can use pieces)

Saute above ingredients in ¼ c of butter and combine with:

1 c day old bread crusts
½ c waterchestnuts (sliced)

3 c of cornbread or Pepperidge
Farm cornbread stuffing

Salt and use poultry seasoning to your taste, if not using Pepperidge Farm stuffing. Use a rich poultry stock and melted butter to moisten dressing. This should really be used for a turkey or a large hen.

Quick Rolls
Taste just like homemade!

1 pan of Mrs. Baird's Biskrolls

1 stick of butter

Take the foil pan of Mrs. Baird's Biskrolls and pour melted butter over rolls and bake at 350° until golden. Serve immediately. (Don't tell anyone they are not homemade!)

Banana Loaf

⅔ c sugar
⅓ c shortening
2 eggs
3 tbsp sour milk or buttermilk
1 c bananas (mashed)

2 c sifted flour
1 tsp baking powder
½ tsp soda
½ tsp salt

Mix together thoroughly the first 3 ingredients. Stir in the next 2 ingredients. Sift together and stir the rest of the ingredients. Blend in ½ c of chopped nuts if desired. Pour into bread pan and let stand for 20 minutes before baking. Bake 50–60 minutes at 350°.

Super Group Coffee Cake

4 c Bisquick baking mix
⅔ c sugar
2 eggs
1⅓ c milk

¼ c butter or margarine (melted)
2 tsp vanilla
1 tsp cinnamon

Preheat oven to 400°. Combine Bisquick, ⅓ cup of sugar, eggs, milk, 2 tablespoons of butter, and vanilla. Beat vigorously 1 minute. Spread batter in greased, oblong pan 13 × 9 × 2. Drizzle remaining butter over batter. Sprinkle remaining sugar and cinnamon over batter also. Lightly swirl batter several times for a marbled effect. Bake 25–30 minutes. Serves 15 to 18.

Boiled Peach Halves with Marshmallow

1 peach half per person

1 marshmallow per person

Lay each peach half in a 6 oz pyrex dish and top with marshmallow. Set dishes on a small pan with sides. Set aside until ready to eat. Turn broiler on and have rack adjusted so direct flame is several inches from dishes. Set pan under direct heat for about 2 minutes until marshmallows brown slightly. Remove and eat.

Quick Strawberry Ice

4 boxes frozen
   strawberries

¼ c lime juice
¼ c lemon juice

Place all ingredients in a blender at high speed until pureed. Pour into container and freeze. Cut into squares. Serves 12.

Lemon Ice

4 c water
2 c sugar

1 c fresh lemon juice
1 tbsp grated lemon rind

Boil water. Add sugar and cook until sugar dissolves, about 5 minutes. Cool. Stir in lemon juice and grated lemon rind. Freeze to a mush. Remove from freezer, beat with electric mixer and refreeze. Serves 8 to 12.

Amaretto and Pineapple Parfait

1 large fresh pineapple
3 jiggers amaretto liqueur

1 pint vanilla ice cream
2 c crushed ice, optional

Twist crown from pineapple. Cut pineapple into quarters. Remove fruit from shells. Core and cut pineapple into chunks. Add 4 cups pineapple to blender along with liqueur, whip until pureed. Add ice cream. Blend until smooth. For a frosty less rich parfait, add 2 cups crushed ice and blend until smooth. Makes 4 to 5 cups.

Country Vanilla Ice Cream

½ c sugar
1 egg well beaten
1½ c milk or Half & Half
1 dash salt

1 c heavy cream or
* whipping cream*
1 tsp vanilla

Add sugar gradually to the beaten egg, beating well. Add remaining ingredients and mix thoroughly.

For fruit: Reduce milk to ½ cup. Add 1 cup of fresh or frozen fruits puree to country cream. If you double this, it fills an electric freezer ¾ full. Ice cream is much richer when you add Half & Half or whipping cream.

Apricot Torte

2 (½ oz) packages of slivered
  almonds
2 c of sugar cookie crust or
  enough to line entire pan

¾ stick butter
1 quart vanilla ice cream
  (softened)
10 oz jar of apricot preserves

Melt butter in a 9 × 9 pan in a 350° oven. Add almonds to melted butter and cook until lightly brown. Remove almonds with slotted spoon and drain thoroughly on paper towel. Add cookie crumbs to butter and mix. Press crumbs in pan. Layer vanilla ice cream and sprinkle half of the almonds on top. Then place whole jar of preserves on top of almonds. Top with another half of ice cream. Sprinkle remaining almonds over top. Freeze and when ready to serve, cut into squares. Serves 8 to 10.

Cookie Crumb Crust

18 sugar cookies
½ stick butter

1 c chopped pecans

Crush cookies very fine. Melt the butter and chop the pecans. Add all ingredients together and press into a 10" pie shell. Mold *to* the pie shell with a fork for the bottom and sides.

Blueberry Cream Cheese Tart

1½ c of graham cracker crumbs
⅓ c sugar

⅓ c of melted butter

Combine all ingredients. Press firmly into bottom and sides of a 9 × 9 × 2 pan.

Cream Cheese Layer:

1 8 oz package of cream cheese
2 eggs
½ c sugar

1 tsp vanilla
¼ c cornstarch

Cream cheese in mixing bowl. Add 1 egg at a time, stirring constantly. Add vanilla and pour into a crumb lined pan. Bake at 350° for about 30 minutes. Cool. Drain 2 #303 cans of blueberries. Combine ¼ cup of cornstarch and two tablespoons of sugar. Add juice and cook at medium temperature until thick. Add 2 tablespoons of lemon juice. Cool. While still warm, add blueberries. Spoon over top and add whipping cream if desired. Serves 8 to 10.

Apple Crisp Pie

8 large firm apples
1½ c light or dark brown sugar
1 c all-purpose flour

1 tsp salt
¾ c chopped pecans
½ stick butter

Peel and core apples. Place in shallow rectangular dish and spread half of the sugar on top. Combine remaining sugar, flour, salt and pecans. Cut butter into mixture with pastry blender until crumbly. Spread entire mixture over apples, pressing down around edges so topping completely covers apples. Bake for 1 hour at 350°. Serve warm. Serve with whipping cream on top or for less calories, serve with Cool Whip. Absolutely DELICIOUS! Serves 8.

Peach Crumb Cobbler

10 to 12 large peaches
½ c butter
1½ c brown sugar, packed
2 tsp grated lemon peel
2 eggs
2 c granulated sugar

½ c boiling water
2 tsp vanilla
½ tsp nutmeg
2 c sifted flour
1 tsp baking powder
dash salt

Peel peaches, cut in quarters and arrange in 9 by 13 inch baking pan. Dot peaches with butter, then sprinkle on brown sugar and lemon peel. Beat eggs until light in color. Gradually add sugar and beat thoroughly. Stir in boiling water and vanilla. Sift together flour, baking powder, nutmeg, and salt. Add to egg mixture and blend well. Pour batter over peaches. Bake at 375° 55 to 60 minutes or until crust is lightly browned and stiff to the touch. Serve warm with ice cream or whipped cream. Serves 10 to 12.

Double French Silk Pie

1 10″ cookie pie crust
1 c butter
1½ c sugar

2 squares unsweetened
   melted chocolate
2 tsp vanilla
4 eggs

Cream butter and sugar thoroughly. Add vanilla and chocolate. Add eggs, 1 at a time, beating 5 minutes between each egg. Pour mixture into 10″ pie shell. Refrigerate at least 1 hour. Top with whipping cream or Cool Whip to provide fewer calories. Then add additional cookie crumbs left over from pie shell. Serves 8.

Rocky Road Freezer Pie

1 pie shell
¼ stick butter
1½ c vanilla wafers (crumbled)

1 can coconut
1 box of Rocky Road Icing Mix
whipping cream

Mix thoroughly coconut and vanilla wafers. Pour melted butter over this mixture and bake at 350° for about 15 minutes. Prepare icing as directed on box, then pour into pie shell over coconut mixture and freeze. Top with whipping cream when ready to serve. Serves 6 to 8.

Lemon Eagle Brand Pie

2 cans Eagle Brand milk
2 eggs
1 10" pie pan

¾–1 c of fresh lemon and
    lime juice mixed

Mix Eagle Brand milk with eggs, lemon and lime juice and beat with mixer until thoroughly mixed. Pour into 10" pie crust, chill until set. Top with whipping cream or Cool Whip.

Crust: You may use girl scout butter cookies. These make an excellent crust. Crumb crust: ½ box of cookies. Crush cookies and pour melted butter into crumbs until crumbs can be molded into pie pan. Serves 6 to 8.

Hershey Bar Pound Cake

½ lb butter
2 c sugar
4 eggs
2 tsp vanilla
½ tsp salt
8 regular size Hershey bars

2 tbsp water
2½ c sifted cake flour
1 c buttermilk
¾ tsp soda
½ c chopped nuts

Melt candy bars in top of double boiler. Cream butter and sugar. Add eggs, 1 at a time, beating after each. Add vanilla, salt and melted candy bars. Mix buttermilk with soda. Add flour and buttermilk alternately. Fold in nuts. Bake in a greased tube or bundt pan for 1 hour at 350°. You may have to cook it a little longer. Sprinkle cake with powdered sugar. Serves 12 to 14.

Cheese Cake

3 large packages of soft
   cream cheese
4 eggs
¾ c sugar

1 tsp vanilla
1 pint sour cream
1 box of Zwieback, or any crumb
   crust of your choice

Cream the cheese and then add ¾ cup of sugar and each egg 1 at a time. Add vanilla. Pour into greased 10″ spring pan, lined with the crumb crust, and bake for 30 minutes at 350°. Whip 1 pint of sour cream with ¼ to ½ cup of sugar and pour over cake. Return to oven for 10 minutes. Put into refrigerator and chill at least 2 hours or until completely hard. Serves 10 to 12. A great dessert.

Chocolate Ladyfinger Molded Cake

½ lb butter
3 c powdered sugar
6 eggs, separated
3 squares of unsweetened
   chocolate (melted)

1 tsp vanilla
½ tsp of almond extract
2 dozen ladyfingers, split
whipping cream

Cream butter and sugar thoroughly with blender. Add egg yolks, 1 at a time, beating well after each. Blend in melted chocolate, vanilla, and almond extract. Beat egg whites until stiff. Fold in by hand. Line buttered 12″ springform pan with ladyfingers. Spoon in some of the chocolate mixture and then more ladyfingers to form as many layers until mixture is gone. Refrigerate overnight or you may also freeze. Before serving, unmold and top with whipping cream. This may be frozen ahead. Delicious but extremely rich. Serves 12.

Milky Way Cake

8 (1¾ oz) Milky Way bars
3 sticks butter
2 c sugar
4 well beaten eggs
2½ c flour

¼ tsp baking soda
1¼ c buttermilk
1 tsp vanilla
1 c chopped pecans
powdered sugar

Melt milky ways with 1 stick of butter. Remove from fire and let cool. Cream remaining 2 sticks of butter with sugar. Add well beaten eggs and cooled chocolate mixture. Sift flour and baking soda together. Alternate flour and buttermilk to the batter, blending well. Then add vanilla and nuts. Grease and dust with powdered sugar 3 9″ cake pans or 1 long 16 × 12 or 8 × 17 pan. Bake at 325° for 30–45 minutes.

Icing:

2½ c sugar
1 c evaporated milk
1 stick butter

1 c chopped pecans
1 c marshmallow cream
1 6 oz package of chocolate chips

Combine sugar and evaporated milk. Cook to a soft ball stage. Remove from heat and add butter, marshmallow cream and chocolate chips, stirring until all ingredients have melted. PUT ON HOT CAKE. This is a great dessert that everyone will enjoy! Serves 12 to 14.

Quick Fudge Frosting

2 packages of semi-sweet chocolate pieces (2 c)

3 c sifted confectioners sugar
¼ c hot milk

Melt chocolate in double boiler over hot boiling water. Add all ingredients and beat with the electric beaters. This will frost 2 layers of a cake or a sheet cake generously.

Blender Quick Fudge Sauce

1 (8 oz) package semisweet
   chocolate chips
¼ c light cream
3 tbsp water

Place chocolate chips into a blender. Bring light cream and water to a boil, then add to chips. Cover and blend at highest speed for at least 1 minute. This recipe may be doubled if desired. Make sure you blend at *highest speed.*

Lemon Lime Bars

1 c of flour
½ c of butter (softened)
¼ c of powdered sugar
2 eggs beaten
1 c of sugar
2 tbsp lemon juice
2 tbsp lime juice
1 tsp grated lemon rind
1 tsp grated lime rind

Combine flour, butter and powdered sugar and mix thoroughly. Spread in a 9" square pan. Bake at 350° for 15 minutes. Meanwhile, mix eggs, sugar, lemon and lime juice, lemon and lime rind and spread over first layer in pan. Return to oven for 25 minutes. When cool, frost with Lemon Lime glaze. Cut into bars. Makes 2–3 dozen. See Lemon Lime glaze, next recipe.

Lemon Lime Glaze

½–¾ c of powdered sugar
1 tsp lemon juice
1 tsp lime juice
1 tsp water

Mix powdered sugar, lemon juice, lime juice and water together. Make sure you spread thinly over bars or any other dessert. This glaze would be so good on a lemon pound cake

Brownies for 30–40

*3 boxes of Duncan Hines
    Brownie Mix (family size)*
2 boxes of Rocky Road Icing mix

*1 extra packet of chocolate
    sauce from another box*

Follow directions on back of brownie box although adding extra packet of chocolate mixture to the ingredients. Bake 40 minutes at 350°. Bake in large roasting pan. Before removing, test with toothpick. Follow sauce directions on the box of frosting and place on brownies as soon as they are removed from the oven. This amount will serve 30–40 people. The secret to making good, chewy brownies, is to remove them from the oven about 5 minutes before time!

Tip for Bundt Cake Pan

After you grease pan, dust thoroughly with powdered sugar—cake will never stick.

Rules for Refrigerator Cookies

Combine all the ingredients as directed and shape the dough into long rolls about 2″ in diameter. If the dough is too soft to roll, chill it until it can be handled easily. Do not use the additional flour. Cover the rolls with waxed paper and place them in the refrigerator for about 24 hours until they are thoroughly chilled. Cut the rolls into the thinnest possible slices. Bake them on a greased sheet in an oven heated to 400° for about 10 minutes. The whole nut meats may be combined with the dough or they may be used to garnish the slices, or the entire roll of dough may be rolled in chopped nuts so as to make a border when the cookie is cut.

Butterscotch Refrigerator Cookies

Follow the recipe for Vanilla Refrigerator Cookies. Substitute for the white sugar: 1¼ cups of firmly packed brown sugar.

Coconut Refrigerator Cookies

Follow the recipe for Butterscotch Refrigerator Cookies. Omit the nut meats. Substitute 1 cup of grated coconut.

Cream Cheese Refrigerator Cookies

Makes about 60 2″ cookies.

½ c butter	1 tsp vanilla
1 c sugar	2 c all-purpose flour
1 well beaten egg	⅛ tsp soda
1 package of cream cheese (3 oz)	½ tsp baking powder
2 tbsp sour milk	½ tsp salt

Beat the first 3 ingredients until creamy. Soften the cream cheese, and beat into the butter mixture, the next 2 ingredients. Beat in the rest of the ingredients. Follow the rules for refrigerator cookies. Be sure to sprinkle the cookies with sugar, to which you may add cinnamon. This dough, after being chilled, may be rolled to paper thinness, cut into shapes and baked. Bake them in a moderate oven (350°) from 12 to 15 minutes.

Vanilla Refrigerator Cookies

1 c of sugar
½ c of butter
1 egg
1 tsp vanilla

½ tsp grated lemon rind
1¾ c of all-purpose flour
¼ tsp of salt
1½ tsp baking powder

About 40 2″ cookies. This cookie resembles a sand tart and is less troublesome to prepare. Sift the sugar. Beat the butter until soft. Add the sugar gradually. Blend these ingredients until they are very light and creamy. Beat in 1 egg and add the vanilla and the lemon rind. Sift the flour before remeasuring. Resift with the salt and the baking powder. Stir the sifted ingredients into the butter mixture. Add ½ cup of nut meats if desired. After slicing, sprinkle cookies with sugar to make them sandy. Bake as directed on rules. You will find rules above.

Oatmeal Refrigerator Cookies

This makes about 56 2″ cookies:

½ c white sugar
½ c brown sugar
¾ c sifted all-purpose flour
½ tsp soda
½ tsp salt
½ c soft butter

1 egg
1½ tsp grated orange or
  lemon rind
½ tsp of almond or vanilla
  extract
1½ c of rolled oats

Stir in the first 9 ingredients until well blended. Work in with hands, the last ingredient. To vary the flavor, you may use 1½ tablespoons of molasses and 2 additional tablespoons of flour. Follow the rules for refrigerator cookies.

Christmas Wine Jelly

¾ c apple juice
1 bay leaf
5 cloves
1½ c Burgundy wine
1 tbsp lemon juice (strained)

1 tbsp lime juice (strained)
3 c sugar
1 (6 oz) bottle pectin
1 box of Gulfwax

Combine apple juice, bay leaf and cloves. Simmer. Remove cloves and bay leaf. Add burgundy, lemon juice, lime juice and sugar. Bring to a rolling boil and stir in pectin. Pour into large wine glasses and cover with melted Gulfwax when jelly is cool. Decorate wine glasses with ribbons for a great Christmas gift.

Auntie's Fig Preserves

1 lb of fresh figs
½ lb of sugar

2–3 c of water
1 lemon (sliced thin)

Boil sugar, water and lemon until it turns to syrup. Add figs and cook until tender. This should take about 30 minutes. Put in canning jars, top with wax and chill. May be kept 6 months.

Cheese or Plain Omelette

5 eggs, well beaten
salt and pepper

butter
grated cheese (optional)

Take a divided skillet of 3 sections. Beat 5 eggs well. Add salt and pepper to your taste. Butter sections with large pats of butter. When butter starts sizzling, pour eggs into each section. Cook eggs until thoroughly formed on bottom. Loosen eggs from bottom with spatula. Move around until all loose eggs are cooked. Put grated cheese or any other ingredients you may desire in center and flap over. Cook 1 minute and serve immediately. Serves 3.

AN ELF'S WORK IS NEVER DONE
John
Thomas
James
Carroll
Stephen
Cliffe
Chrissy
Doug
Randa
Isla
T.R.
Boo
A.T.Λ.
ST Thomas

Oh, Heavenly Father,
We thank Thee for food, and
remember the hungry.
We thank Thee for health, and
remember the sick.
We thank Thee for friends, and
remember the friendless.
We thank Thee for freedom, and
remember the enslaved.
May Thy gifts to us be used
for others—Amen.

Inell's Iced Tea

6 c boiling water
4 tea bags

1½ c sugar
lemon, lime, pineapple and mint

Steep tea in boiled water for 5 minutes. Remove tea bags. Add sugar to hot tea. Stir. Let tea cool. When serving, fill tall glasses with crushed ice. Squeeze 1 lemon and 1 lime over ice. Add tea. Garnish with orange, lemon, and lime slices. Add fresh mint and fresh pineapple if available. Serves 12.

Lemon-Orange "Aid"

This is "sick bay" drink—but delicious anytime. To make 1 glass:

juice of 1 orange
juice of ½ lemon

sugar or Sweet n Low to taste

Mix in glass. Fill glass with ice and water.

Easy Daiquiris

1 (6 oz) can frozen limeade or
    pink lemonade

1 c of rum
ice (to fill blender)

Mix together in blender. Serve in champagne glasses. Banana: Add 1 large or 2 small ripe mashed bananas. Strawberry: Add 1 ten ounce package frozen strawberries. Try with apricots or peaches.

Bellini

6 peaches

1 bottle chilled Champagne

Crush peaches in blender. Divide peach puree into eight fluted champagne glasses. Fill each glass with champagne. (Serves 8.)

Sangria

4 c red wine
2 (6 oz) cans frozen limeade
4 c water

orange, lemon, lime slices
strawberries
cherries

Mix together wine, limeade, water. Put into clear pitcher or bowl. Add fruit slices and whole berries. Let stand for an hour or two. When serving, add ice and you may also add a bottle of soda, Champagne, 7-Up or ginger ale. For a virgin sangria, substitute grape juice for wine.

Sister Aldea's Hot Toddy

6 c apple cider
1 c golden rum
¼ c maple syrup
2 tbsp lemon juice
12 whole cloves

½ tsp whole allspice
2 sticks cinnamon
orange and lemon slices studded
  with cloves

Tie allspice, cloves and cinnamon in cheese cloth bag. Mix cider, syrup and lemon juice. Add spice bag. Heat to boiling. Reduce heat and simmer 15 minutes. Remove spices and stir in rum. Serve in mugs garnished with orange and lemon slices.

Egg Nog
Christmas Tradition

12 egg yolks
12 egg whites
13 tbsp fine sugar

20 tbsp bourbon or brandy
1 quart whipping cream

Separate eggs. Beat egg yolks (use mixmaster). Add sugar and bourbon alternately, 1 tablespoon at a time. Bourbon will "cook" egg yolks. Let mixture stand. Before serving, beat egg whites stiff. Fold into egg yolks. Beat cream until thick but not stiff. Mix into egg mixture. Serve with fresh grated nutmeg on top. This is thick—eat with a spoon.

Elegant Kir

chilled Champagne   Cassis or Framboise liquor

Put one ounce of liquor in wine glass. Fill with champagne.

Cheese Ball

1 lb sharp cheddar cheese   2 tsp worcestershire
1 large package cream cheese   salt
12 bacon slices—cooked   cayenne
   and crumbled   6 tbsp sour cream
2 tsp onion juice

Grate cheddar. Mix cheeses until creamy. Add other ingredients. Mix well. Roll into 1 large ball or small cheese balls. Refrigerate

"Potato Stuffing" Dip

1 small can Wilson's Bacon Bits or   2 c grated cheddar cheese
  1 c chopped cooked bacon   ½ c green onions chopped
½ pint sour cream   (optional)

Toss all together lightly and serve as a dip. Use crackers, rye bread, potato chips or crisped potato skins as dippers.

Crisp Potato Peels

Bake potatoes until done. Lower oven to 275°. Cut potatoes into quarters lengthwise. Scoop out pulp leaving a little clinging to skin. Cut peels into strips. Place them, peel down, in a shallow buttered baking dish. Drizzle melted butter over them and sprinkle with salt and pepper. Bake at 275° for 10–15 minutes until crisp. This makes a super hors d'oeuvre or snack.

Cream Cheese Dip

*1 large Philadelphia cream
    cheese*
¼ small white onion
1 tsp worcestershire

3 drops Tabasco
1 (4 oz) sour cream
juice of 1 lemon
salt and pepper to taste

Mix all ingredients together until creamy.

Serving Suggestions:

1. with Fritos and potato chips
2. fill scooped out cabbage with dip and serve with carrot and celery sticks, cherry tomatoes, zucchini and yellow squash strips, snow peas, cauliflower buds, cucumber
3. add 1 can tuna fish, and serve in fresh tomato
4. add 1 can crabmeat or ground smoked salmon
5. stuff celery, cherry tomatoes, jalapenos

Raymond's Picante Dip

3 large packs cream cheese

8 oz Paces picante sauce

Mix together. Serve with Doritos. You may add some chopped jalapenos. Put some in flour tortilla. Roll up in paper towel and place in microwave for 1 minute. Delicious with flank steak (see index).

Doug's Deviled Eggs

12 eggs
4 heaping tbsp mayonnaise
1 tsp yellow or Dijon mustard
2 tbsp Durkees

onion juice (optional)
salt
pepper
1 tsp worcestershire

Have eggs at room temperature. Place eggs in pan of cold water. Put eggs on fire and bring to a boil. Remove from fire. Cover and let stand 20 minutes. Remove eggs and cool. Peel eggs. Slice eggs in half. Mash egg yolks with all other ingredients. Stuff back into white halves. Sprinkle with paprika. Chill. Leftover deviled eggs make great egg salad sandwiches. Chop up and spread on bread or toast.

Seafood Dip

1 can lump crabmeat
1 lb cooked shrimp
2 pints sour cream
6 tbsp lemon juice
salt, pepper, cayenne

6 oz frozen king crab
6 oz frozen snow crab
16 oz cream cheese
½ grated onion
worcestershire

Mix sour cream, cream cheese, and seasonings. Cut seafood into small pieces. Add to cheese. Hollow a large round loaf of crusty bread, leaving a rather thick part on the bottom. Fill hole with dip. Use hunks of bread for dippers.

Randa's Guacamole

8 ripe avocados
½ white onion grated
juice of 3 lemons
garlic salt (or 1 fresh garlic clove)
salt

pepper
seasoning salt
2 fresh or canned green chile,
    seeded and chopped fine
few drops of Tabasco

Mash avocados well and add seasonings to taste. If avocados aren't real tasty, a few drops of Tarragon Vinegar help. Save 4 seeds and keep in bowl to keep dip from turning dark. To make more guacamole, if you don't have enough ripe avocados, you can add the frozen guacamole mix or cream cheese. Serves 16.

Chili Con Queso

1 large Velveeta cheese
½ lb sharp cheddar
1 can Rotel Tomatoes and Chiles
1 white onion

Tabasco
jalapenos
1 garlic pod

Melt Velveeta and cheddar in top of double boiler. Add Rotel. Grate in onion. Add a few drops of Tabasco and juice of one garlic. Slice jalapeno strips and add. Let stand several hours. Serve with fried tortillas, Doritos or Fritos. Keep hot.

Green Enchiladas

2 dozen fresh tortillas
1 fryer
2 chicken breasts
4 small cans or 2 pints fresh
  green tomatillos (Mexican
  green tomatoes)
2 hot green chiles (fresh)

1 onion
2 c grated Monterrey Jack cheese
  (you can use Swiss, cheddar or
  American cheese if you prefer)
½ pint sour cream
2 c Wesson or Mazola
2 garlic cloves or garlic salt

Cook tomatillos, onion, green chiles (remove the seeds if you don't want real hot sauce) salt, pepper, garlic about 30 minutes. (If using fresh tomatoes, add one cup water.) Put in blender. Return to skillet. Cook chicken in water with celery, parsley, salt and pepper. When chicken is tender, remove from stove and pick meat from bone. Run tortillas through hot grease, then through sauce. Place some shredded chicken and a spoon of cheese in each tortilla. Roll up and place side by side in 2 (9 × 12) baking dishes. Pour remaining sauce over top. This may all be fixed early in the day. When ready to serve, place in 350° oven until hot. Add the rest of the grated cheese and sour cream and return to oven until cheese is melted. This is trouble, but worth it! Delicious served with guacamole salad. Serves 12.

Mexican Chalupas

1 pork roast or 2 pork tenders
1 lb pinto beans
8 c water
1 large onion
2 garlic cloves

2 jalapeno peppers
3 tbsp chili powder
1 tbsp comino
salt and pepper

Wash beans and soak overnight. Chop onion and jalapenos. Drain beans, mix with onion, jalapeno, 1 teaspoon salt, 1 tablespoon chili powder and comino. Pour in bottom of roaster pan. Season meat with garlic, salt, pepper, 2 tablespoons chili powder. Place meat on beans and pour in 8 cups water. Cover and roast at 325° for about 5 hours. When done, pull meat apart in strips and semi-mash beans. Serve on hot chalupa shells with following: grated Monterrey Jack cheese, Rat and Romano cheese, chopped avocado, tomatoes, onions, guacamole, hot sauce and sour cream. Serves 12.

Chiles Rellenos Tomas

4 cans Ortega whole chiles
6 eggs
2 tbsp flour
salt
pepper

Rat cheese or American cheese
or cream cheese (combination
of 3 cheeses is good)
cooking oil

Drain chiles. Slice "fingers" of cheese (American, cheddar, cream or Swiss). Stuff each chile with cheese. Handle carefully as they tear easily. Beat egg whites until stiff. Add 2 tablespoons of flour. Beat yolks and fold into whites. Salt and pepper chiles, dip in egg mixture and fry in hot grease until batter looks crispy and golden and cheese has melted. Serve with Salsa Fria. All the boys in the family love these and can fix them! Serves 8.

Chile Relleno Casserole

2 (4 oz) cans Ortega Whole Green
  Chiles
1 small can evaporated milk
4 eggs
salt
pepper

garlic salt
1 lb grated Monterrey Jack cheese
1 lb grated cheddar cheese
1 tbsp flour
sour cream

Cut chiles into strips or bite size chunks. Mix the 2 kinds of cheese and chiles. Heavily butter long pyrex baking dish. Place chile-cheese mixture into dish. Separate eggs. Mix flour, milk, and seasonings into egg yolks. Whip egg whites stiff and fold into the yolk mixture. Pour over chiles and cheese. Bake at 325° for 30 minutes. Serve with hot sauce and sour cream. (Chopped onion is good on it, too.) Serves 6.

Salsa Fria
(Hot Sauce)

6 fresh tomatoes
1 large onion
1 garlic pod (optional)

2–4 fresh green chile peppers
  (more if you want hotter sauce)

Chop all fine. Do not use blender. If you can find Cilantro (fresh coriander), add this to sauce. Salt and pepper to taste. Use canned firm tomatoes if fresh ones aren't tasty.

James' Chili Pie

Fritos or Doritos
chili

cheese—Velveeta or rat

Put chips in bowl. Heat chili *real hot*. Pour over chips. Top with grated cheese. Add chopped onions if desired.

Tortilla Soup

1 onion, chopped
1 jalapeno, chopped
2 garlic cloves, mashed
2 tbsp oil
1 lb can stewed tomatoes
1 can chicken broth
1 can water
1 tsp comino
1 can beef bouillon

1 tsp chili powder
1 tsp salt
1 tsp pepper
2 tsp worcestershire
½ tsp Tabasco (optional)
8 corn tortillas, fried
   or nacho chips
1 c cheddar or white cheese,
   grated

Combine first 5 ingredients and saute in large kettle. Add the next 10 ingredients and simmer for 1 hour. Cut tortillas into strips and add to soup. Simmer 10 minutes. Serve in bowls and pass cheese and extra hot sauce, or put in bowls and bake. Serves 10.

Vegetable Soup

1 large meaty soupbone
2 lb stew meat
1 (28 oz) can tomatoes
1 bunch carrots
4 potatoes
2 onions
2 turnips
salt and pepper

2 zucchini
2 yellow squash
½ lb green beans
1 pack frozen lima beans
1 pack frozen green peas
1 pack frozen cut corn
1 tbsp celery salt
1 jalapeno pepper

Place bone, meat and 1 gallon of water in giant pot. Add a splash of vinegar and seasoning salt. Cover pot and simmer for 3–4 hours. Cut vegetables in bite size pieces. Add tomatoes and fresh vegetables to stock. Cook 40 minutes. Add frozen vegetables and seasonings. Cook 10 minutes. This freezes well. Serves 10.

Cold Avocado Soup

1 large ripe avocado
2 green onions
1 tsp salt
1 tsp seasoning salt
3 or 4 drops of Tabasco

1 envelope dried vegetable broth
1 c whipping cream
1½ c milk

Put avocado, onion, cream in blender. Mix well. Add seasonings, dried broth, and milk. Blend until smooth. Taste for seasoning. Chill well. To keep from turning dark, put seed in soup until serving time. Serve in small cups and top with fresh chopped chives. Serves 4.

Quick Oyster Stew

1 c fresh oysters
1 tbsp onion
salt, pepper

1 can celery soup
1 c cream
2 tbsp butter

Chop oysters. Saute onions until soft. Add oysters and saute five minutes. Add soup. Mix well. Add cream and seasoning. Heat until hot but not boiling. You may put a whole oyster in each cup of soup. Serves 4.

Onion Soup

2 quarts water
6 onions
1 stick butter
6 tbsp flour

3 c grated Swiss cheese
French bread
salt and pepper
dash of sugar

Slice onions in thin strips. Saute onions in butter until golden. Sprinkle onions with flour and saute until lightly browned. It is easier if you do this in two pans—the onions will saute more evenly. Combine all onions, add water, salt, pepper, and sugar. Simmer for 30 minutes. Cut *crisp*

crusty French bread into thin slices. Place bread in bottom of deep casserole or in individual casseroles. Pour soup over bread and cover top with cheese. Bake in hot oven until cheese is melted and slightly browned. This soup is better if it stands several hours. Add bread and cheese when serving. If too thick add water or clear broth. Serves 10.

Gumbo

5 lb raw shrimp	4 bouillon cubes
4 onions	1 #2 can tomatoes
1 green pepper	3 #2 cans water
3 stalks celery	1 small can tomato sauce
1 lb okra (frozen or fresh)	1 tbsp chili powder
3 tbsp butter	1 can lump crabmeat (fresh)
3 tbsp bacon grease	1 can crab claws (fresh)

Shell and clean shrimp. Chop onion, green pepper and celery. Saute chopped vegetables in 3 tablespoons of bacon grease. Add canned tomatoes and okra and cook until done. Salt and pepper to taste. Saute shrimp in 3 tablespoons butter. When golden, add 4 bouillon cubes, water, salt, pepper and chili powder. Cook until shrimp are done. Mix vegetables and shrimp together. Add tomato sauce. If you want to freeze some, take it out now. Simmer remainder for 10 minutes. Add crabmeat just before serving and get it *real hot*. Serve with rice. Serves 12.

Baby John's Pizza

1 package English Muffins—split	salami rounds or thin slices of hot dog
2 packages grated Mozzarella cheese	1 jar Ragu (Italian tomato sauce)

Place cheese, Ragu and salami rounds on English muffin halves. Broil until cheese melts. Serve immediately. Small children can fix this, and they are really delicious. You can make Ragu with a small can of tomato sauce and dry spaghetti seasoning.

Carroll's Fried Baloney

baloney   mayonnaise or A-1 sauce
bread

Grill baloney in skillet or griddle until real hot. Put baloney on bread with mayonnaise or A-1 sauce on it.

Thomas' Supersonic Sandwich

3 slices bread   mayonnaise
2 slices American cheese   pickles (hot—Rainbo garlic dills)
2 slices each—baloney, salami,   mustard (optional)
   ham

Put mayonnaise on bread. Put 1 slice cheese, baloney, ham and salami and lots of pickles on 1 slice. Then, make another layer. You can grill or serve plain. Fun for children to make. Good on French bun.

Canadian Bacon Sandwiches

To cook Canadian bacon, see index for recipe for Canadian bacon. You may use any kind of bread. Sometimes you can find a round sliced bread which fits the bacon perfectly. Onion rolls are delicious. Put mayonnaise, mustard, hot mustard, sour cream and purple onion, relish, cheese, pickles and cracked pepper out in bowls. Let everyone create their own delight! This also makes a delicious *hot* sandwich.

Croissant Wiches

Fill french croissants with ham, cheese, cream cheese. Serve hot or cold. Delicious with brie cheese.

French Dip Sandwich

1 roast with natural gravy
French bread or rolls

mustard, mayonnaise,
horseradish

Cook any kind of roast. Slice meat and serve on French bread or rolls. Give each person a small bowl of natural gravy from the meat to dip the sandwich in. Serve with other sandwich fixings. Boys love this.

Sunday Burgers

hamburger patties
hamburger buns

sliced onions (optional)
cheese (optional)

Cook hamburgers in *butter* on griddle. Grill thinly sliced onions on same griddle. Grill buns in butter on same griddle. Serve meat and onions on buns with mustard, mayonnaise, pickles, etc. Another way to serve hamburgers is to make a mixture of: cream cheese, horseradish and bacon and spread on buns (especially good on rye buns). Add meat and other fixings.

Tuna Salad

3 cans white tuna
1 jalapeno pepper
grated onion

¼ tsp jalapeno juice (optional)
lemon juice
3 heaping tbsp mayonnaise

Do not drain all oil from tuna. Mix tuna, mayonnaise. Add onion and lemon to taste. Chop jalapeno fine (remove seeds if you do not want it hot). Add jalapenos and juice. Hors d'oeuvre idea: Stuff seeded jalapenos with tuna and chili.

Spinach Salad

fresh spinach
green onions
cream cheese
rat cheese

bacon bits
fresh black pepper
seasoning salt
lemon juice

Lemon Dressing:

1 c olive oil
½ c lemon juice
salt
pepper

dry mustard
worcestershire (optional)
3 garlic pods (place whole in jar)

Wash and dry spinach well. Put in plastic bag. Chill and crisp. Chop green onions, grate rat cheese, cut cream cheese in small pieces, break up bacon (or use Bac-Os or Wilson's Bacon Bits). Break spinach in bowl. Squeeze some fresh lemon juice over leaves. Sprinkle with seasoning salt. Add salad dressing. Toss with bacon, cheeses and green onions. Top with cracked pepper.

Variations: Sliced turkey or chicken, small pieces of ham or Canadian Bacon, Swiss cheese or Rondole cheese, mushrooms, tomatoes. Any or all, added to salad, are delicious.

Cucumbers or Jicama

4 cucumbers
lemon or lime juice

seasoning salt

Peel and slice cucumbers. Squeeze lemon or lime juice over cucumbers. Sprinkle with seasoning salt and refrigerate. Good "snacks." To crisp cucumbers, peel and place whole in ice cubes. Then slice. These are good with lime juice and a little cayenne. Also with white vinegar and a tablespoon of dill and salt to taste. There is a mexican turnip type vegetable called Jicama which is delicious and crunchy and can be fixed in the same way as cucumbers. Children love it. It is good chopped in chunks and put into salad.

Crunchy Cole Slaw

cabbage
1 pint sour cream
1 c mayonnaise
½ c white vinegar
pepper

1 heaping tsp celery salt
1 tsp seasoning salt
grated onion to taste
1 tbsp dill pickle juice

Shred cabbage. Put in plastic bag and keep *real* cold. Mix all other ingredients and let stand all day. Mix cabbage and dressing just before serving. People that "hate" slaw seem to like this. It is crunchy and tart. Also
good with shredded cucumber or tomato added. Serves 6.

Variation: 1 small jar chopped pimento olives, 3 whole green onions
chopped, ¼ cup ketchup, ¼ cup mayonnaise, salt, pepper, 1 teaspoon
vinegar. Mix together and toss with shredded cabbage.

Grapefruit, Avocado, Orange Salad

4 grapefruit
4 oranges

3 avocados
10 lettuce cups

Peel grapefruit and oranges whole. Section out in whole sections. Peel
avocados. Slice avocados in lengthwise slices. Arrange lettuce cups with
avocado, orange and grapefruit slices. You may serve with oil and vinegar or poppy seed dressing. This will make 10 salads, but I always have
to make more because they get gobbled up!

Poppy Seed Dressing

1 c sugar
2 tsp dry mustard
2 tsp salt
⅔ c vinegar

3 tbsp onion juice
2 c Wesson Oil
3 tbsp poppy seeds

Mix first 5 ingredients. Beat in oil. Add poppy seeds. Store in refrigerator.
This is also good on shredded cabbage. If you don't want to make dressing, La Martinique Poppy Seed dressing is excellent.

Green Bean Salad

2 cans Blue Lake green beans
  (vertical pack)
1 large onion

1 tbsp olive oil
1 tbsp vinegar
salt and pepper

Arrange beans and thinly sliced onions in dish in layers. Mix oil, vinegar, salt and pepper and dribble over beans. Refrigerate at least 4 hours. Serve in lettuce cups topped with dressing. Mix all following ingredients together:

½ pint sour cream
½ c mayonnaise
1 tbsp lemon juice

¼ tsp dry mustard
2 tsp horseradish
few drops onion juice

Holiday Cranberry Salad

1 (10 oz) package frozen sliced
  strawberries
1 can whole cranberry sauce
1 tsp lemon juice

1 (10 oz) package frozen red
  raspberries
2 (3 oz) packages any red Jello
1 c water

Mix Jello with cup of boiling water. Add thawed berries. Mix well. Add cranberry sauce. Chill until firm. Serves 10 to 12.

Cherry Jello Salad

1 large box black cherry Jello
1 large box cherry Jello
2 c boiling water
1 c Coke

1 large can Bing cherries
juice from cherries to make 1 c
  (add water if not enough)

Fix jello as directed on package, substituting Coke and cherry juice for cold water. Add Bing cherries. Pour into mold or 9 × 12 pyrex. Chill until firm.

Zucchini-Avocado Salad

½ c sour cream
¼ c mayonnaise
½ tsp Italian seasoning
¼ tsp garlic salt

1 tsp salt
3 avocados
2 zucchini

Mix all ingredients except avocado and zucchini. Cut avocado into bite size pieces. Slice zucchini into rounds. Mix gently into dressing. Add 1 tablespoon vinegar and serve in lettuce cups. Serves 8.

Tomato Aspic

18 oz can tomato juice
1 14 oz can tomatoes
3 fresh tomatoes
3 carrots
4 stalks celery
1 fresh green chili pepper or
   4 drops Tabasco

juice of 2 lemons
1 onion
2 tsp worcestershire sauce
salt and pepper
1 tbsp Picka-peppa
3 packages Knox gelatin

Boil all but gelatin. Let simmer for 1 hour. Remove from heat and force through sieve. Soften gelatin in 1 cup water, V-8, or tomato juice. Add to hot tomato mixture. Pour into glass mold which has been "greased" with mayonnaise. Chill until firm. You may add: olives, cream cheese balls, artichoke hearts, avocado, hearts of palm, cocktail onions or shrimp to partially congealed aspic. Serve on lettuce leaf with homemade mayonnaise.

Blender Mayonnaise

2 whole eggs
1 c Wesson oil
1 tsp salt

2 tbsp lemon juice
1 tsp dry mustard

Beat eggs at high speed in blender, add mustard and salt. Add oil in steady stream. Add lemon juice

Variations: *1 tsp onion juice or*
1 tsp curry powder or
½ c finely chopped watercress

Stephen and T.R.'s Salad Dressing

2 tsp Dijon mustard
½ tsp cayenne
2 tsp salt

1 tsp pepper
⅓ quart salad oil
⅓ quart vinegar

Mix seasonings and vinegar in quart jar. Stir in oil. You may use part olive oil. This is tart but very tasty. If dressing is too oily add water. Add crumbled roquefort or blue cheese for a taste treat.

John's Salad Dressing

Mix lemon juice, seasoning salt, worcestershire and maggi sauce to taste. Pour over salad greens.

Hofbrau Dressing A La Bynum

2 crushed garlic pods
1 tsp pepper
½ tsp salt
1 tsp worcestershire sauce

⅔ c olive oil
4 tbsp lemon juice
24 finely chopped pimento olives

Mix all ingredients except oil and olives. Add oil slowly, blending well. Add chopped olives. Pour over finely cut lettuce.

Creamy Roquefort Dressing

1 small package cream cheese
1 c oil and vinegar French
   dressing
½ c mayonnaise

½ c Roquefort cheese (or Blue)
½ pint whipping cream
¼ tsp garlic salt
1 tsp onion juice

Blend all together until smooth. Serve over greens.

Guadalupe Fish Fry

red fish, snapper, trout or catfish,
   oysters, scallops
cornmeal
oil

lemon juice
paprika
dry mustard
salt and pepper

Buy a fish for each two people you plan to serve (more if fish fillets are small and you have big eaters!) Skin and fillet fish. Cut fish into finger strips. Soak fish in lemon juice. Lightly salt and sprinkle with paprika. Pour cornmeal in large brown bag. Season meal with salt, black pepper and dry mustard. Heat oil in *big* iron skillet. Put fish in bag, shake, and drop fish in hot fat. Fry until golden. You can't cook it fast enough! We cook this on the river in Hunt, and it disappears like popcorn! Serve with a bottle of ketchup and a bottle of Tabasco. Jalapeno corn bread and slaw are perfect with it. Also, some cold white wine.

Madora's Quick Curry

1 ½ lb raw fresh or frozen shrimp
  (peeled and cleaned)
2 tbsp butter
¾ c sour cream

1 (10¾ oz) can cream of shrimp
  soup
1 (10¾ oz) can cream of mushroom soup
1 ½ tsp curry powder

Thaw shrimp if frozen. Stir and cook shrimp in butter for 3–5 minutes. Add soups and stir until smooth. Stir in sour cream. Add curry powder. Squeeze ½ lime over curry. Serve with rice and pita bread. Chopped onion, peanuts, eggs, coconut, chutney for condiments. Serves 6.

Quick Red Sauce

1 c ketchup
2 tbsp Mr. Mustard

juice of 1 lemon

Mix together. Tasty and quick!

Shrimp or Crab Sauce

1 ½ c mayonnaise
¼ c chili sauce
¼ c ketchup
2 tbsp lemon juice
1 tbsp vinegar
1 tbsp worcestershire sauce

1 tbsp onion juice
2 tbsp horseradish or
  Mr. Mustard
½ tsp seasoning salt
Tabasco

Mix all ingredients. Let stand a few hours before serving to let flavor meld.

Oyster Fritters

1 c chopped oysters
4 eggs
salt
pepper

cayenne
6 tbsp flour
grated onion (about 1 tbsp)

Beat egg yolks until they thicken. Add seasonings. Add flour, mixing it in well. Beat egg whites stiff. Fold egg whites into yolk mixture. Fold in chopped drained oysters. Drop by spoonfuls into hot fat. Fry until golden and crunchy.

Barbecue Shrimp

3 dozen shrimp
1 jar Woody's Cooking Sauce

½ c butter
1 lemon

Peel and clean shrimp. Put 6 shrimp on each skewer. Coat shrimp with Woody's Cooking Sauce. Cook over hot coals. Baste for last 2 minutes with butter and lemon. Serve for hors d'oeuvres or as a main course. Do not overcook.

Shrimp in Liquid Smoke

Boil shrimp (shelled or unshelled) in water with Liquid Smoke and salt. Serve with Barbecue Sauce for dipping.

Sauteed Lump Crabmeat

Saute fresh lump crabmeat in butter until hot. Serve with hot bread.

Chicken Kiev Casserole

8 chicken breasts, boned and
  pounded thin
8 (1") squares of butter
1 c milk
1 egg
juice of ½ lemon

1 tsp salt
1 c sliced mushrooms
2 c sour cream
¾ c chives or ½ c very finely
  chopped green onion tops

Wash, dry and split chicken breasts. Pound until thin. Season with salt, pepper and garlic salt. Insert pat of butter in each breast. Fold together. Press and pound edges together. Dip in batter made with milk, egg, lemon and salt. Roll in flour and fry in butter or deep fat until tender, about 5–7 minutes. Drain fat. Saute mushrooms. Add chives and sour cream. Put chicken in casserole. Pour sauce over top and bake, covered, at 350° until hot. When you cut into the chicken, the butter should squirt out. This can be serve without the sauce. Good with brown rice.

Chicken Salad

5 boned chicken breasts
chicken broth
3 oz package cream cheese
1 c mayonnaise

½ c sour cream
1 tsp dill seed (optional)
salt to taste
fresh ground black pepper

Cook chicken breasts in broth seasoned with celery, parsley, carrot and onion. When tender, remove chicken and cut into chunks. Reserve broth for consomme or freeze to eat or cook with later on (good for "sick" days). Cream together cheese, sour cream, mayonnaise, salt and dill seed. Mix with chicken and cracked pepper. Chill. Serve on tomato, lettuce cup, or avocado. Serves 10.

Variation: Toasted almonds, water chestnuts and curry powder, chopped celery, green onions, capers.

"Munchen" Chicken

This is a simple roasted chicken from "Octoberfest." They were roasted on a spit and served whole. We ate them with our hands with a giant mug of cold beer. This is as close as we've come at home.

6 whole young fryers　　　　　*fresh parsley*
coarse ground salt　　　　　*paprika*
coarse ground pepper

Wash and dry fryers. Grind rock salt and black pepper. Rub chicken inside with salt and pepper. Stuff chicken with parsley. Sprinkle outside of chicken with paprika. Rub chicken, covering well, with coarse salt and pepper. Preheat oven to 425°. Roast chickens on a rack for 1½ hours. Turn chicken every 20 minutes so they brown evenly. The coarse salt and high temperature are the secret to the juicy inside and crunchy outside. This is really better done with young fryers, 2 pounds or under.

Easiest Chicken

2 fryers (cut up) or 10 breasts　　　*1 package onion soup mix*
　or 6 thighs & 6 breasts　　　　*1 can of beer*
1 pint sour cream　　　　　　*2 cans mushroom soup*
1 c uncooked rice

Mix onion soup with beer. Season chicken with salt, pepper, and garlic salt. Place chicken in baking dish, on top of rice, cover with beer, soup, sour cream and bake at 350° for about 1½ hours. If you like mushrooms, add to casserole for last 15 minutes. Serves 10.

"Backhendl"
Austrian Fried Chicken

5 boned chicken breasts
½ c flour
3 eggs
½ c oil
paprika

2 c bread crumbs (Italian are best)
½ c butter
salt
pepper

Pound chicken breasts until flat. Split in half. Mix flour, salt, pepper and paprika. Cover breasts lightly with flour, dip in egg, and then into bread crumbs. Place in refrigerator for at least 1 hour. Heat oil and butter. Fry chicken about 5 minutes a side. Children love this! Try fixing chicken by dipping it in fine cracker crumbs and frying in butter. Serves 10.

Dove Casserole

1 can mushroom soup
1 can mushrooms—undrained
4 or 5 whole garlic cloves
1 can beer
12 to 15 doves

salt and pepper
flour
1 small can jalapenos
12 to 15 bacon slices

Combine soups, garlic, beer in deep casserole. Cover and place in 450° oven. Bring to a boil. Salt and pepper doves. Roll in flour. Place ½ jalapeno in each wrap with bacon. Put doves in casserole. Reduce oven to 250°. Bake at least 2 hours.

Squab

This is fun—like having your "own" little chicken. Good to eat with your fingers! Tender.

8 squab   worcestershire sauce
salt and pepper   parsley

Wash and dry, and rub squab with salt, pepper and margarine. Stuff with parsley. Sprinkle with worcestershire. Put in roasting pan, pour a cup of white wine over birds, cover and bake until tender, about 1½ hours. If you like them browner, turn broiler on for a few minutes before serving. These are so tender, tasty and *easy* to fix! I like to stuff them with dressing. (See dressing recipes.) Squab may also be split in half and broiled with butter and lemon juice, salt, pepper and worcestershire. Broil about 30 minutes. Do not overcook.

Wild Duck

10 ducks—clean, clean, clean!   3 apples
1 bottle worcestershire   3 stalks celery
salt to taste   10 buttons garlic
pepper to taste   10 strips bacon
3 onions

Sprinkle ducks inside and out with vinegar. Rinse and dry. Salt and pepper ducks inside and out. Quarter onions, apples and celery. Put 1 button of garlic and 1 piece of apple, onion and celery in each duck. Pierce breast with fork. Place ducks in roasting pan. Put 1 slice of bacon over each one and pour bottle of worcestershire over ducks. Add 1–2 cups of water to bottom of roaster. Cook uncovered for 15 minutes at 400°. Lower oven to 325° and cover pan. Bake until tender, about 2 hours. Remove bacon and stuffing before serving ducks. Serve with wild rice. A treat in our house, but Mama doesn't cook unless the ducks come in clean.

Barbecued Wild Duck and Dove

Place onion and garlic pod in cavity of clean duck. Salt and pepper each bird. Saturate birds with Louisiana hot sauce (not Tabasco). Wrap each in a strip of bacon. Wrap in foil. Cook in oven for 4½ hours at 250° or on smoke pit for 5 hours.

To cook 6 doves, melt 1 stick of butter, add juice of 1 lemon, 4 tablespoons A-1 sauce. Add worcestershire and seasoning salt to taste. Place birds in sauce. Cook birds directly over coals, basting until brown on both sides.

Smoked Turkey—Tamale Stuffed

Stuff turkey with hot tamales. Mix 2 tablespoons salt, 1 tablespoon black pepper, 1 tsp red pepper, 1 garlic pod. Rub on turkey. Cover entire turkey with foil. Cook on pit 8–12 hours. The secret of good barbecue is slow cooking. Be sure to use enough coals. Keep fire hot.

Pepper Corn Steak

steaks—Strip, Club, New York cut or Rib-Eye	*salt*
pepper corns	*butter*

Salt both sides of steak. Grind pepper coarse. Press pepper into both sides of steak. Broil steak under broiler (leave door partially open), or on red hot coals. Remove steak when done and spread a heaping spoonful of butter over steak. The butter and pepper give this steak a super flavor! If broiling a plain steak in the oven, let the steak marinate 5 minutes a side in butter. Then salt and pepper meat and broil. The butter keeps meat from hard searing.

Cliffe's T-Bones

10 thin (¼") young beef T-bones   salt
   (not heavy beef)   pepper
worcestershire sauce

Heat skillet. Rub bottom of skillet with fat trimmed from T-Bones. Salt and pepper meat. Fry steaks on one side, about 4 minutes. Turn steaks and pour worcestershire sauce all over steaks. Continue frying until done. You can only fit 3 or 4 steaks in the skillet at a time, so serve right out of pan onto hot plate and eat immediately.

Oven Brisket

5 lb beef brisket   garlic salt
1 (4 oz) bottle Smoke Worcester-   salt
   shire or Liquid Smoke   pepper
plain worcestershire   1 large chopped onion
celery salt

Night before, rub brisket with celery salt, garlic salt. Sprinkle with onions. Marinate in Smoke Worcestershire. Before cooking, remove from marinade. Salt, pepper and sprinkle with plain worcestershire. Wrap in foil. Seal. Roast in pan 5–6 hours at 225°. (I like to do two 4 pound briskets.) Good with barbecue sauce. Leftovers make such great hot barbecue sandwiches.

Barbecue Sauce

1 bottle ketchup
1 cup vinegar or 6 lemons, juiced
2 beef cubes or 2 chicken cubes
1 c beer
1 tbsp worcestershire sauce
1 garlic clove
1 onion in quarters

1 tsp chili powder
1 tsp prepared mustard
salt
pepper
Tabasco
celery salt to taste
½ c Tequila

Simmer all together for at least 20 minutes.

Beef Tartar

2 lb ground round—raw
½ c onion—minced
½ c capers
8 anchovies—minced
paprika

2 eggs slightly beaten
salt and pepper
worcestershire
Tabasco
2 tsp parsley—minced

Blend all ingredients together. Form into a ball. Chill. Serve with toast or bread.

Stew

4 lb lean stew meat
3 c water
1 c tomatoes or tomato juice
6 carrots
2 turnips
2 zucchini
2 yellow squash
2 onions

1 package green peas
12 new potatoes
salt
pepper
Lawry's Seasoning Salt
garlic salt
½ c of Sauce Robert, A-1, or
   other brown meat sauce

Season meat with salt, pepper and garlic salt. Flour lightly and brown in small amount of fat. Put meat in large Dutch oven or roasting pan. Add 3 cups of water, meat sauce and 1 cup of tomato juice or canned tomatoes. Simmer covered on top of stove or cook in oven for 1½ hours. While stew is cooking, peel vegetables. Quarter onions, leave new potatoes whole, and cut carrots, squash, zucchini and turnips in bite size pieces. Sprinkle vegetables with seasoning salt. Add potatoes, carrots and onions to stew. Continue cooking 30 minutes. Then add turnips, squash and peas. Cook 20 more minutes. Add water if liquid is not enough. Keep hot until ready to serve. This is delicious with hot biscuits or a crusty French bread, red wine and a cheese platter.

"Little League" Stew

3 lb stew meat	*1 c Burgundy wine or beer*
1 envelope onion soup mix	*salt*
2 cans mushroom soup	*pepper*
2 cans drained mushrooms	*garlic salt*

Mix in casserole or roasting pan. Cover and bake at 300° for 3 hours. Do not peek! Good with brown rice.

Leg of Lamb

1 large or 2 small lamb legs	*salt*
garlic	*pepper*
worcestershire sauce	

Rub lamb with crushed garlic, salt and pepper. Cover generously with worcestershire sauce. Add 2 cups of water to roasting pan and bake in 375° oven for 3 hours. This is for well done lamb. Some prefer it pink, so cut down on cooking time. To cook outside, smoke in pit for 6 hours (not over coals.) Makes a real crusty skin. Season ½" T-Bone lamb chops with same seasonings and broil for about 4 minutes a side. Serve at least 3 per person.

Lamb Shish-Kabob

1 leg of lamb	*¼ c worcestershire*
fresh mushrooms, whole	*1 bay leaf*
cherry tomatoes, whole	*3 cloves garlic*
onions, quartered	*1 chopped onion*
½ c oil	*salt*
1 c red wine vinegar	*pepper*
½ c soy sauce	*paprika*

Have lamb cut in cubes. Marinate overnight in vinegar, soy sauce, oil, onion, worcestershire, garlic, bay leaf and paprika. Prepare skewers with lamb, onion, tomato and mushrooms. Salt and pepper meat and vegetables. Cook over charcoal for about 20 minutes—turn every 5 minutes. Zucchini chunks are good on this.

Barbecue Weiners

½ c chopped onion	*16 frankfurters*
½ tsp salt	*¾ c ketchup*
1 tsp dry mustard	*¾ c water*
3 tsp sugar	*6 tbsp vinegar*
½ tsp pepper	*4 tsp worcestershire sauce*
1 tsp paprika	*3 drops Tabasco*

Saute onion in ¼ cup oil. Add all ingredients and simmer 15 minutes. Split weiners and place in baking pan. Cover with sauce. Bake in 375° oven for 30 minutes. Baste while baking.

Outside Ribs

4 sides lean spare ribs
meat tenderizer
vinegar

salt and pepper
garlic salt (Lawry's)
worcestershire

Wash off ribs. Sprinkle with meat tenderizer. Pour over ribs: vinegar and worcestershire. Rub with: salt, pepper, garlic salt (Lawry's). Put on barbecue pit (not over flame), and let cook 5 hours or until tender. Turn every hour. The last hour, baste with barbecue sauce. Wrap in foil and keep in warmer or warm oven until ready to eat. Wrapping any barbecue meat in foil for at least 20 minutes will make it juicier.

Inside Ribs

Fix ribs the same as for outside. Bake in oven for about 4 hours at 350°. Check for tenderness, as texture and thickness of meat changes cooking time. After ribs have cooked for an hour, baste with barbecue sauce.

Barbecue Sauce: 1 bottle of store bought barbecue sauce
       Add: ¼ c vinegar or lemon juice
            5 dashes Smoky Worcestershire
            1 bouillon cube
            ½ c water
            2 tbsp brown sugar

Canadian Bacon

1 whole or ½ Canadian bacon
1 can beer (Coors)

1 tbsp mustard
1 c brown sugar

Pour ¾ can of beer over bacon. Bake at 350° for 20 minutes, basting 2 or 3 times. Combine mustard, brown sugar and ¼ can of beer to make a paste. Spread on bacon and cook for 1 hour.

Weenies and Kraut

1 jar Jamison Sauerkraut
2 packages Kosher Knockwurst
1 tbsp tarragon vinegar
1 tsp celery seed

½ tsp pepper
1 tbsp bacon grease
1 onion

Saute chopped onion in bacon grease. Drain sauerkraut and add to onion. Add seasonings. Brown weiners under broiler about 2½ minutes a side. Add weiners to kraut and simmer about 30 minutes. This is fun to fix with an assortment of sausages and weiners. Browning in broiler enhances flavor. Serve with rye, brown or pumpernickle bread, Dijon mustard and cold beer.

T.R.'s Venison Chili

2 lb chili cut meat
1 onion, chopped
1 jalapeno, chopped
2 cloves garlic, minced
paprika

1 14 oz can tomatoes, chopped
1 c water
5 tbsp chili powder
5 tbsp cumin
salt and pepper

Brown meat. Add everything else and let simmer about 1 hour. To make thicker add 2 tablespoons of masa flour mixed with warm water the last 15 minutes.

Venison Jerky

3 lb lean venison
1 tbsp salt
2 tsp pepper
1 tsp garlic powder

1 tsp onion powder
½ c worcestershire
¼ c soy sauce
1 tbsp prepared mustard

Cut venison in ½" wide and ¼" thick strips. Mix all ingredients. Marinate meat overnight. Remove from marinade. Dry with paper towels. Place a drip pan in bottom of oven. Hang strips of meat over oven rack. Let meat dry and cure. Electric oven should be at 200°. Leave hanging until jerky is of right consistency. In gas oven, meat will cure in 4 days using only the heat from pilot light. This can also be made with flank steak.

Weiner Schnitzel or Veal Milanesa

20 paper thin slices white veal
5 eggs, beaten
bread crumbs

salt and pepper
paprika
flour

Salt and pepper veal lightly—dip in flour, then in beaten egg and then in bread crumbs mixed with paprika. This can be done early in the day, then refrigerate. When ready to eat, fry veal slices in Mazola and olive oil about 3 minutes (or until golden brown). This deserves a cold glass of Soave Bolla (white Italian wine) or Moselle. Try this with *raw* turkey or chicken breast or pork. Pound thin and flat. Cook as above.

Inell's Apple Sauce

Cook 6–8 peeled tart apples in ½ cup water for five minutes. Add 1 heaping teaspoon cinnamon, 1¼ cups sugar. Cook over low heat until soft, mash and serve hot or cold.

Apple Rings

3 tart apples
1 c sugar
¾ c water

½ tsp red food coloring
¾ tsp cinnamon

Core apples. Slice apples into rings (leave skin on). Boil sugar and water until syrup spins a thread. Add cinnamon and food coloring. Add apple rings. Leave rings in hot syrup about 10 minutes. Serve with pork dishes. Another way is to combine 1 package of Red Hots candy with 3 tablespoons butter and ¾ cup water. When Red Hots have melted, add apple rings and cook about 10 minutes.

Eggplant Casserole

2 eggplants
1 lb ground beef
2 strips bacon
2 onions, chopped
2 garlic pods, chopped

salt and pepper
2 eggs
bread crumbs or cracker crumbs
2 c Velveeta cheese, grated

Steam eggplant until tender. Slice and coat with bread or cracker crumbs. Fry and drain. Fry bacon until slightly crisp. Chop bacon. Add chopped onion and garlic and saute until golden. Stir in ground beef and cook until done. Slightly beat 2 eggs. Cut up fried eggplant. Mix eggplant, meat, eggs and 1 cup of cheese together. Put in casserole, top with other cup of cheese and bake until hot and cheese is melted. Serves 10.

Jalapeno Spinach

4 packages frozen chopped
  spinach
8 tbsp butter
4 tbsp flour
1 small finely chopped onion
1 c evaporated milk
1 c vegetable liquor
1 tsp pepper

dash cayenne
2 tsp celery salt
2 tsp garlic salt
1 tsp salt
2 6 oz rolls Jalapeno cheese
2 tsp worcestershire
2 tbsp lemon juice

Cook spinach. Drain well and reserve liquor. Melt butter, add onions and saute until tender. Add flour and mix until smooth. Add liquid slowly, stirring constantly to avoid lumping. Cook until it thickens. Add seasonings and cheese. Stir until it is melted. Combine with spinach and place in casserole. Top with buttered bread crumbs. Before serving, heat until bubbly. This is better if made the day before. It also freezes beautifully.

Good Luck Black-Eyed Peas

1 large piece smoked ham   *black pepper*
1 onion   *salt*
1 garlic   *2 packages frozen, black-eyed or*
1 jalapeno pepper   *   1 lb fresh peas*

Cook ham and onion in boiling water about 30 minutes. Add peas, garlic, jalapeno, salt and pepper. Cook until tender. Keep pot on stove all New Years Day so everyone can have a bite.

Cauliflower

1 whole cauliflower   *water*
1 c milk or skim milk   *salt*

Soak cauliflower head down in cold, salted water for 15 minutes. Place cauliflower in boiling water, salt and 1 cup milk. This keeps cauliflower white. Cook uncovered for about 15 minutes. Drain. Serve covered with hollandaise, buttered bread crumbs or cheese sauce.

Cheese Sauce:

2 tbsp butter   *1 c grated yellow cheese*
2 tbsp flour   *dash cayenne*
1 ½ c milk   *dash paprika*
½ tsp dry mustard

Melt butter. Stir in flour until well blended. Stir in milk slowly. When sauce is smooth and hot, add seasonings and cheese Stir until cheese is melted.

Spinach With Cream Cheese

3 packages frozen spinach
1 (8 oz) package Philadelphia
   cream cheese
½ stick butter
2 tsp lemon juice

1 small chopped onion (or
   ½ c green onions
Tabasco
salt
pepper
bread crumbs

Cook spinach as directed on package. *Drain well*. Combine butter, cream cheese, onion and spinach and lemon juice. Season to taste. Put in casserole and top with bread crumbs. Bake at 350° for 10 minutes, or until hot and bubbly. Try this with ½ cup sour cream and 1 packet onion soup dip (omit fresh onion).

Stuffed White Squash

12 summer squash
1 chopped onion
½ stick butter
1 c cracker crumbs (Escort
   are best)

1 c cheddar cheese, grated
salt to taste
pepper to taste
seasoning salt

Boil whole squash (or steam) until barely done (about 10 minutes). Scoop out pulp and reserve. Save shells. Brown onion in butter, add pulp, crumbs, salt, pepper and cheese. Mix and stuff back into shells. Place in baking dish. Cover and heat about 20 minutes in 350° oven.

Squash and Cream Cheese

10 yellow squash
1 (8 oz) package cream cheese
6 tbsp butter

salt
pepper

Cook squash in tiny amount of water (or steam) until tender, about 10 minutes. Halve squash and drain well in colander. Place halves on pan. Salt and pepper halves. Place a wedge of softened cream cheese on each half—top with other half. Pour butter over squash. Cover tightly and bake until cheese begins to melt. A few chopped green onions sprinkled over cheese add flavor.

Zucchini Mexicani

4 lb zucchini squash	*2 (4 oz) cans diced green chilies*
¾ stick butter	*2 c sour cream*
1 c diced onion	*1 tsp salt*
3 c jack or cheddar cheese	*1 tsp pepper*
2 c bread crumbs	*1 tsp garlic salt*

Scrub zucchini. Soak 10 minutes in salted water. Slice and saute with onions in 3 tablespoons of butter. Drain. Drain chilies. Mix all ingredients together except bread crumbs. Put in 9 × 12 casserole. Sprinkle with crumbs and dot with remaining butter. Bake at 350° for 20–25 minutes. Serves 12.

Corn on Cob

corn	*salt*
butter	*pepper*

Wrap each buttered, seasoned ear in a separate piece of foil. Bake in 350° oven for 30 minutes.

Carroll's Mushrooms

Saute fresh mushrooms in butter and a few drops of Liquid Smoke. Salt and pepper to taste.

Bacon Wrapped Corn

8 ears corn	*8 slices bacon (thin)*

Wrap ears of corn with bacon. Place on grill and cook about 20 minutes or until bacon is cooked and corn done. Turn often.

Baked Beans

1 large can pork and beans
½ c brown sugar
1 tsp yellow mustard
2 tsp worcestershire sauce

½ onion
¾ c ketchup
4 slices bacon

Mix beans, mustard, ketchup, worcestershire and sugar in casserole. Grate onion into beans. Spread bacon across top. Bake at 350° for about 45 minutes. Good with barbecue ribs, chicken or weiners.

Beer Batter

2 c flour
1 can of beer (Coors, of course)

salt
pepper

Just mix together and use for frying any vegetable. Green pepper rings are great. Onions, zucchini, yellow squash, parsley and okra. A very light, tasty batter and easy. Onion rings are good dipped in sour cream and flour, then fried.

Easy Batter

1 package pancake mix
½ c milk
½ c water
1 egg

salt
pepper
1 tsp worcestershire sauce

Dip sliced vegetables in batter and fry in deep fat. Try canned asparagus tips fried in olive oil.

Blender Hollandaise

3 egg yolks
1 tbsp cream
1 c melted butter

1 tbsp lemon juice or white wine
vinegar
dash cayenne pepper

Place egg yolks, cream and pepper in blender and blend at high speed for a few seconds until smooth. Melt butter. At high speed, add warm butter thin, steady stream. When half of butter has been added, pour in lemon juice or vinegar. Continue blending until all butter is added.

To make a *Mock Bernaise,* add: 2 tablespoons tarragon vinegar in place of lemon juice, 1 tablespoon chopped parsley, 1 teaspoon chopped chives or green onion and fresh black pepper. Serve with beef tender or Tournedos.

Potato Casserole

12 red or new potatoes
6 strips cooked bacon or ½ c
bacon bits

2 c sharp cheddar, grated
½ stick butter

Boil potatoes, with skins on, until done. Drain and let cool. Slice thin. Butter bottom of 9 × 12 baking dish. Put one layer of potatoes, salt, pepper, half of cheese and bacon in casserole. Dribble ½ butter over layer. Make another layer the same way. Bake in 350° oven until bubbling hot (about 15 minutes).

Roasted New Potatoes

Wash small new potatoes. Rub with butter. Cover with coarse salt. Roast in 400° oven for 1½ hours. These are really crunchy.

Greatest Au Gratins

6 medium California or
  red potatoes
1 stick butter
1 c flour
1½ tsp salt
pepper

4 c milk
2 c cream
1 c sour cream
1 c grated American cheese
bread crumbs

Boil potatoes in jackets in salted water. Cool, peel and *cube*. Melt butter, add flour and salt and stir into smooth paste. Scald milk and cream and add to butter and flour, stirring constantly. Cook for 10 minutes. Cool and add sour cream. Add potatoes. Pour into 9 × 12 buttered casserole, or individual casseroles. Sprinkle cheese over top. Add thin layer buttered bread crumbs over top. Bake at 375° for 20 minutes or until hot and bubbly. This is a lot of trouble, but so good, it's worth it. It does not freeze well. Serves 12.

Easy Au Gratins

1 (2 lb) package frozen
  hash browns
½ c melted butter
1 tsp salt
1 tsp pepper
1 can cream of chicken soup

1 pint sour cream
2 c grated cheddar cheese
1 c Velveeta cheese, grated
½ c finely chopped onion
  (optional)

Thaw potatoes. Grease baking dish. Mix all ingredients well. Pour into baking dish. Cover with buttered bread crumbs and bake at 350° for about 45 minutes.

Cliffe's Sweet Potatoes

3 c mashed sweet potatoes
1 c sugar
¼ tsp salt
½ stick butter

½ c milk
2 eggs
½ tsp vanilla

Mix all ingredients together. Pour into casserole and bake at 350° for ½ hour. Cover top with marshmallows for last 10 minutes of baking.

Variation: Add ¼ teaspoon cinnamon to first mixture. Omit marshmallows. Combine ½ cup flour, 1 cup brown sugar, ½ stick butter and 1 cup chopped pecans. Top potatoes with this and bake 30 minutes.

Brown Rice

2 c rice
2 chicken bouillon cubes
4 c water

½ stick butter
1 tsp salt
1 can mushrooms (optional)

Brown raw rice in butter. Dissolve bouillon cubes in water, add salt. Pour rice and bouillon into oven casserole. Add mushrooms. Bake covered at 350° about 1 hour. This is good using 2 cups onion soup and 2 cups consomme.

Jalapeno Rice

1 c uncooked rice
1 small can chopped green chilies
1 c sour cream
½ c salad oil

1 garlic clove
2 jalapenos, seeded and chopped
  (optional)
1 lb sharp cheese, grated

Cook rice. Add other ingredients to rice. Mix well. Bake at 275° for 1 hour. This is also good with Monterrey Jack cheese, or combine both cheeses. Good to make with leftover rice. Freezes well. Serves 6.

Wild Rice

1 c wild rice
2 tbsp salt
1 stick butter
¼ c flour

2 c milk
1 (8 oz) package cream cheese
1 c mushrooms

Wash wild rice well. Stir rice into 4 cups boiling water and 1 teaspoon of salt. Cook without stirring for 40 minutes to an hour. Drain. Melt butter, and stir in flour. Slowly stir in milk. When sauce is smooth and hot, stir in cream cheese and other teaspoon of salt. Stir until cheese is melted. Butter a 2 quart casserole. Make layers of rice, mushrooms and cheese sauce, ending with good amount of sauce. Bake at 325° about ½ hour or until hot, bubbly and golden brown. Serves 6.

Turkey Dressing

4 c dry lightly toasted bread
4 c crumbled cornbread
4 c biscuits, crumbled
¾ c chopped onion
½ c green onions
¼ c chopped parsley
1 c chopped celery

1½ tsp salt
½ tsp Lawry's garlic salt
1 tsp black pepper
1 tsp sage
1 c broth
½ c butter
2 beaten eggs

Combine all ingredients. Mix well. Stuff turkey and bake.

Sausage Dressing

¾ c yellow cornmeal
1 c flour
1 tbsp baking powder
1 tsp salt

1 c milk
1 egg, beaten
2 tbsp butter or bacon grease

Preheat oven to 425°. Sift dry ingredients together. Add liquids. Mix and bake in greased pan for 20 minutes. Crumble cornbread in bowl and add:

1 lb ground sausage (hot is best)	*3 tbsp worcestershire sauce*
6 ribs finely chopped celery	*2 eggs*
1 bunch chopped green onions	*½ tsp garlic salt*

Mix all well and bake at 350° for about 40 minutes.

Fettucine

2 lb fettucine noodles	*1 egg, beaten*
1 stick butter	*¼ lb fresh Parmesan cheese*
½ carton whipped butter	*1 wheel Gruyere cheese (6 oz)*
3 c heavy cream or creme fraiche	

Boil very large pot of water with 1 tablespoon olive oil, 1 tablespoon salt—drop in fettucine and cook 2–3 minutes (if fresh), 5–7 minutes if dry. I always test pasta by throwing one piece on a tile wall. If it sticks, it's "al dente." Pour noodles in colander. Drain. Return noodles to *hot* casserole and toss with sauce.

Sauce:

Blend butter, grated Parmesan and grated Gruyere. This can be prepared early. At serving time, warm egg and cream in saucepan. Add cream and cheese mixtures to hot fettucine. Toss well and serve immediately. (Warm plates because noodles cool very quickly.) Serve with fresh ground pepper.

Canneloni

1 box canneloni or manicotti
   noodles
1 lb ground round
2 tbsp olive oil
1 small, finely chopped onion
5 tbsp fresh, grated Parmesan
   cheese

1 tsp finely chopped garlic
½ tsp oregano
salt and pepper to taste
3 jars of baby strained spinach
2 slightly beaten eggs
2 tbsp heavy cream

Saute onion and garlic in olive oil. Add meat and cook until done. Add spinach and mix well. Then add eggs, cheese and seasonings. Boil water with some celery salt in large kettle. Cook noodles. Drain well. Stuff noodles with meat mixture.

Sauce 1: Tomato

2 cans Italian tomatoes
1 package Lawry's plain
   spaghetti mix

fresh black pepper
Mix and simmer for 20 minutes.

Sauce 2: Besciamella

6 tbsp butter
6 tbsp flour
1 c milk

1 c heavy cream
1 tsp salt
⅛ tsp white pepper

Melt butter. Stir in flour. Pour in milk and cream, stirring constantly with a whisk. Whisk over heat until sauce comes to a boil. Simmer, still stirring, 2 or 3 minutes or until sauce coats whisk heavily. Season with salt and pepper. Preheat oven to 375°. Pour a thin layer of tomato sauce in bottom of two rectangular baking dishes. Lay stuffed noodles side by side on sauce. Cover with rest of tomato sauce and pour Sauce 2 over top. Sprinkle each casserole lightly with grated Parmesan and dot with butter. Bake for 20 minutes or until hot and bubbly. This can be made the day before. Cover tightly in refrigerator. Freezes well. Serves 8 to 10. This is good meatless. Stuff noodles with Mozzarella, cream cheese and Ricotta. Cover with sauces and bake.

Mexican Macaroni

3 c cooked macaroni
3 c sour cream
1 lb Monterrey Jack cheese
cheddar cheese

2 small cans Ashley's green,
  chopped chiles
1 seeded & chopped jalapeno
salt and pepper

Cook and drain macaroni. Cut Monterrey Jack cheese into strips. Mix sour cream, chiles and seasonings. Butter casserole. Make 2 layers of macaroni, sour cream, cheese strips. Cover with grated cheddar. Bake at 350° about 30 minutes or until hot and bubbly. Serves 6.

Manicotti "Mama"

1 package manicotti noodles
1 lb ground beef
1 package Lawry's Spaghetti
  sauce seasoning
1 #2 can tomato sauce
3 c Mozzarella cheese

1 onion, chopped
1 garlic pod or garlic salt to taste
salt and pepper
1 tbsp celery salt
8 oz Ricotta cheese

Brown meat and onions. Add spaghetti sauce, garlic and tomato sauce. Cook noodles in boiling water with 1 tablespoon celery salt and 1 tablespoon olive oil "al dente." Rinse noodles in colander. Stuff with grated Mozzarella cheese. Spread thin layer of meat sauce on bottom of pyrex dish. Place stuffed manicotti on top of sauce. Sprinkle 8 ounces of Ricotta cheese on top. Cover with remaining meat sauce. Sprinkle with Parmesan cheese. Bake at 350° until hot and bubbly. You can also cover with cheddar cheese at last 5 minutes. Tastes like Italian enchiladas. Serves 8 to 10.

Garlic Bread

1 loaf crusty Italian or French
   bread
2 sticks butter

2 buttons garlic
grated Parmesan cheese

Melt butter. Squeeze garlic into butter with garlic press. Mix well. Slice bread into ¾" slices. Dip completely into butter. Coat completely with cheese. Broil on both sides until golden.

Thomas' Quick Garlic Bread

Spread bread with butter. Sprinkle with garlic salt and any cheese. Run under any broiler.

Jalapeno Cornbread

1 c yellow cornmeal
1 tbsp baking powder
1 (8 oz) can yellow creamed corn
⅔ c Mazola
2 eggs
½ pint sour cream

½ tsp salt
1 c grated rat cheese
1 small onion, grated
4 jalapeno peppers, seeded
   and chopped

Preheat oven to 400°. Combine all ingredients. Pour into well greased baking pan (12 × 8 × 2). Bake 20–25 minutes. This is good with ½ cup chopped bacon added.

Bread Stix Trix

½ c melted butter
1 package bread sticks

½ c Parmesan cheese or
½ c cinnamon sugar

Pour butter over bread stix. Roll them in cheese or sugar mix. Place on cookie sheet. Bake 10 minutes at 350°.

Coors Beer Biscuits or Bread

1 (12 oz) can Coors beer
3–5 tbsp sugar

3–4 c Bisquick or self-rising flour

Mix together thoroughly. Grease muffin cups (12). Fill halfway. Bake at 350° for 15–20 minutes, or pour into greased loaf pan, cover with ¼ cup butter and bake at 350° for 40 minutes.

Christiana's Bran Muffins

1 15 oz box Raisin Bran
3 c sugar
5 c flour
5 tsp soda

2 tsp salt
4 beaten eggs
1 quart buttermilk
1 c vegetable oil

Mix all dry ingredients. Mix eggs, oil and milk. Add to dry ingredients and stir well. Pour into greased muffin tins. Bake at 350° for 15 minutes. You may add 5 tsp of cinnamon. Makes 3 dozen muffins. Mix will keep for 6 weeks in refrigerator.

Banana Muffins

1 egg
⅓ c salad oil
½ c sugar
4 very ripe bananas

1¾ c flour
¼ tsp salt
2 tsp baking powder
¼ tsp soda

Beat egg slightly, add sugar and oil. Add mashed bananas and mix well. Sift dry ingredients into banana mixture. Stir until just blended. Mixture will be lumpy. Fill 12 greased muffin cups ⅔ full. Bake at 375° about 15 minutes.

Randa's Blueberry Muffins

1 c sugar
⅔ c shortening
3 eggs
3 c flour

1 tsp salt
2 tsp (heaping) baking powder
1 c milk
1 can blueberries or 1 c frozen

Preheat oven to 375°. Drain blueberries. Cream shortening and sugar. Add eggs, 1 at a time. Sift dry ingredients. Add dry ingredients and milk alternately to shortening and sugar. Fold in blueberries. Bake in muffin tins greased only on bottom. This batter will keep a couple of weeks in the refrigerator. Really light!

Dell's Bread
(Originally my great grandmother's)

4 c milk
2½ c sugar
3 fresh yeast cakes

¼ c Crisco
2 tbsp salt

Heat these ingredients together until Crisco melts. Crumble 3 fresh yeast cakes on top of warm milk mixture. (You may use 3 packages of dry yeast.) When this mixture gets puffy, add 2–3 cups of flour. This mixture should be about the consistency of pancake batter. Beat this until smooth. Beat in 2 eggs. Cover. Let mixture rise until double. Push down and add 5–7 cups more of flour. Beat in well. This takes lots of arm power. Spread top of dough with lots of melted butter. Cover and let rise again. When mixture rises to top, it is ready to work. (If mixture is ready and you aren't, just punch dough down and let rise again.) To make loaves of bread, take out a big spoonful and work it with hands until it stays together. You might have to work more flour into dough to get it to the right consistency. This is the hard part—something that takes practice to get the right feel. Dell could just put it all together. She would tell me "Don't be scared of it, work it!" I still get tunnels in my loaves. Form your loaves and place in bread pan which is covered on bottom with butter. Cover pans with dish cloth. Let dough rise over pan. Preheat oven to 450°. Place pans in oven, lower heat to 350°. Bake 30–40 minutes. This

sounds hard, but if you ever have time, and you want to really feel close to earth—try it! You will never taste anything better. Good luck! And, if it doesn't turn out, the smell of bread baking will make everyone love you anyhow. This also makes the most divine hot rolls.

Dell's Bun

Fix bread as in previous recipe. Roll out dough and sop with butter. Soak 1 cup raisins in milk. Sprinkle raisins, cinnamon and sugar over dough. Roll up dough into roll. Put in bread pan or casserole. Pour butter over top. Let bun rise to double. Bake in 350° preheated oven about 40 minutes. Do not overcook. This can be made, rolled up and sliced into rounds. Place rounds in buttered cake pans and bake for sweet rolls. Gooey and good.

Leftover Bread, Bread Crusts or Dried Bread

1. Make French toast.
2. Cube and freeze for dressings.
3. Toast slightly and grind in blender for bread crumbs.
4. Split and slice hamburger and hot dog buns in strips. Dip in melted butter. Bake in 250° oven until crisp—good bread sticks. Before baking, roll in seame seeds for a crunchy treat.

Bread Pudding: I love this!

1½ c milk	1 c bread cubes
1 c sugar (white or brown)	1 c raisins
2 eggs	½ c pecans
½ stick butter	1 tsp vanilla
1 tsp baking powder	

Mix all together and bake at 325° for ½ hour. Add 1 cup coconut if you like. Nutmeg and cinnamon may be added for a spicier taste. Brown sugar makes a more "caramely" pudding. Serves 6.

Gooey Rolls

16 large marshmallows
2 cans Pillsbury Icebox
   Crescent Rolls

½ c sugar
½ c melted butter (or margarine)
1 tsp cinnamon

Mix sugar and cinnamon. Dip marshmallows in melted butter. Roll in sugar mixture. Separate dough into triangles. Wrap 1 triangle around each marshmallow and pinch dough together. Dip in butter. Place in muffin tins or cake pans and bake at 375° for 10–15 minutes. *Glaze:* 1 cup powdered sugar, 2 tablespoons butter and 1½ tablespoons milk (more if needed), ½ teaspoon vanilla. Serves 8.

Pumpkin Bread

5 c flour
4 c sugar (you can use ½ brown,
   ½ white)
4 c pumpkin (canned)
1 c oil
1 tsp cloves

2 tsp cinnamon
1 tsp salt
4 tsp baking soda
1 tsp vanilla
1 c chopped pecans
1 box raisins or chopped dates

Mix all ingredients. Grease and flour five 1 pound coffee cans. Fill cans half full. Bake at 350° for 1 hour. Remove from oven. When cool, use coffee can lids to cover and store. This bread gets more moist after a couple of days. Bread will come out of can easily. This freezes well.

Rice Muffins

1 c cold, cooked rice
2 eggs
1 c milk
1½ c flour

¼ tsp salt
3 tsp baking powder
12 slices bacon (thin)
3 tsp sugar

Beat eggs and milk together. Add rice. Sift dry ingredients together. Mix into egg and milk. Put a strip of bacon around each muffin cup. Fill each cup half full of batter. Bake at 400° for 25 minutes. This is a good recipe for leftover rice.

Tommy's Bananas

1 stick butter
1¾ c light brown sugar
½ lemon

1 oz banana Liqueur
5 bananas

Melt butter in large skillet. Add sugar. Stir until melted. Add liqueur and juice of ½ lemon. Cook until sauce is bubbly. Slice bananas in half, then lenthwise, so each banana makes 4 pieces. Add bananas to syrup mixture. Turn bananas in syrup for about 4 minutes. Do not overcook. Pour sauce and bananas over vanilla ice cream. These are so good and so rich!

Crunchy Apple Betty *Good*

8 tart apples
1 c brown sugar
½ c white sugar
1 c flour

1 tsp vanilla
½ c butter or margarine
1 tsp cinnamon
1 tsp nutmeg

Peel, slice apples. Place apples in buttered casserole. Sprinkle with white sugar, cinnamon, and nutmeg. Add ¼ c water. Mix brown sugar, flour, vanilla and butter until crumbly. Cover top of apples. Bake at 400° for 15 minutes. Reduce heat to 350° and bake 25 minutes. Serve with ice cream or whipped cream or just plain. Rich but delicious and easy. This can be made with peaches or 2 cans sour pie cherries. Substitute 1 teaspoon almond extract for cinnamon. Increase white sugar to 1 cup when using cherries.

Salzburg Nockerl
Vanilla Souffle

2 egg yolks	*4 egg whites*
1 tsp vanilla	*pinch salt*
½ tsp grated lemon peel	*2 tbsp sugar*
1 tbsp flour	*powdered sugar*

Preheat oven to 350°. Mix egg yolks with a fork and stir in vanilla and lemon peel. Sprinkle flour over yolks. Beat egg whites with salt until they cling to beater. Add sugar and beat until stiff. With spatula, stir part of egg whites into yolk mixture, then fold back into rest of whites. Do not over fold. Butter an oval or oblong (8 × 10 × 2) baking dish. Sprinkle with powdered sugar. Make 3 mounds of mixture (touching) in dish. Bake in middle of oven 10–12 minutes or until it is lightly brown on outside, but still soft inside. Sprinkle with powdered sugar and serve immediately. Good "Mit Schlag" (whipped cream).

Cinnamon Pudding

1 c brown sugar	*2 tsp baking powder*
3 tbsp butter, melted	*2 tsp cinnamon*
¾ c water	*1 c milk*
2 c flour	*1 tsp vanilla*
1 c sugar	*1 c chopped pecans*
¼ tsp salt	

Bring water, 1 tablespoon butter and brown sugar to a boil. Pour into square baking pan. Sift flour, sugar, baking powder, salt and cinnamon. Add milk, 2 tablespoons butter and vanilla. Beat real well. Pour over mixture already in pan. Sprinkle chopped pecans over top. Bake at 350° for about 40 minutes. Serve with whipped cream or pudding sauce.

Date Pudding

1 c dates, chopped
1 c pecans, chopped
1 c sugar

2 eggs
3 tbsp flour
1 tsp baking powder

Preheat oven to 325°. Sift flour and baking powder together. Add to dates and nuts. Beat eggs and sugar together. Add to other mixture. Bake in a greased pan, set in water, for 45 minutes. Serve with whipped cream or pudding sauce.

Pudding Sauce

3 eggs, separated
⅔ c butter
1½ c sugar

2 tsp boiling water
1 tsp vanilla

Cream butter and sugar. Add boiling water. Add egg yolks and beat until creamy and smooth. Add vanilla. Beat egg whites stiff and fold into mixture. Add bourbon to this if you like a hard sauce taste.

Mother's Dessert

1 c brown sugar
1 egg, beaten
⅓ c sifted flour
1½ c broken pecans

½ tsp baking soda
1½ tsp vanilla
1 c whipping cream

Mix all ingredients except cream. Bake at 325° for 25 minutes. Remove from pan and crumble into bowl. Cool. Whip cream. Fold into cookie mixture. Chill and serve. This is a real favorite! Serves 6.

Chocolate Sin

1 stick margarine
1 c flour
½ c chopped pecans
1 large Cool Whip
1 tsp vanilla

1 (8 oz) cream cheese
2 small instant chocolate
  pudding
1 c powdered sugar
2½ c milk

Mix flour, margarine, pecans, and press into 9 inch pie pan. Bake at 350° for 10–15 minutes. Combine cream cheese, powdered sugar, 1 cup Cool Whip and vanilla. Mix until smooth. Spread over crust. Mix pudding with milk. Add 1 cup Cool Whip. Spread over cheese mixture. Cover with remaining Cool Whip or ½ pint of fresh whipped cream. Refrigerate.

Almeta's Strudel
Biscuit Dough Scraps (see Almeta's Biscuits)

6 tart apples
1 c stewed apricots
1 c raisins
1½ c sugar

1 tsp cinnamon
½ tsp nutmeg
1 tsp vanilla
1 stick butter

Take leftover biscuit dough pieces and put into 2 pans. Slice apples. Mix apples, apricots and raisins. Place on pans. Mix sugar and spices. Sprinkle over fruit. Put more biscuit dough scraps on top. Melt butter, add vanilla and pour over pies. Bake at 350° until apples are done.

Amaretto Freeze

Amaretto Liqueur (or
  Creme de Noyaux)

vanilla ice cream

Fill blender with vanilla ice cream. Add 1 cup liqueur and blend. Serve in champagne glasses. This is good as a dessert or an after dinner drink.

Chocolate Chantilly

1 c sugar
7 squares unsweetened chocolate

½ c water
1¾ c whipping cream

Dissolve sugar in water in top of double boiler. Add chocolate and melt over simmering water. Remove pan and *completely* cool chocolate mixture. Whip cream until it holds peaks. Gradually add chocolate and beat until stiff. Chill. This may be served out of 1 big bowl or put in individual pots de creme or parfaits. It will seem as though it is too soft, but it will become firmer after chilling for several hours.

Thomas' Mousse

A quick chocolate mousse the children can whip up. Put a big spoonful of chocolate or fudge syrup into a bowl. Add a couple of large squirts of canned, whipped cream and mix well with a spoon and eat. So easy and really tasty.

Microwave S'mores

2 graham cracker squares
1 large marshmallow

½ (1.5 oz) chocolate bar

Place marshmallow on 1 cracker square. Place on paper towel. Microwave high 15–25 seconds (until marshmallow puffs). Top with chocolate candy bar and other cracker square. Yummy!

Flo's Lemon-Orange "Shuffle"

juice of 2 large oranges
juice of 1 large lemon
4 eggs, separated

2 packages Knox gelatin
⅔ c sugar
½ pint whipping cream

Beat egg yolks and sugar until smooth. Dissolve gelatin in ¼ cup cold water. Add ¼ cup boiling water. Alternately, add juices and ½ of gelatin to egg yolks, beating constantly. Beat egg whites until stiff. Add other ½ of gelatin. Fold in yolk mixture. Pour into cold, rinsed mold and refrigerate until firm. Unmold and serve garnished with whipped cream.

Strawberry Romanoff

3 pints fresh strawberries
⅔ c powdered sugar
½ c Cointreau or Amaretto

¼ c fine sugar
1 pint whipping cream

Wash and hull berries. Put berries in crystal bowl. Cover with liqueur and powdered sugar. Let stand in refrigerator until serving time. Whip cream and fine sugar until thick. Serve berries with side bowl of cream or fold in together and serve. An elegant but easy dessert. You may serve over ice cream or beat ½ pint vanilla ice cream into whipped cream.

Grandmother's Raspberry Cooler Dessert

2 pints Raspberry Ice

2 cartons frozen raspberries

Thaw raspberries. Serve scoop of ice covered with raspberries in a glass bowl. Very refreshing, light, pretty and simple!

Ice Cream Clowns

Fun for children's parties. Make ice cream balls. Put cone on ball so it looks like a clown hat. Make faces in ice cream balls with M & M candies, red hots or any other small decorative candies. Keep in freezer until serving time.

"Fredericksberg" Peach Ice Cream

2 pints whipping cream
1 pint Half & Half
1 large mixing bowl of peaches,
  sliced

2 c sugar
2 tsp vanilla
2 tsp almond extract

Chill ice cream container to electric freezer. Slice peaches. Cover with 2 cups sugar (this makes juice come out). If peaches are not real tasty, squeeze a lemon over them. Let this stand at least 2 hours. Combine cream, Half & Half, vanilla and almond extract. When ready to freeze, mash peaches and taste for sweetness. Combine peaches and cream mixture in cold freezer container. Churn in mixer until done. Remove dasher and pack in ice. Use 6 parts ice to 1 part ice cream salt. When packing, use 8 parts ice to 1 part salt. Substitute strawberries for peaches; or use juice of 6 lemons, 3 cups sugar, no almond for a good lemon ice cream.

Apricot Cream

2 c stewed, strained apricots
  with juice
1 c sugar
3 tbsp lemon juice

1½ tsp gelatin
¼ c cold water
1 pint whipping cream

Soak gelatin in water. Bring apricots to a boil. Dissolve gelatin in hot apricot. Add sugar and lemon juice. Chill until almost set. Whip cream until stiff. Fold in apricot mixture. Freeze or refrigerate.

Three Fruit Sherbet

4 oranges
3 lemons
3 mashed bananas

1 pint milk
½ c sugar
½ c white corn syrup

Squeeze lemons and oranges. Add milk, sugar, syrup and bananas. Put in bowl in freezer. When partially frozen, stir well. Return to freezer and serve when solid.

Orange Ice

6 c fresh orange juice
3 c water

½ c sugar (more or less depending on sweetness of oranges)

Mix all together in large bowl. Place in freezer. Stir several times while freezing. Pretty to stuff into hollowed out orange shells and top with a sprig of mint.

Grapefruit Ice

1 c sugar (you can substitute
    Sweet & Low for sugar—
    about 6 packs)

6 c fresh grapefruit juice
3 c water

Prepare the same as Orange Ice. This is really refreshing. Ices can be made with any fruit—just add water and sugar to taste: cantaloupe, watermelon, pineapple, lemon, lime, strawberry, peach, apricot, etc.

Angel Food Cake

13 egg whites
2 tsp cream of tartar
1½ c sugar (sifted or superfine)
¼ tsp salt

1 c flour (sifted 6 times)
2 tsp vanilla (or 1 almond,
  1 vanilla)

Preheat oven to 375°. Beat egg whites and salt until thick. Add cream of tartar and beat 4 minutes in electric mixer. Add sugar gradually. Add flour. Add vanilla. Rinse Angel Food pan in cold water. Dry and pour in batter. Bake 40 minutes. Remove pan and invert on bottle until cool. For chocolate angel food cake: add ¼ cup cocoa sifted with flour.

Icing:

3 c whipping cream
1½ c powdered sugar

¾ c cocoa
dash salt

Whip cream. Sift in cocoa, sugar and salt. Blend and ice cake.

Stephen's Birthday Cake

1 Angel Food cake
2 pints fresh strawberries
1 pint whipping cream

1 tsp vanilla
¼ c sugar
¼ c powdered sugar

Buy or bake 1 Angel Food cake. Wash and trim berries, reserving 6–8 of the prettiest ones. Slice the rest and cover with sugar. Beat cream until thick enough to spread on cake. Add powdered sugar, vanilla and strawberries. You may also add a drop of red food coloring to make icing pink. Ice entire cake with this. Place whole strawberries around top. Refrigerate. This may also be fixed with a pound cake. Split and ice layers as well as top.

James' Birthday Cake

2 c sugar
2 c flour
1 stick butter
½ c shortening
4 tbsp cocoa

1 c water
2 beaten eggs
½ c buttermilk
1 tsp soda
1 tsp vanilla

Sift together sugar and flour. Bring butter, shortening and water to a boil. Add cocoa, flour and sugar. Mix well. Add eggs, milk, soda, vanilla. Pour into greased and floured 9 × 12 pan. Bake at 400° for 30 minutes. Leave cake in pan. Ice while warm. (See Icing—following recipe.)

Chocolate Icing

1 stick butter
4 tbsp cocoa
6 tbsp milk

1 box powdered sugar
1 tsp vanilla
1 c pecans (optional)

Melt butter, add cocoa and milk. Bring to a boil. Sift powdered sugar. Add sugar to hot mixture. Stir until smooth. Add vanilla and pecans. Spread on cake while hot. This cake gets more moist after a couple of days, so it can be made ahead of time.

Diane's Oatmeal Chocolate Cake

1 c oatmeal
1 stick butter
½ bar German chocolate
1 c white sugar
1 c brown sugar

2 eggs
1 tsp vanilla
1⅓ c flour
1 tsp soda

This is a super quick cake to make. Preheat oven to 350°. Pour 1½ cups boiling water over 1 cup oatmeal. Add 1 stick butter and ½ bar German chocolate. Let stand 20 minutes. Mix 1 cup white sugar, 1 cup brown sugar, 2 eggs, 1 teaspoon vanilla, 1⅓ cups flour and 1 tablespoon soda to oatmeal mixture. Bake in greased sheet cake pan 35 minutes. Dust with powdered sugar or use same icing as on James' Birthday Cake.

Prune Cake

1 c sugar	*2 tsp cinnamon*
¾ c butter	*1 tsp allspice*
3 eggs	*1 tsp soda*
1 c prunes (cooked, seeded and mashed)	*pinch of salt*
3 tbsp sour cream	*flour to make a stiff batter (about 2 c)*

Cream butter and sugar. Add eggs, prunes, sour cream. Gradually mix in dry ingredients which have been sifted together. Bake at 350° in greased and floured tube pan about 40–45 minutes.

Icing:

1 c sugar	*½ c sour cream*
3 eggs	*lump of butter*
1 c prunes (cooked, seeded and mashed)	*1 c pecans*
	1 tsp vanilla

Mix all ingredients in order listed. Stir over stove until thick enough to cover cake. Very rich. You can split cake into layers and put icing in between.

Prune Whipped Cream

Soak pitted prunes in Amaretto (overnight). Cut up and fold into whipped cream. Serve over plain cake, or as a dessert.

Apricot Whipped Cream

Mix stewed, strained apricots with sweetened whipped cream, almond and vanilla extract. Serve over Angel or pound cake.

Cliffe's Birthday Cake
1 Angel Food Cake, Fudge Filling, White Icing

Prepare 1 white Angel Food cake—you may make it from scratch, use Angel Food Cake Mix or buy an Angel Food cake from the store or bakery. Cut center hole slightly larger. Prepare fudge filling.

Fudge Filling:

1 box powdered sugar
1 stick butter
¼ c cocoa

¼ c milk
2 tsp vanilla

Bring butter, cocoa, milk to a boil. Add powdered sugar (put sugar through a strainer or sifter to prevent lumping). Blend well. Add vanilla. Fill hole of Angel Food cake with chocolate mixture. Ice cake with white icing.

White Icing:

2 egg whites
1 c white corn syrup
4 tbsp white sugar

½ tsp almond extract
½ tsp vanilla
¼ tsp salt

Beat egg whites with salt until they form soft peaks. Mix syrup and sugar in pot over fire until sugar dissolves and mixture boils. Beat egg whites and pour syrup over slowly in thin stream until all is gone. Continue beating until consistency is good for spreading. Add vanilla and almond. Spread on cake. This will not harden or crack. Be sure to ice cake when no one is around or there won't be enough left to cover the cake.

Mother's Spice Cake

½ c butter
1½ c sugar
1 tsp baking powder
3 eggs, separated
2 c cake flour

1 tsp cinnamon
¾ tsp nutmeg
1 tsp soda
pinch of salt
1 c sour milk

Cream butter and sugar. Add baking powder and beat well. Beat egg whites stiff. Add this to sugar mixture. Add 3 egg yolks. Sift together flour, spices and soda. Add dry ingredients and milk alternately to first mixture. Beat well. Bake in greased layer pans at 350° about 30 minutes. This cake is good with either of the following icings.

Icing 1: White

2 c sugar
⅔ c water
2 egg whites
1 c raisins

2 tsp corn syrup
1 c pecans
1 tsp vanilla

Soak raisins and pecans overnight in bourbon. Mix sugar, water and syrup. Cook until firm ball stage. Beat egg whites stiff. Pour syrup over egg whites, beating constantly. Add *well drained* raisins and pecans. Add vanilla. Dribble a little of drained bourbon over cake layers. Ice layers and cake.

Icing 2: Caramel

1 stick margarine
1 c brown sugar, sifted
¼ c milk

1¾ c powdered sugar, sifted
1 tsp vanilla

Stir sugar and margarine over low heat 1 minute. Add milk and bring to a boil. Remove from fire and add powdered sugar until right consistency to spread on cake.

Peggy's Rum Cake

1 golden butter cake mix
1 small package vanilla or lemon
   instant pudding mix
½ c Wesson Oil

½ c water
½ c rum (dark is best)
4 eggs

Combine first 5 ingredients. Add eggs, beating in 1 at a time. Grease and flour bundt or tube pan. Cover bottom of pan with 1 cup chopped pecans. Pour batter over pecans. Bake at 325° for 50–60 minutes. Punch holes in hot cake with ice pick. Pour rum sauce over.

Rum Sauce:

1 c sugar
1 stick butter or Oleo

¼ c water
¼ c rum

Bring to a boil. Boil 1 minute. Remove from heat, and add ¼ cup rum. Let sauce soak in well. Do not remove cake from pan until completely cool. Cake keeps well and gets more moist. Can be made 1 or 2 days before needed. Also freezes well.

Variations:

Chocolate Rum Cake: substitute a butter fudge cake mix and chocolate instant pudding.
Amaretto Cake: fix as a rum cake, substituting Amaretto (Italian almond liqueur) for rum and use 1 c sliced almonds instead of pecans.
Grand Marnier Cake: fix as rum cake, substituting 1 small package of lemon pudding for vanilla and use Grand Marnier (orange liqueur) instead of rum, and use almonds or pecans.
Top Banana Cake: fix as rum cake, substituting 1 small package of instant banana pudding for vanilla pudding. In place of rum, use banana liqueur (Creme de Banana) and use pecans.

MY MOM'S THE FINEST COOK ON EARTH
AND SHE TOLD ME LONG AGO
THE BREAD'S NO GOOD UNLESS
YOU ADD SOME LOVING TO THE DOUGH

Florence's Pie Crust

4 c flour, sifted
1½ c Crisco

1 c ice water
1 tsp salt

Blend all ingredients well with hands. Roll out and place in pie pans. I keep pie crusts in freezer, so when you want to make a pie, all you have to do is prepare filling. Fit pastry in pan loosely. Flute edge of pie up high. Prick a few holes with a fork in bottom crust. In top crust, make small slits to allow steam to escape.

Strawberry Pie or Tart

1 pie shell or 12 tart shells
1 c sugar
1 c water
2 tbsp cornstarch
1 tbsp flour

1 tbsp lemon juice
2 pints strawberries (whole
    or sliced)
½ pint whipping cream

Combine sugar, cornstarch and flour in saucepan. Add water and cook over medium heat until it thickens. Add lemon juice and a couple of drops of red food coloring. Place berries in pie shell or tarts. Cover berries with glaze. Chill. Whip cream with 1 tablespoon of powdered sugar. Serve on top of pie. This is also good in a meringue shell. Slice bananas into pie shell and top with whipped cream.

Pumpkin Pie

1 (9") pastry shell (make with ¼ c
    chopped pecans)
1 (30 oz) can pumpkin
1 egg
1 can sweetened condensed milk
½ c brown sugar

¼ c flour
¼ c chopped pecans
¼ c firm butter
½ tsp cinnamon
¼ tsp nutmeg

Blend egg, pumpkin and condensed milk. Pour into pie shell. Mix brown sugar, flour, butter and spices with fork until crumbly. Sprinkle over top of pie. Bake 50 minutes. Cool. Chill. Serve with whipped cream.

Rich Apple Pie

Filling:

3 lb tart apples
½ c flour
3½ c sugar

4 eggs
2½ tsp vanilla
3 c sour cream

Topping:

2¼ c sugar
1½ c flour

2 sticks butter

Makes 2 thin, flaky crusts or 1 deep dish. Chop apples fine. Mix sugar and flour. Add sour cream, eggs, vanilla and pinch of salt. Beat real smooth. Add apples. Pour into pie crust. Mix topping until crumbly and place on top of filling. Bake at 350° for 30 minutes. Cover and bake for 10 minutes longer. This is full of calories, but out of sight!

Quick Coconut Cream Pie or Banana Pie

1 (¾ oz) coconut
  instant pudding
1¾ c milk
½ tsp almond extract

1 (8-oz carton) Cool Whip
½ c shredded coconut
1 cookie crumb pie shell

Mix pudding and milk for 1 minute. Add ½ of Cool Whip and extract. Pour into crust. Top with rest of Cool Whip. Sprinkle coconut over top. Chill.

Substitute banana pudding and vanilla for coconut and almond. Slice 3–4 bananas into pie shell. Prepare filling as above. Pour over bananas. Top and chill.

Caramel Pie

1 (9″) pie shell
1 c sugar
½ c boiling water
2 tbsp butter
5 tbsp flour
¼ tsp salt

½ c milk
3 egg yolks, slightly beaten
3 eggs whites
¼ tsp cream of tartar
½ c sugar

In iron skillet, stir cup of sugar until it caramelizes (turns golden brown). Turn off heat. Add boiling water and stir until dissolved. In saucepan, melt butter over low heat. Stir in flour and salt. Add ¼ cup milk, stirring constantly. Add remaining milk and caramel sugar. Cook until thick, stirring constantly. Add some of mixture to egg yolks and beat. Return this to caramel mixture. Cook 1 minute. Pour into baked pie shell. Beat 3 egg whites with cream of tartar. Add ½ cup sugar, slowly, beating until stiff. Pour on warm filling and bake at 400° until lightly browned. Chill. This takes time, but, if you are a caramel lover, it's worth it.

Lemon Angel Pie

4 eggs
½ tsp cream of tartar
1½ c sugar

2 tsp finely grated lemon rind
3 tbsp lemon juice
1 pint whipping cream

Beat egg whites until foamy. Add cream of tartar and beat until they stiffen. Gradually add 1 cup of sugar and continue beating until meringue is stiff and glossy. Spread into lightly buttered 9″ pie plate. Make outside rim come up higher. Bake this at 300° for 40 minutes. Cool. Beat egg yolks until thick and lemon colored. Beat in ½ cup sugar, lemon juice and rind. Cook this in double boiler until thick. Cool. Whip ½ pint cream. Fold into lemon mixture. Fill meringue with mixture. Chill at least 8 hours. When serving, whip other ½ pint of cream with 2 tablespoons sugar and cover pie. This is dreamy!

Old Timey Cherry Pie

1 (16 oz) can red sour pitted
   cherries
1 c sugar
1 c juice from cherries
2 tbsp flour

2 tbsp butter
½ tsp vanilla
½ tsp almond
¼ tsp red food coloring
pinch of salt

Mix flour, sugar, salt. Add juice. Stir until smooth. Cook over slow flame until thick. Stir constantly. Add flavorings and coloring, butter and cherries. Pour into *unbaked* pie shell (see index). Make strips of pastry and criss-cross over top of pie. Bake at 350° for 40–45 minutes.

Lemon Cherry Pie

1 vanilla wafer crust
1 can pie cherries
1 can Eagle Brand
   Condensed milk

½ pint whipping cream
⅓ c sugar
1 c pecans (optional)
1 lemon

Pie Crust:

1⅓ c vanilla wafer crumbs or
   Girl Scout "Scot Teas"
½ stick margarine

¼ c powdered sugar
¼ tsp vanilla

Melt Oleo. Mix in other crust ingredients. Press into pie plate and bake at 350° for 5 minutes. Beat whipping cream until thick. Beat in sugar. Combine cream and condensed milk. Add juice of 1 lemon. Drain cherries, chop, drain again and add to cream mixture. Chop pecans and stir in. Pour into pie shell and chill for 12 hours.

Tip: Superfine sugar makes finer pie crust.

Heath Bar Pie

2 pie plate meringues
15 Heath Bars

1 pint whipped cream
vanilla

Grind up Heath Bars. Whip cream until stiff. Add vanilla. Reserve ⅓ of whipped cream. Add Heath Bars to other ⅔ of cream. Mix well and spread between 2 meringues. Top meringue with rest of whipped cream. Refrigerate 24 hours before serving. Shave a few chocolate "curls" over top.

Grandmother Libbie's Zwiebach Pie

Crust:

2 c Zwiebach crumbs	½ c sugar
1 c melted butter	2 tsp cinnamon

Make crumbs by crushing 1 box of Zwiebach toast in blender. Mix crumbs, butter, cinnamon and sugar. Press in oblong pyrex. Bake at 300° for 15 minutes. Reserve some crumbs to sprinkle over top of pie.

Custard:

6 egg yolks, beaten	2 tsp vanilla
1 c sugar	2 c milk
6 tbsp flour	

Mix all ingredients and cook until mixture thickens. Stir constantly.

Topping:

6 egg whites	6 tbsp sugar
pinch salt	

Beat eggs stiff. Add sugar slowly and beat until blended in. Pour custard into pie shell. Put egg white on top. Sprinkle with reserved crumbs. Bake at 375° about 10 minutes to lightly brown meringue. Refrigerate and serve when cold.

Tips On Cookies

To crisp cookies that soften, put in a 300° oven for 5 minutes.

Place a slice of bread in cookie can to keep soft cookies soft.

Do not bake meringue type cookies on rainy days.

Date Chewies

3 egg whites
1 c sugar
2 tbsp flour

1 c dates, chopped
1 c pecans, chopped
1 tsp vanilla

Beat egg whites until stiff. Add sugar and beat well. Mix flour into chopped dates. Add to egg white mixture. Add pecans. Line cookie sheets with wax paper. Drop teaspoons of batter on cookie sheets. Bake at 300° for 10–12 minutes. You may substitute 1 6 oz package Butterscotch or Chocolate Chip morsels for dates. Tip—when "chopping" dates, use scissors. Dip scissors in warm water to keep from sticking. (Also works for marshmallows.) Make these when you have hollandaise—use up egg whites.

Christiana's Cinnamon Cookies

1 c butter
1 c sugar
1 egg, separated

2 c flour
1 tbsp cinnamon
1 c pecans (finely chopped)

Cream butter and sugar. Add beaten egg yolk. Mix in flour and cinnamon. Lightly butter 10" × 15" baking pan. Spread on mixture, covering pan. Brush slightly beaten egg white over batter. Sprinkle with finely chopped pecans, and pat lightly. Bake for 30 minutes at 325°. Cut into bars while warm. Do not remove from pan until cool. For a crisper cookie, use same recipe but only use 1 cup flour and 3 tablespoons cinnamon.

Sand Tarts

2 sticks butter
½ c sifted powdered sugar
1½ tsp vanilla

2 c sifted cake flour
1 c finely chopped pecans

Cream butter. Add sugar. Stir well. Add flour, nuts and vanilla. Shape dough into crescents and bake on ungreased cookie sheet at 325° for 20 minutes. Roll warm cookies in powdered sugar.

Dell's Icebox Cookies

½ c shortening
½ c brown sugar
¾ c white sugar
1 egg
1 tsp vanilla

2 c flour
¼ tsp salt
2 tsp baking powder
¾ c chopped pecans

Cream shortening and sugars. Add egg, vanilla and beat well. Sift together flour, salt and baking powder. Blend in. Add pecans. Roll dough into logs. Wrap in wax paper. Refrigerate. When well chilled, slice in thin slices and bake at 400° about 10 minutes. These can be rolled out and cut into shapes for children.

M & M Cookies

1 c shortening
1 c brown sugar
½ c sugar
2 eggs
2¼ c sifted flour

1 tsp baking soda
½ tsp salt (if using butter,
    eliminate salt)
1 tsp vanilla
¾ lb sack M & M candies

Cream shortening and sugars. Beat in eggs and vanilla. Sift dry ingredients into mixture. Mix well. Stir in ½ c M & M's. Drop batter by teaspoons onto ungreased cookie sheet. Decorate tops with remaining M & M's. Bake at 375° about 10 minutes.

Cheesecake Cookies

12 oz Oatmeal Cookie Mix
1 tbsp water
2 (3 oz) packages of softened
*   cream cheese*
1 egg

¼ c sugar
2 tbsp milk
1 tbsp lemon juice
½ tsp vanilla

In small bowl, combine cookie mix and water. Stir until mixture is coarse crumbs. Reserve ¾ cup crumbs. Press remaining crumbs into lightly greased square baking pan. Bake for 5 minutes at 350°. Combine softened cream cheese, sugar, egg, milk, lemon juice and vanilla. Beat until creamy. Pour over crumb crust. Sprinkle ¾ cup crumbs over top. Bake at 350° 25–30 minutes. Cool completely. Slice and chill.

Carroll's Fortune Cookies

These are fun for girls to make. They make up fortunes and write them on ¼" strips of paper, then make cookies. This makes about 20 cookies.

½ c flour
¼ c sugar
2 tbsp cornstarch
⅛ tsp salt

¼ c vegetable oil
2 egg whites
3 tbsp water

In a small bowl, combine flour, sugar, cornstarch, salt—mix well. Stir in oil and egg whites until smooth. Add water, mix well. Lightly grease and heat 2 crepe pans. Put 1 tablespoon batter in pan. Tilt pan to spread batter into 3½" thin circle. (If batter seems too thick, add a few drops of water at a time.) Cook until edges begin to brown, about 2 minutes. Turn and cook 1 minute. Working quickly, place hot cookie on flat surface, put fortune in center, fold cookie in half. Fold cookie again over edge of water glass. Place upside down in muffin tin to retain shape until cool. Lightly grease crepe pan in between cooking each cookie.

Turtles

Crust:

½ c softened butter

2 c flour

1 c brown sugar

Top Layer:

⅔ c butter

½ c brown sugar

1 c pecan _halves_

1 c milk chocolate chips

Combine crust ingredients. Mix 3 minutes at medium speed. Pat firmly into ungreased 13 × 9 × 2 pan. Sprinkle pecans evenly over crust. Combine butter and brown sugar for top layer. Cook over medium heat until mixture boils. Stir constantly. Boil about 1 minute. Pour evenly over crust and pecans. Bake at 350° for 15–20 minutes (until crust is golden and caramel is bubbling). Remove from oven and sprinkle chips on top. Lightly swirl chips—do not spread. Cool and cut into squares.

Marshmallow Bars

½ c shortening

¾ c sugar

2 eggs

¾ c flour

¼ c cocoa

¼ tsp baking powder

¼ tsp vanilla

¼ tsp salt

miniature marshmallows

Cream shortening and sugar. Add eggs. Sift dry ingredients. Add to egg mixture—mix well. Spread batter into greased and floured 12 × 8 pan. Bake at 350° for 25 minutes. Remove from oven and spread with marshmallows. Return to oven for 3 minutes. Cool and frost.

Frosting:

½ c brown sugar

¼ c water

2 squares chocolate

1½ c powdered sugar

2 tbsp butter

1 tsp vanilla

Combine butter, brown sugar, water, chocolate, and vanilla. Boil 3 minutes. Add powdered sugar, thinning with milk if necessary. Spread over cookies. Sprinkle with nuts if desired.

Almeta Scott's Brownies

2 sticks butter

4 squares Bakers unsweetened
  chocolate

2 c sugar

4 eggs

1 c flour

1 tsp vanilla

1 c pecans

1 tsp baking soda

Melt butter and chocolate in double boiler. Add sugar and eggs. Beat well. Add soda, flour and vanilla and pecans. Bake in 9″ × 12″ cake pan at 350° for 25–30 minutes.

Icing:

1 stick butter

2 squares semi-sweet chocolate

1 box powdered sugar

¼ c of hot cream or coffee

1 tsp vanilla

Melt chocolate with cream or coffee and butter. Add sifted sugar. Mix until smooth. Add vanilla. Beat until creamy. Pour on brownies while hot.

Apricot Dreams

1 c flour
½ c butter
¼ c powdered sugar
2 eggs beaten
1 tsp vanilla

1 c sugar
2 tbsp stewed apricot juice
6 apricots—mashed
1 tsp lemon juice

Combine flour, butter, powdered sugar. Mix thoroughly. Spread in 9 inch square pan. Bake at 350° for 15 minutes. Mix eggs, sugar, juice, and apricots. Spread over crust layer. Return to oven for 25 minutes. Cool slightly and glaze.

Glaze:

½ c powdered sugar
4 tsp apricot juice

½ tsp lemon juice

Easy Cookies

1 lb box light brown sugar
2 c biscuit mix
4 eggs, well beaten

2 c chopped pecans
2 tsp vanilla

Combine all ingredients and mix well. Pour into greased 13″ × 9″ pan. Bake at 325° for 30–35 minutes. Remove from oven and cool thoroughly before slicing. Dust with powdered sugar. Chewy and good and quick!

Nanoo's Cream Candy

2 c sugar
1¾ c white Karo syrup
1 pint heavy cream

2 sticks butter
1 tsp vanilla
1 c broken pecans (optional)

In a deep pan, mix sugar, Karo and cream. Stir until mixture reaches a boil. Add butter. Cook until soft ball stage. Beat candy, add vanilla. Add pecans. Pour into buttered pan. Let stand several hours before cutting.

Divinity

3 c sugar
¾ c water
¾ c white corn syrup
3 egg whites

⅛ tsp salt
1 tsp vanilla
1 c chopped pecans (optional)

Stir sugar, water and corn syrup until sugar dissolves. Then cook over medium heat to crack stage. While syrup is cooking, beat egg whites and salt until stiff. Put electric mixer near stove and pour syrup over egg whites gradually, beating constantly. Keep syrup hot on flame, and add it little by little. When all is beaten in, add vanilla. Beat in nuts with a spoon and continue beating until mixture stands up and does not look glossy. Drop by spoonfuls on waxed paper. Store in tin. I have been making this since I was about 8 years old. Do not make divinity on a rainy day.

Granny's Pull Candy or Taffy

1¼ c sugar
¼ c water
2 tbsp white vinegar

1½ tsp butter
½ tsp vanilla (or peppermint)

Combine everything but vanilla and stir over heat until sugar dissolves. Then cook quickly to light crack stage. Add vanilla. Pour candy onto oiled platter and let cool until a dent can be made in it. Gather into lumps and pull it until it is light and porous. You can roll it into strips and cut it into pieces. We always play with it so much and eat as we go along. For the kids, this is a must for Thanksgiving weekend in Hunt, Texas.

Mother's Fudge

2 c sugar	*2 squares bitter chocolate*
1 c milk	*1 tsp vanilla*
1 hunk butter	*1 c broken pecans*

Put sugar, milk, chocolate in deep pan. Stir over flame until mixture comes to a boil. Continue cooking without stirring until soft ball stage. Remove from stove. Add butter and vanilla. Let cool. Beat until creamy. Add pecans and beat until it begins to set. Pour in buttered pan and cut in squares.

Candy Apples on a Stick

3 c sugar	*2 tsp vanilla*
⅔ c white corn syrup	*10–12 tart apples*
⅔ c butter	*10–12 sticks*
1 c water	*red food coloring*
1 tsp salt	

Spear apples with sticks. Cook all ingredients, (except apples) to hard ball stage, stirring constantly. Add 10 drops red food coloring. Cool until thick. Dip and coat apples quickly. Let harden and cool on waxed paper.

Holiday Fake Buñuelos

Large flour tortillas or lebanese mountain bread. Cut shapes into bread or tortillas—use cookie cutters, trace your hands, or any inventive design, fry in hot grease. Sprinkle with powdered or cinnamon sugar, or bake on greased cookie sheets for 2–3 minutes at 425°. Before baking brush each shape with following glaze:

1 egg yolk	*¼ tsp almond extract*
2 tsp sugar	*food coloring*

Enough for 10 buñuelos. Much fun for the kiddies.

Eggs in the Basket

Cut hole in bread slices with biscuit cutter. Place bread on well buttered griddle. Break egg into hole. Cook until firm enough to turn. Turn and cook on other side. Fun and good!

Eggs in Muffin Cups

10 thin slices bacon   *10 eggs*

Cook bacon slightly. Put 1 slice of bacon around inside of muffin cup. Break eggs into cups. Bake eggs and bacon in 350° oven until eggs are done. When using a 12 muffin cup tin, put a little water into unfilled cups.

Pan Frito

thin sliced bread   *butter*

Buy crustless, sliced party bread. Melt butter, dip bread in butter, covering both sides. Cook on griddle until slightly crisp. Fattening and so good. *Any* bread is good this way.

Children's Cinnamon Toast

2 pieces bread for each person   *melted butter*
sugar   *cinnamon*

To make cinnamon sugar, put 3 teaspoons cinnamon to 1 cup of sugar. Blend well with fork. Keep in covered container or sugar shaker. Toast bread on one side under broiler. Remove bread and cover untoasted side with butter. Sprinkle well with cinnamon-sugar and toast until bubbly.

French Toast

12 slices bread or English muffins
3 eggs
2 c milk

2 tbsp sugar
2 tsp vanilla

Beat eggs, milk, sugar, vanilla until frothy. Dip bread into mixture and cook on well buttered griddle. Sprinkle with powdered sugar or cinnamon sugar. This is delicious made with leftover French bread or English muffins. Also good to deep fat fry. Add 1 teaspoon baking powder to batter. Fry 3–5 minutes a side, turning only once.

Waffles

2 c flour
1 c milk
1 tbsp baking powder
1 c cream

2 eggs
2 tbsp sugar
1 tsp vanilla
½ stick melted butter

Mix flour, sugar, baking powder, milk and cream. Separate eggs. Combine egg yolks and butter. Add to first mixture. Beat egg whites fluffy. Fold into mixture. Add vanilla. Beat until creamy. Cook on waffle iron. If you use a mix to make waffles or pancakes, always add a full teaspoon of vanilla to the batter. It makes them so tasty.

Tommy's Sourdough Pancakes

Starter:

1 package dry yeast
2½ c warm water
2 tbsp sugar

1 c instant non-fat dry milk
4 c flour

Stir yeast, water, milk and sugar in bowl (non-metalic). Stir in flour and beat until it makes a smooth batter. Let stand loosely covered (dish cloth makes a good cover) 3–5 days. Stir occasionally. Store in a crock or jar in refrigerator. This will be your "starter" which is the base for any sourdough recipe. It will not spoil. If liquid comes to top, just stir it in.

Pancakes: Prepare the evening before.

1 c starter　　　　　　　　　　　　*2½ c flour*
2 c warm water

Mix and cover bowl. Set in warmest spot in kitchen. Allow at least 10–12 hours of fermenting. Before preparing pancakes, be sure to return 1 cup starter to crock and put back in refrigerator for next time.

To remaining batter, add:

1 egg　　　　　　　　　　　　　　*¼ c evaporated milk*
2 tbsp cooking oil

Blend:

1 tsp baking soda　　　　　　　　*2 tbsp sugar*

Sprinkle this blend over batter and fold in. Let set for 5 minutes. Then drop by spoonfuls on a hot griddle. For waffles, add 2 tablespoons butter to above and cook in waffle iron. The griddle and waffle iron need to be a little hotter than for regular pancakes.

Crepes

2 c sifted flour　　　　　　　　　*⅛ tsp salt*
4 eggs　　　　　　　　　　　　　　*(For dessert crepes, add*
2 c milk　　　　　　　　　　　　　　*½ c sugar and ¼ tsp vanilla)*
¼ c melted butter

Mix sifted flour and salt in bowl (add sugar if for dessert). Stir in eggs, 1 at a time (add vanilla). Add warmed milk, stirring constantly with wooden spatula. Batter should coat spatula and be smooth. Add melted butter and stir in well. Cover and chill at least one hour. Have small crepe pan well buttered. Put in enough batter to cover bottom. Brown slightly. Turn and brown other side. Keep warm in pie plate in 325° oven. Do not be discouraged if first few crepes stick—just throw away and keep trying. You have to get pan "seasoned." For Crepes Suzette batter, add ¼ cup Cognac to batter and cut ¼ cup of milk.

Creme Fraiche

This is a heavy cream to use over fruits, or for cooking.

1 c whipping cream   *1 tsp buttermilk*

Pour cream into a jar. Add buttermilk. Cover and let stand at room temperature for 24–48 hours (or until cream thickens). Refrigerate. This will keep 2–3 weeks.

Almond-Apricot Jam

2 (18 oz) jars apricot jam   *⅓ c Kirsch (cherry liqueur)*
1 tbsp almond extract

Heat jam in pan. Stir in Kirsch and almond extract. Cook until bubbly. Pour into jars and refrigerate. Makes 4 cups.

Margaritas

1 oz fresh lime juice
2 oz tequila

2 oz Triple Sec

Place all in blender and add 12 ice cubes. (This will vary according to how thick you like your margaritas.) Blend until frothy. Pour into salt lined, chilled glasses. (Wipe used lime around edges of chilled glass and roll in salt.) Serve with a small wedge of lime. Glasses can be prepared ahead of time and put in freezer. Makes 2 or 3 drinks—depending on size of glasses.

Cheese Biscuits

4 sticks butter
4 c flour, sifted
1 lb sharp cheese

¼ tsp salt
1 tsp red pepper

Grate cheese and mix together with butter and rest of ingredients. Place in refrigerator until chilled. Roll in balls and place on cookie sheet. For biscuits, press with spoon or fork until flattened. Bake at 350° for 20 minutes. To stuff with olives: roll dough around a Spanish olive and cook for 15 minutes. Makes 6 dozen.

Cheese-Onion Dip

2 (3 oz) packages cream cheese
2 beef bouillon cubes
boiling water

mayonnaise
5 green onions, minced
⅛ tsp Beau Monde seasoning

Cream cheese. Dissolve bouillon in smallest amount of water (¼ cup). Add to cheese. Add onion and Beau Monde. Mix and refrigerate. Add mayonnaise to taste until dip is right consistency for vegetable dipping. Makes 2 cups.

Hot Crabmeat Dip

3 lb lump crabmeat
½ c horseradish mayonnaise
½ c regular mayonnaise
1 tbsp mustard
1 tbsp salt
½ tsp white pepper

¼ c chopped pimento and
  green peppers
capers to taste
dash of Tabasco
2 eggs, beaten

Mix all and top with extra mayonnaise. Bake at 350° for 15–20 minutes. Delicious as a main course with salad and french bread. Serves 12 to 16 people.

Margie's Hot Sauce

Use very ripe tomatoes, Serrana chilies and Jalapeno peppers.

6 chilies
4 jalapeno peppers
6 tomatoes
8 oz can tomato juice

2 tbsp salt
1 tbsp pepper
1 8 oz can hot water

Put pepper and chilies on a cookie sheet and run under the broiler to make skins turn black. You will have to turn them once or twice. Do tomatoes the same way. Peel the skins from the peppers and chilies. Do not peel tomatoes. Put everything into blender and mix well—if it is too hot or not hot enough, subtract or add jalapeno peppers to taste. Makes approximately 1½ quarts.

Easy Chili

2 lb ground meat *-chili meat*
1 tbsp shortening
4 tbsp chopped garlic
2 tbsp ground cumin seed
1 small bottle chili powder

1 tbsp salt
3 c water
2 tbsp flour
¼ tsp pepper *too thin*

added more thickening (flour/water)
10 min before end of cooking

Cook meat and garlic in hot grease. Cook slowly 15 minutes. Add chili powder, flour and cumin seed. Stir, add water, salt and pepper. Cook 45

minutes over low heat. Makes 2 quarts. This is good to use for any recipe calling for chili.

Tamale Pie

jalapeno cornbread mix
crisp, crumbled bacon
corn (see cornbread mix)

1 chopped onion
1 can chili
1 c grated, sharp cheese

Add mix and bacon and corn (according to directions on mix). Pour into a greased baking dish. Place 1 chopped onion over cornbread batter. Add 1 can of chili over onion and 1 cup grated sharp cheese on top. Bake according to cornbread directions. Serves 6 to 8.

Chalupas

This is fun to have for teenage parties.

Make the Easy Chili recipe (see index).

1 can refried beans
1 tbsp oil
1 onion, grated
shredded lettuce

chopped tomatoes
sharp cheese
chopped jalapeno peppers
tortillas (homemade or bought)

Put oil in skillet and add beans. Mash until very smooth. Grate 1 onion and cook until fairly dry. Shred lettuce, chop tomatoes. Grate cheese and chop jalapeno peppers.

Make Guacamole:

4 ripe avocadoes
8 cherry tomatoes
6 green onions

1 lemon (juice)
salt and pepper
hot sauce to taste

Mix all in blender.

Buy prepared chalupa shells or use flat tortillas (fried). Spread beans on shells, then add chili meat, cheese, lettuce and tomatoes. Top with guacamole and chopped peppers. This recipe makes 12–16 chalupas.

Cacerolo

1 ½ lb lean ground beef
1 onion, chopped
2 tsp powdered instant coffee
1 tsp chili powder (more if
   desired)
1 tsp salt

¼ tsp pepper
2 8 oz cans tomato sauce
8 tortillas
1 (3 oz) package cream cheese
grated Parmesan cheese

Brown beef and onion in skillet; pour off fat. Stir in coffee, chili powder, salt and pepper and 1 can of tomato sauce. Simmer 3 minutes. Spread tortillas with soft cream cheese, then top with meat mixture. Fold in half, overlap in baking dish open side up (like a taco). Fill in spaces around tortillas with remaining meat. Pour on remaining can of tomato sauce. Sprinkle with Parmesan cheese. Bake at 350° for 20 minutes. Serves 6 to 8.

Fajitas

The secret to good fajitas is *good*, well prepared meat. It should be seasoned well and marinated for 12 hours or overnight. It is also very necessary that it be cooked over the correct fire. We have tried many ways and this is our favorite.

Have your butcher trim all visible fat from a skirt steak and slice to ¼" thick. Have him run the steak through the meat tenderizer once. Then cut it into 3" or 4" pieces. You can also prepare the steak yourself but it will take longer. After you have cut your steak into pieces, you use a meat pounder to tenderize each piece. Now you are ready to marinate the meat.

Fajitas Marinate Sauce:

1 large bottle Wishbone Dressing
½ c worcestershire sauce

1 garlic clove, crushed
salt & lots of pepper

This will marinate 4 to 6 prepared steaks, probably about 30 to 40 pieces. Be sure each piece is covered on both sides with sauce. I use a glass casserole dish and stack pieces after saturating in sauce. Then I

pour remaining sauce over all. Cover with clear wrap and refrigerate. Remove and let the meat get to room temperature before cooking. Be sure you have a good hot fire. Place meat on grill to sear each side. Then let meat remain on part of grill that is not as hot for about 5 minutes. Remove and serve immediately. It is wise not to cook too many pieces at one time.

We eat fajitas just like this served with Mexican Rice, refried beans, guacamole and soft tortillas and Margie's hot sauce.

It is also very good cut up in bite size pieces and rolled in a soft flour tortilla, served with guacamole on top.

One skirt steak will serve 3 or 4 people.

Fajitas can be used cut up for tacos and chalupas. It also makes wonderful nachos.

Fajitas Nachos

Cover tortilla chips with cut up cooked meat. Cover with grated rat cheese and top with jalapeno pepper slices. Run under the broiler for about 2 or 3 minutes. Top with guacamole. Variations: sour cream or chopped onions on top, or spread refried beans on chip before adding meat. Top everything with Margie's hot sauce. And don't forget to serve margaritas with all your Mexican dishes.

Hot Pimento Cheese and Green Pepper Sandwich

1 c grated sharp cheddar cheese
½ grated onion
½ grated green pepper

½ small jar pimentos
mayonnaise to taste

Mix above ingredients. Spread on bread which has been toasted. Slide under broiler for a few minutes. Cover with toasted bread. Serve hot. Makes enough for 4 sandwiches.

Gazpacho Salad

3 c chopped fresh cabbage
1 c diced fresh tomatoes
½ c sliced radishes
¼ c sliced scallions
1 tsp powdered mustard
½ c olive oil

1 tsp warm water
2 tbsp fresh lemon juice
1 tbsp white vinegar
1 tsp salt
⅛ tsp ground, black pepper

Place cabbage in salad bowl. Top with other vegetables. Blend in warm water and let stand 10 minutes for flavor to develop. Add lemon juice, vinegar, salt and pepper and mix well. Add oil and mix. Place over vegetables in salad bowl. Toss lightly just before serving. Serves 6.

Mixed Bean Salad

1 can green beans (#303 size
   or 2 c)
1 can wax beans
1 can red kidney beans
½ c chopped green pepper

¾ c sugar
⅔ c cider vinegar
⅓ c salad oil
1 tsp pepper
1 tsp salt

Drain beans *well*. Add chopped green pepper to beans. Combine remaining ingredients and mix. Mix all and let stand refrigerated for 24 hours. Drain off excess juice. Serves 8 to 10.

Caesar Spinach Salad

3 c torn spinach leaves
3 c torn Boston lettuce
1 c sliced cauliflowerets
½ lb cooked and crumbled bacon

4 hard boiled eggs (cooled and
   quartered)
½ c Caesar dressing

Combine spinach and lettuce in salad bowl. Add cauliflower, bacon and eggs. Add dressing and toss. Serves 4–6.

Shrimp Louie

4 c cooked shrimp, chilled

1 head lettuce

Sauce:

1 c mayonnaise
¼ c heavy cream
¼ c chili sauce
1 tsp worcestershire sauce

salt and pepper
¼ c chopped green pepper
½ c chopped green onions
2 tbsp lemon juice

Combine sauce ingredients and chill. Put lettuce (shredded) in salad bowl. Place chilled shrimp on top. Cover with sauce. Serves 8.

Seafood Caesar Salad

6 c lettuce greens
¾ c croutons
2 c cooked and cooled shrimp
   (or crab or lobster or all)
¾ c Caesar dressing

1 avocado, peeled and sliced
1 tomato, peeled and cut in
   wedges (or cherry tomatoes
   cut in half)

Place all in bowl and add dressing. Lightly toss. Serves 8 to 10.

Perfection Salad

1 envelope unflavored gelatin
¼ c sugar
½ tsp salt
1¼ c water
¼ c mild vinegar
1 tbsp lemon juice

½ c shredded cabbage
1 c chopped celery
1 pimento cut in small pieces
   or 2 tbsp chopped red or
   green pepper
spinach or lettuce

Mix the gelatin, sugar and salt together in saucepan. Add water and stir over medium heat until gelatin and sugar are thoroughy dissolved. Remove from heat and add vinegar and lemon juice. Chill to unbeaten egg white consistency. Fold in cabbage, celery and pimento or pepper. Turn into a 2 c mold or individual molds and chill until firm. Unmold on fresh spinach or romaine lettuce. Top with mayonnaise. Serves 4 to 6.

Kraut Salad

1 (1 lb) jar sauerkraut
1 shredded onion
1 c shredded celery
2 tbsp pimento

1 c sugar
½ c vinegar
¼ c oil

Bring sugar and vinegar to hard boil. Pour this mixture over the rest of the ingredients. Refrigerate in jars for 24 hours or more before serving.

Hot Cabbage Salad

1 medium cabbage
1 medium onion
3 tbsp butter
1 pint sour cream

1 medium green pepper
scant more than 1 c of water
salt to taste

Saute finely chopped onion and green pepper in butter. Add shredded cabbage, salt and water. Cook until cabbage is tender but not limp (approximately 5 minutes). Drain and top with sour cream. Serve immediately. Serves 6 to 8.

Chicken Salad

3 c diced cooked chicken
1½ c celery cut into ½" slices
2 tbsp chopped parsley
1 tsp salt
½ tsp pepper

½ c heavy cream, whipped
1 c mayonnaise
2 tbsp lemon juice
½ c toasted almonds, coarsely chopped

In a large bowl, toss chicken with celery, parsley, salt and pepper. Gently fold in whipped cream, mayonnaise, lemon juice and almonds. Refrigerate until chilled, about 1 hour. Serves 6 to 8.

Hot Chicken Salad

3 c cooked chicken, chopped
½ c chopped almonds
1 tbsp minced onion
1½ tbsp lemon juice
½ tsp pepper

1 c mayonnaise
1½ c grated cheddar cheese
1½ c crushed potato chips
  (barbecued)
1½ c diced celery

Combine chicken, celery, almonds, onions, lemon juice and pepper in mixing bowl. Add mayonnaise and toss. Divide into individual casseroles or put in 1 large one. Sprinkle top generously with grated cheese and finish with the potato chips. Bake in preheated oven, 375° for 25 minutes, uncovered. Serves 8.

Whipped Cream Fruit Salad

1 c pineapple chunks, drained
1 c halved orange sections,
  drained
½ c chopped pecans
¼ c mayonnaise

1 c pitted Queen Anne cherries,
  drained
2 c tiny marshmallows or 16
  large (cut up)
½ c whipped cream

Combine fruits, pecans, marshmallows and mayonnaise. Fold in whipped cream and chill 2 hours. Serves 8.

Congealed Avocado Salad

2 packages lime Jello
2 packages Philadelphia cream
  cheese (3 oz)
1 c mayonnaise

2 c avocado pulp
  (mashed)
1 tsp onion juice

Dissolve Jello in 2 cups hot water. Add ½ cup cold water. Mash avocados to a pulp. Mash cream cheese and cream it well. Add mayonnaise. When Jello thickens, add by the tablespoonful to avocado, cream cheese and onion mixture. Add ½ teaspoon salt and mix well. Pour in greased mold and refrigerate. Serves 10.

Avocado Fruit Freeze

1 large avocado
2 tbsp lemon juice
1 (3 oz) package cream cheese, softened
2 tbsp sugar
¼ c mayonnaise

¼ tsp salt
1 (1 lb) can pears, drained and diced (1½ c)
¼ c well drained chopped maraschino cherries
½ c whipping cream, whipped

Halve, peel and dice avocado and sprinkle with 1 tablespoon of lemon juice. Blend cream cheese, remaining lemon juice, sugar, mayonnaise and salt. Add avocado, pears and cherries. Fold in whipping cream. Pour in 3 cup ice box tray. Freeze until firm, about 6 hours. Let stand 15 minutes before serving. Serves 8.

Waldorf Salad with Cranberries

2 c raw cranberries
3 c miniature marshmallows
¾ c sugar
2 c diced unpeeled tart apples

½ c seedless green grapes
½ c broken walnuts
¼ tsp salt
1 c whipped cream, whipped

Grind cranberries and combine with marshmallows and sugar. Cover and chill overnight. Add apple, grapes, walnuts and salt. Fold in whipped cream and chill. Serve in large bowl and garnish with green and red grapes. Serves 8 to 10.

Easy Hollandaise

4 egg yolks
½ tsp salt

4 tbsp lemon juice
½ lb butter

Beat egg yolks and lemon juice in blender on low speed. Slowly add melted butter at high speed until thickened. Makes 1½ cups.

Parsley Dressing

2 c fresh parsley
½ c chopped chives
1 c sweet pickles, drained and
*   chopped*

2 cloves garlic
salt and pepper to taste
*   (I like lots of pepper)*

Cut chives very fine with scissors. Put all ingredients together through a food grinder twice or chop them for a very long time. Then add:

½ c olive oil
½ c red wine vinegar

¼ c tarragon vinegar

Mix all and keep at room temperature for 24 hours in a covered jar. Then refrigerate. Serve over cold, peeled and sliced tomatoes.

Avocado Cream Cheese Dressing

3 tbsp light cream
2 packages (3 oz) cream cheese
3 tbsp lemon juice
2 tbsp vinegar

½ tsp salt
⅛ tsp dry mustard
¾ c mashed avocado (1 large or
*   2 small)*

Beat cream with cream cheese. Gradually add next 4 ingredients and fold in avocado. Makes 2 cups.

Mary's Salad Dressing

juice of 1 lemon, strained
6 tbsp olive oil (no substitute)
1 tsp salt

1 tsp pepper
½ clove garlic

Mix and stir. Let stand at room temperature for several hours, then refrigerate. Remove garlic before serving. Makes approximately ½ cup.

Shrimp Creole

¼ c diced green pepper
½ c diced celery
1 tbsp flour
½ tsp salt
¼ c minced onion
4 tbsp melted butter
1¾ c canned tomatoes

½ tsp pepper
1 tsp sugar
1 bay leaf
parsley sprig
2 c (1 lb) cooked shrimp
¼ tsp Lea & Perrins
1⅓ c cooked rice

Saute green pepper, onion and celery in butter in skillet until tender. Add flour, blend. Add tomatoes gradually, stirring constantly. Add salt, pepper, sugar, bay leaf and parsley. Cook gently 30 minutes. Remove bay leaf and parsley. Add shrimp and Lea & Perrins sauce. Heat. Serve over rice. Serves 4.

Shrimp Rolled Crepes

Crepes:

1 c cold water
1 c cold milk
4 tbsp melted butter

4 eggs
½ tsp salt
2 c flour (sifted)

Blend all for 1 minute on high speed in a blender. Refrigerate 2 hours or more before cooking crepes. Makes 12 6½" crepes. Cook crepes on very hot griddle—pour 2 tablespoons butter and spread with spoon very thinly to size of salad plate. Turn when bubbles show. Do not stack crepes.

Shrimp Filling:

2 tbsp butter
3 tbsp green onions, chopped
salt and pepper

1½ c diced, uncooked shrimp
¼ c dry white vermouth

Saute shrimp in hot butter with green onions for 1 minute. Add salt and pepper, vermouth and boil rapidly until liquid is almost gone. Put in bowl.

Sauce:

½ c dry white vermouth
2 tbsp cornstarch blended with
    2 tbsp milk
¼ tsp salt

white pepper
1½ c cream
½ c grated Swiss cheese

Add vermouth to saucepan and boil rapidly until it is only 1 tablespoon. Stir in cornstarch mixture, cream and seasonings. Simmer 2 minutes, stirring. Blend in cheese and simmer 1 minute. Blend ½ of sauce into shrimp. Place big spoonful of shrimp on lower third of each crepe. Roll crepe into cylinders and arrange in buttered dish. Pour over rest of sauce, sprinkle with grated cheese, dot with butter and refrigerate until serving time. Cook under slow broiler for several minutes until bubbling and sauce is browned slightly on top. Makes 12 crepes.

Cheese and Shrimp Casserole #1

1 c raw rice
¾ c Swiss Gruyere cheese
4 tbsp butter

2 c diced, cooked shrimp
Parmesan cheese
paprika

Wash and drain rice. Mix Swiss cheese and shrimp. Place layer of rice, then cheese mixture, then rice. Dot with butter and sprinkle with Parmesan cheese and paprika. Bake in pan of hot water for 35 minutes at 400°. Serves 8.

Cheese and Shrimp Casserole #2

6 slices white bread
1½ lb cooked shrimp
½ lb Old English cheese
    (comes sliced)
3 whole eggs, beaten

¼ c butter, melted
½ tsp dry mustard
salt
1 pint milk

Break bread in pieces about the size of a quarter. Break cheese in bite size pieces. Arrange shrimp, bread and cheese in several layers in greased casserole. Pour on butter. Beat eggs. Add mustard, salt and milk. Mix and pour over shrimp mixture. Let stand overnight or at least 3 hours in refrigerator, covered. Bake 1 hour at 350° covered. Serves 8.

Cold Crab or Lobster

4 oz mayonnaise
3 oz catsup
½ jigger of chives (cut into bits
    with scissors)
1 tsp paprika

½ c lemon juice
1 jigger brandy
1 lb prepared lobster or fresh
    lump crabmeat

Mix and store in refrigerator. Serve over spinach leaves. Serve cold. Serves 4. Delicious served in the hot summer.

Shrimp Casserole

1½ lb cooked shrimp
¾ c rice (cooked)
1 can mushroom soup
½ tbsp lemon juice
½ large chopped onion
1 tbsp butter
dash garlic salt

salt
pepper
¾ c grated sharp cheddar cheese
½ bell pepper in rings (parboil
    2 minutes)
½ c sour cream

Saute onions in butter until tender—make sauce by adding soup, lemon juice and seasonings. Fold rice and shrimp into sauce. Fold sour cream in last. Pour into buttered baking dish. Sprinkle grated cheese on top. Place pepper rings on top and bake in 325° oven for 30 minutes. Serves 6 to 8.

Crab and Spinach Casserole

2 packages frozen chopped
    spinach
1 lb lump crabmeat
1½ c grated, sharp cheese
1 small can tomato paste

1 c finely chopped onions
1 c sour cream
dash nutmeg
salt
pepper

Thaw spinach (or use fresh). Grate cheese. Layer: spinach, then onions, then crab, and last, cheese. Add nutmeg, salt and pepper. Repeat all. Refrigerate. When ready to bake, mix sour cream and tomato paste and put on top. Bake at 325° for 45 minutes. Serves 4.

Crab and Shrimp Casserole

1 ½ lb lump crabmeat
1 lb shrimp (small)
½ green pepper, chopped
⅓ c parsley
2 c cooked rice

1 ½ c mayonnaise
1 package frozen peas, if desired
   (thawed but not cooked)
salt and pepper

Toss lightly. Place in greased casserole and refrigerate, covered. Bake 1 hour at 350° covered. Serves 6.

Barbecued Fish

3 lb red snapper, trout or red fish
   fillets
½ c oil
¼ c tarragon red wine vinegar
½ tsp ginger

1 tbsp sugar
2 tbsp sherry
1 tsp M.S.G.
2 tbsp soy sauce

Place fish in glass casserole. Mix and pour rest of ingredients over fish. Let sit for 1 hour. Barbecue on grill over hot coals for 12 minutes on each side. Brush with marinade. Serve with lemon juice and butter. Serves 6.

Sauteed Trout Fillets

Fresh trout
salt to taste
pepper to taste
egg white (1 for each fish)
milk

flour
4 tbsp butter
4 tbsp oil
fresh lemon
fresh parsley

Buy fresh trout and have it halved and cut into fillets. Salt and pepper heavily. Brush with egg and milk and heavily flour. Mix butter and oil in skillet. Heat until very hot. Add fish and cook on 1 side for 2 minutes. Turn and cook 2 more minutes. Squeeze fresh lemon on one side and sprinkle with fresh parsley. Do not let the butter burn, but the hotter the oil and butter the crisper the fish.

Lisa's Broiled Fish Fillets

2 tbsp finely chopped onions
1 medium carrot, cleaned and
    chopped
1 lemon, sliced
pinch of thyme
1 small bay leaf
1 tsp salt

½ tsp pepper
1½ lb fish fillets, either trout or red
    fish is best
½ c dry white wine
1 tbsp vermouth
1 tbsp chopped parsley

Heat oven to 400°. Place onion, carrot, lemon, thyme, bay leaf, salt and pepper in a well buttered baking dish. Place fillets on top of vegetables. Lightly salt and pepper again and dot with butter. Combine wine and vermouth and pour over fish. Bake 20 minutes or until fish flakes easily when tested with a fork. Sprinkle with parsley and serve with juices. Serves 4–6.

Salmon Mousse

1 envelope unflavored gelatin
¼ c cold water
¼ c vinegar
1 tbsp sugar
1¼ tsp salt
⅛ tsp dry mustard

1 tbsp capers
2 c flaked, cooked salmon
1 c finely diced celery
½ c heavy cream, whipped,
    or ⅓ c icy cold evaporated
    milk, whipped

Mix gelatin and water and vinegar in top of double boiler. Dissolve gelatin over boiling water. Stir in 1 tablespoon sugar, salt and dry mustard. Remove from heat and chill. Stir in salmon, celery and capers. Fold in heavy cream or evaporated milk. Turn into 3 cup mold or individual molds and chill until firm. Unmold on lettuce or fresh spinach. Serve with mayonnaise sprinkled with red pepper. Serves 8.

Salmon Casserole

1 large can pink salmon
1 c grated cheddar cheese
1 c bread crumbs
1 tbsp minced onion
1 tbsp butter
½ tsp salt

½ tsp celery salt
pepper
1 beaten egg
⅔ c milk
1 tsp paprika

Combine ingredients and bake at 350° for 30 minutes. Serves 6 to 8.

Stuffed Crab

2 tbsp butter
1 small onion, diced
3 tsp flour
1 c milk or water
4 eggs (hard boiled and sieved)
1 tsp lemon juice

bread crumbs
salt and pepper
1 lb fresh lump crabmeat
1 small can diced mushrooms
crab shells

Melt butter in a saucepan. Add onion (don't brown). Add flour, stir until smooth. Add cup of water and stir until thickened. Add eggs, lemon juice, seasoning, crabmeat and mushrooms. The mixture shouldn't be too soft. Fill shells, add bread crumbs. Dot with butter and brown in 350° oven for about 25 minutes. Serves 4 to 6.

Chicken Casserole

3 or 4 cups quarter size pieces
   of chicken (boiled)
1 c sliced celery
4 tsp chopped onion
3 c cooked rice
2 c cream of chicken soup
1 tsp salt

½ tsp pepper
½ c water
2 tsp lemon juice
1½ c mayonnaise
6 hard boiled eggs, sliced
4 c crushed potato chips

Combine chicken, celery, onion, rice, soup, salt, pepper and lemon juice. Mix mayonnaise with water and stir in. Gently stir in egg slices. Put in buttered casserole and top with crushed potato chips. Bake 450° for 15 minutes. Serves 10 or 12.

Chicken and Rice

1⅔ c thinly sliced carrots
2 tbsp butter
¼ c sliced onion
1⅓ c orange juice
⅔ c water
2 tbsp sugar

1 tsp salt
¼ tsp pepper
½ tsp grated orange rind
½ tsp poultry seasoning
2 c cooked, cut up chicken
1⅓ c cooked rice

Saute carrots in butter in large skillet until almost tender. Add onions and saute until clear. Add remaining ingredients except chicken and rice. Bring to a boil. Add chicken and rice—cover and simmer about 5–10 minutes. Serves 6 to 8.

Fried Chicken

medium chicken pieces
buttermilk
pepper
garlic salt

salt
paprika
flour
Crisco oil

Soak chicken in buttermilk for 2–3 hours. Mix pepper, garlic salt, salt, paprika and flour in a paper bag. Heavily coat buttermilk chicken in flour and add immediately to hot Crisco oil. Cook until light brown, turning often. Do not let the chicken get too brown. Reduce heat if necessary, but always keep grease hot enough to insure crispy chicken.

Chicken and Rice Croquettes

2 c finely chopped cooked
  chicken
2 c cooked rice
1 egg

4 tbsp lemon juice
grated rind of 1 lemon
salt

Mix, spread out on a flat pan or platter and chill several hours. Form into croquettes, dip in beaten egg and fine white bread crumbs. Fry in deep hot fat for 4 minutes. Serve with thin cream sauce with capers and grated lemon peel added to sauce.

Cream Sauce:

4 tbsp butter
4 tbsp flour
2½ c boiling milk

½ tsp salt
¼ tsp black pepper or white
   pepper for a white, white sauce

Blend flour and butter for 2 minutes in heavy pot. Remove from heat and blend in milk, salt and pepper. Simmer mixture, stirring constantly for 2 minutes or until creamy and smooth. If a thinner sauce is desired, add more milk.

Sesame Chicken

1 fryer or whatever pieces
   you like
1 tsp paprika
2 tbsp sesame seeds
2 tbsp butter

2 tbsp salad oil
½ c dry white table wine
¼ c finely chopped green onion
salt, pepper and flour

Sprinkle chicken with salt and pepper to taste. Shake in a paper bag containing flour mixed with paprika. Shake off excess flour. Melt butter in shallow glass baking dish (12 × 8). Add oil. Turn chicken in mixed butter and oil until coated all over. Lay pieces in single flat layer, skin side down. Sprinkle with half the sesame seeds. Bake in hot oven, 400° for 30 minutes. Turn chicken skin side up. Pour wine and onion over it. Sprinkle with rest of sesame seeds. Cook at 350° for 30 minutes longer or until golden brown and tender. Serves 4.

Chicken in Cream

2 lb boneless chicken
flour
salt
white pepper
2 oz butter

2 oz brandy (optional)
10 oz fresh mushrooms, sliced
1 tbsp chopped green onions
1½ c heavy cream

Roll each piece of chicken in flour. Salt and pepper. Place in a skillet with butter. Saute chicken until golden brown on both sides. Cover and cook over low heat 12–15 minutes or until done. Add mushrooms and onions and cook a few minutes more. Add brandy and cream and boil a few minutes until sauce thickens. Serve. Serves 6.

Turkey Spaghetti Curry

1 tbsp salt	3 tbsp flour
3 quarts boiling water	1 c milk
8 oz spaghetti	1 c cream
¼ c butter	2 tsp lemon juice
2–3 tsp curry powder	1 lb leftover turkey, cut up
1 tsp salt	

Add 1 tablespoon salt to boiling water. Gradually add spaghetti so water continues to boil. Cook uncovered. Stir and drain. Meanwhile, melt butter; blend in curry, salt and flour. Gradually add milk and cream. Cook over low heat, stirring constantly until thickened. Stir in lemon juice and turkey. Serve over spaghetti. Serves 8.

Doves or Quail

salt	flour
butter	pepper

Salt birds generously and let stand an hour or so for salt to penetrate through birds. Rinse before cooking. Dot each bird with a slice of butter. Pepper and flour heavily. Place in roaster and almost cover with water. Cook at 350° for 2 or 3 hours (depending on size and quantity). Cook covered except for last 30 minutes.

Robert's Doves

1 large bottle Wishbone Italian Salad Dressing	salt pepper

Marinade cleaned doves in Wishbone Dressing overnight in refrigerator. Cover. Remove from refrigerator for several hours before cooking. Remove from marinade and salt and pepper each dove. Barbecue over medium-hot coals for about 15 minutes. Serve immediately.

Wild Duck

6 wild ducks
2 red apples
2 oranges
3 stalks of celery

2 onions
12 strips of bacon
1 c orange juice
1 c red wine (optional)

Clean and skin ducks well. Rub with salt and pepper inside and outside and lightly flour. Brown in skillet in small amount of oil or bacon drippings. Remove from skillet and stuff with large pieces of fruits (skin and peel on), onion and celery. Add 1 cup water to pan drippings and mix well over low heat. Pour in roasting pan with ducks. Cover with bacon strips. Bake in 350° oven for 3–4 hours or until tender. Mix orange juice and wine after cooking 1 hour and pour over ducks and continue baking. Baste often. Reserve gravy for rice.

Artichokes Stuffed with Veal and Peppers

4 large artichokes
2 tbsp lemon juice
1 tsp garlic salt
¼ c olive oil
1½ lb veal (coarsely chopped)
1 onion, chopped

1 large green pepper, chopped
1 clove garlic, crushed
1 tsp salt
¼ tsp pepper
2 medium tomatoes, chopped
⅓ c grated Parmesan

Wash artichokes, trim stem ends to 1″. Pull off tough outer leaves and cut off tips of remaining leaves Place artichokes up side down, press down firmly to loosen center leaves and choke. Turn right side up to remove center leaves and choke. Place artichokes right side up in 1″ boiling water to which lemon juice has been added. Sprinkle ¼ teaspoon garlic salt over each. Sprinkle with cracked pepper. Cover and cook 40 minutes or until stems can be easily pierced with fork.

Heat oil. Add veal—cook over medium heat, stirring occasionally, about 10 minutes. Add green pepper, onion, garlic salt and pepper and mix well. Cook 10 minutes, stirring occasionally. Add tomatoes, cheese and mix. Cover and cook over low heat, stirring often for 20–25 minutes. Turn cooked artichokes upside down immediately and drain well. Fill with veal mixture. Serves 4.

Veal Stroganoff

6 slices cooked bacon
2 lb veal cut in bite size pieces
2 large onions, chopped
½ lb fresh mushrooms

1 pint sour cream
1 c white (cooking) wine
1 c raw white rice

Set cooked bacon aside and brown veal in grease. Remove. Brown onions in pan. Slice mushrooms. Combine veal, onions and mushrooms; add sour cream which you have mixed with wine. Cook covered slowly on top of stove for 2 hours. Stir occasionally. Boil rice and drain. Combine with veal in layers. Crumble cooked bacon on top and bake uncovered at 300° for 1 hour. Serves 6.

Veal Scallopini

8 thin slices of milk-fed veal
flour
2 beaten egg whites
hot butter

juice of 2 lemons
salt and pepper
fresh chopped parsley

Lightly flour the slices of veal. Dip in mixture of beaten eggs and juice of 1 lemon. Swiftly saute in hot butter, both sides. Add salt and pepper. Put veal on serving plate. To the pan in which the veal was cooked, add more butter and lots of fresh lemon juice and let boil until sauce is consistency of a light cream. Pour over veal, sprinkling with fresh, chopped parsley. Serves 4.

Easy Veal Cutlet

4 nice size lean cutlets
1 egg, beaten
2 tbsp milk

salt
pepper
2 tbsp Parmesan cheese

Beat cutlets until very thin (may need to separate each into 2 small). Combine above ingredients and coat both sides of cutlets. Sprinkle

lightly with flour. Place in small amount of heated oil and brown on both sides, about 10 minutes. Squeeze lemon on top and drain. Serve immediately or put in warmer. Serves 4.

Smoked Top Butt Roast
Smoked Brisket
Smoked Chicken Pieces

Marinate roasts, brisket in sauce for 2 hours

1 package meat marinade sauce *½ c water*
½ c olive oil *2 tbsp Kitchen Bouquet*
2 tbsp worcestershire sauce *cracked pepper*

Season chicken with:

seasoning salt *paprika*
pepper *garlic salt*

Let stand for 1 hour. Soak small hickory log in water at least 30 minutes. Add to side of charcoal in cooker. This will smoke instead of burning. Light fire and wait for 30 minutes before adding meats. Put roast and large meat in rear of cooker because they cook longer. Add chicken pieces around beef. *Smoke slowly* for 1½ hours for chicken—turning often, and 2 hours for large roasts (if medium or rare is desired). Turn often. If desired, you can start meat over hot coals to brown but I think it dries it out. Also, if barbecue sauce is desired on chicken, add last 15 minutes only. We also barbecue wild birds this same way, only for shorter cooking time. I use a large smoker and fix a lot of meats and chickens at a time, then freeze them separately in zip-lock bags.

Sirloin Tip or Top Sirloin

Sauce for Marinating:

1 (5 oz) bottle soy sauce
½ c brown sugar, packed
1 tbsp lemon juice

1 tbsp worcestershire sauce
½ c bourbon
1½ c water

For meat 3–3½" thick: Tenderize at room temperature. Marinate for 6 hours. Barbecue for 5 minutes each side over hot coals. Move away from flames and barbecue 25 minutes on each side—1 hour in all.

Sirloin Tip or Top Butt Roast

Marinade Sauce:

¾ c salad oil
¼ c soy sauce
¼ c honey

1 garlic clove
2 tbsp vinegar (white)
2 tbsp chopped onion

24 hours before serving, season meat with pepper. Mix all marinade ingredients and pour over roast. Refrigerate, covered, overnight. (If roast is not a tender cut, try this.) Before baking, cover bottom of medium size baking pan with 1 box rock salt. Remove roast from marinade sauce and place on rock salt. Cover entire surface of meat with additional rock salt. Bake in a preheated oven 500° for 12–14 minutes per pound of meat. Serve immediately after removing from rock salt.

Plain Beef Tender

5 lb tender
vinegar
olive oil

Kitchen Bouquet
seasoned pepper
¼ c worcestershire sauce or less

Have tender at room temperature. Rub with vinegar then olive oil then Kitchen Bouquet. Heavily pepper with seasoned pepper. Sprinkle on worcestershire sauce. Let stand 2 hours. Cook for 15 minutes at 425°, then 25 minutes at 325°. This will be medium rare.

Beef Tender in Sour Cream

1 small beef tender (5 lb) cut in
  1" slices
butter
1 onion, sliced
2 oz sherry

10 or 12 fresh mushrooms
salt and pepper
1 pint sour cream or 2 pints if
  more is desired

Saute tender slices in butter until lightly browned. Remove from pan. Add onions and cook until tender; add mushrooms and cook. Add sour cream and meat and bake 15 minutes at 325°. Serves 8.

Pork Tender

Trim pork tenders very well. Be sure to remove the outside membrane. Marinate overnight before cooking. Cover while marinating.

Marinade Sauce: enough for 2 tenders.

¼ c soy sauce
¼ c worcestershire sauce
¼ c honey

½ c Wishbone Italian dressing
1 clove garlic, crushed

Bake tender at 350° for 45 minutes to 1 hour. You may cook in the marinade sauce if you prefer. Slice after removing from oven for 10 to 15 minutes. 1 tender will serve 4 people.

Texas Hash

1 lb ground beef
1 onion, chopped
1 green pepper, chopped
1 (1 lb 12 oz) can Hunt's
  whole tomatoes

¾ c raw rice
1 tsp chili powder
1½ tsp salt
1 tsp worcestershire sauce

Brown beef in skillet. Add onion and green pepper and cook until tender. Drain fat. Add tomatoes and seasonings and bring to a boil. Stir in rice. Cover and simmer 30 minutes. Makes 4–6 servings. Add cheese on top and bake last 5 minutes if desired. Children love this. A change from spaghetti.

Pepper Steak

1½ lb beef tenderloin (sliced not
  too thin)
½ c chopped green pepper
½ c sliced mushrooms (fresh)
1 tsp cracked pepper
salt

1 tsp beef extract
3 tsp chopped parsley
2 cloves garlic, chopped
10 wedges fresh tomato
6 oz burgundy wine
½ tsp Accent

Season beef on both sides with salt. Saute in small amount of butter quickly until medium rare. Add all except tomatoes, wine and parsley. Cook 2 minutes more—add tomatoes, wine and parsley. Heat thoroughly but do not cook any more. Serve with garlic croutons. Serves 4.

Barbecue Sauce

2 sticks butter
2 large onions (sliced and
  chopped)
1 large clove garlic, minced
1 stalk celery, chopped
1 tbsp mustard
4 tbsp vinegar

2 tbsp chili powder
2 tbsp worcestershire sauce
1 tsp salt
1 bottle catsup
½ bottle water (I use the
  catsup bottle)

Heat all and cook over low heat for 1 hour covered. Makes 2 quarts.

Barbecued Flank Steak

1 2 lb flank steak
1 tsp mustard
1 tsp salt

¼ c red wine
1 tsp cracked pepper
2 tbsp oil

Rub steak with mustard, salt and pepper. Cover with wine and oil and marinate for 2 to 3 hours. Barbecue 5–7 minutes on each side and turn only once. Spoon on marinade while cookng. Cut in thin slices.

Variation: Marinade in Wishbone Dressing instead of mustard, wine and oil.

Chinese Beef and Vegetables

1½ lb trimmed beef tenderloin
  cut in ¼" slices
¾ c soy sauce
5 tbsp salad oil
¼ lb mushrooms, sliced
1 can (5 oz) water chestnuts,
  sliced

1 tsp seasoning salt
1½ c hot chicken broth
2 tbsp cornstarch
2 tbsp water
1 sliced green pepper
1 sliced onion
½ lb bean sprouts

Marinate beef in soy sauce for 3–4 hours. Drain and reserve sauce. Heat vegetables in oil (1 or 2 tablespoons) just until clear and add bean sprouts for 1 minute. Set aside. Heat salad oil in large skillet. Add beef and stir until all slices are covered with oil. Add mushrooms and water chestnuts and chicken broth. Mix. Simmer covered for 1 minute. Blend cornstarch and water. Stir in 1½ tablespoons reserved soy sauce—add to beef mixture the salt seasoning. Add set aside vegetables and mix thoroughly. Serve immediately. Serves 4.

Rice Meatballs

1 c minute rice
1 egg, beaten
1 lb ground steak
2 tsp salt
2 tsp grated onion

⅛ tsp marjoram (if desired)
pepper
2½ c tomato juice
½ tsp sugar

Mix all except 2 cups of tomato juice and sugar. Shape into balls. Brown meatballs in small amount of oil in skillet. Blend rest of juice and sugar. Pour in skillet with meatballs. Bring to a boil. Cover and simmer slowly 15 minutes. Sprinkle with parsley. Serves 6.

Meatballs with Curry Sauce

1 lb ground beef
½ c grated soft bread crumbs
¼ c milk
¼ c sherry
1 egg, slightly beaten
2 tbsp grated onion
salt

2 tbsp bacon drippings
1 (10½ oz) can condensed cream
   of mushroom soup
¼ c sherry
½ tsp curry powder (or to taste)
pepper

Mix beef, bread crumbs, milk, ¼ cup sherry, egg, onion, salt and pepper. Shape mixture into large balls (or small for cocktails). Heat bacon drippings in large skillet, add single layer of meatballs and cook slowly for 10 minutes. Shake pan from time to time. Combine soup, ¼ cup sherry, curry powder and heat. Pour over meatballs or serve separately in a bowl. Serve toothpicks with meatballs if they are small. Makes 2 dozen meatballs.

Meat Loaf

⅔ c dry bread crumbs
1 c milk or tomato juice
1½ lb ground beef
2 beaten eggs
2 bacon strips
butter

¼ c grated onions
1 tsp salt
¼ tsp pepper
½ tsp sage
1 (8 oz) can tomato sauce

Soak bread crumbs in liquid. Add meat, eggs and rest of ingredients. Mix well. Form into individual loaves or 1 loaf. Place in greased pan. Cover with bacon strips, butter or tomato sauce. Bake at 350° for 1 hour (single loaf). For individual loaves, bake for 45 minutes. Serves 8.

Baked Eggplant

5 lb of eggplant	pepper
½ loaf white bread	6 eggs
1 lb American or cheddar cheese	1 c milk
8 slices bacon (fried)	Parmesan cheese
salt	

Peel and dice eggplants. Parboil in salted water until tender. Drain. Add bread, trimmed and diced. Add diced cheese and bacon, salt and pepper. Stir in beaten eggs and milk. Mix and pour in casserole. Sprinkle with Parmesan cheese and dot with butter. Bake at 350° until brown. Serves 20.

Baked Tomatoes

2 large cans solid packed tomatoes	salt
8 whole cloves	½ onion, chopped
8 whole peppercorns	¾ c brown sugar
1 bay leaf	3–4 slices white bread
2 tbsp butter	(dime size pieces)

Put cloves, peppercorns and bay leaf in cheesecloth bag (shrimp boil bag). Cook tomatoes, undrained, cheesecloth bag and salt on top of stove *very* slowly 30 minutes. Stir occasionally. Add onion, sugar, bread and butter. Place in greased baking dish. When ready to bake, remove cheesecloth bag and bake at 400° for 1 hour. Serves 6.

Lemon-Butter Asparagus

1 bunch asparagus
salt
pepper

¼ c butter
1 tbsp lemon juice

Cook asparagus covered, in 1" boiling salted water until tender (12–15 minutes). Remove to serving plate. Add butter, salt, pepper and lemon juice. Serves 4.

Fresh Cooked Spinach

fresh spinach
salt

pepper
butter or bacon drippings

Wash thoroughly. Place in saucepan and add no water except what clings to leaves. Place over heat and turn with a fork frequently. Cook uncovered 6 minutes. Season with salt, pepper, butter or bacon drippings. Serve immediately.

Variation: Cook and drain spinach. Add ½–1 cup sour cream.

Spinach Filled Crepe

See crepe recipe, page 289.

Sauce:

5 tbsp flour
4 tbsp butter
2¾ c boiling milk
½ tsp salt

⅛ tsp pepper
pinch nutmeg
¼ c cream
1 cup grated Swiss cheese

Cook flour and butter 2 minutes slowly. Remove from heat and beat in milk, salt, pepper and nutmeg. Boil, stirring 1 minute. Beat in cream and cheese. Simmer ½ minute.

Filling:

1½ c chopped spinach
1 c cream cheese or cottage
  cheese
crepes (see crepe recipe)

1 c chopped or sliced mushrooms
2 tbsp chopped green onions
  sauteed in butter
1 egg

Blend several tablespoons of sauce into the spinach. Beat cheese with egg, mushrooms and several tablespoons of sauce to make a thick paste. Combine the two mixtures. Center a crepe in the bottom of a lightly buttered dish spread with layer of spinach filling. Continue in layers until all filling is used. Pour remaining cheese sauce over and sprinkle with grated Swiss cheese and dot with butter. Bake at 350° until sauce is lightly brown on top. Serve immediately. Serves 8.

Sweet and Sour Green Beans

1 lb green beans
3 strips bacon
2 onions, sliced
½ tsp dry mustard

2 tbsp vinegar
1 tbsp brown sugar
1 tsp salt
1 c bean liquid

Cut tips off beans, string and cut them in 1″ diagonal pieces. Cook in salted water, covered, for 45 minutes. Drain and reserve liquid. Fry bacon and cut in small pieces. Saute onion in bacon drippings. Smooth in mustard. Mix in vinegar, brown sugar, salt and bean liquid. Add beans and bacon. Let stand at least 1 hour and reheat before serving. Serves 4–6.

Quick Cooked Vegetables

2 sliced green peppers
12 sliced mushrooms
1 sliced onion
butter

bean sprouts (approximately
  ½ lb)
seasoned salt
pepper

Add onions and green pepper to butter in skillet. Saute until clear (3 minutes). Add mushrooms and heat 2 minutes. Add bean sprouts and heat 2 or 3 more minutes. Add seasoned salt and lots of pepper. Serve immediately with or without soy sauce. Serves 8.

Curried Fruit

1 banana cut in chunks
2 canned peach halves
   cut in chunks
¼ c melted butter

2 canned pear halves quartered
¼ c brown sugar
pinch of salt

curry?

Place fruit in ovenproof casserole. Mix butter and rest of ingredients. Pour over fruit, stir. Bake at 375° until sizzling (4–6 minutes). Serves 6.

Fried Rice

2 tbsp salad oil
1 bunch green onions, chopped
   (tops, too)
1 c diced celery
2 c cooked rice

salt
2 tbsp soy sauce (3 if preferred)
chopped blanched almonds
   (browned in butter)

Saute onions and celery in oil, but do not brown. Add rice (dry as possible), salt and soy sauce. Mix and put in casserole. Bake 350° for ½ hour. Toss almonds on top before serving. You can add shrimp, chicken, ham or turkey to make a complete meal. Serves 8.

Green Rice

3 c cooked white rice
2½ c milk
2 c grated sharp cheese
2 eggs, beaten

2 tsp olive oil
1 c chopped fresh parsley
4 green onions, chopped
1½ tsp worcestershire sauce

Mix and season with salt and pepper and place in greased casserole. Bake at 350° for 45 minutes. Serves 8 to 12.

Golden Rice

1 c rice (cooked)
¾ c milk
¼ c oil
garlic salt to taste

½ c parsley flakes
½ c green pepper, chopped
½ lb sharp cheese, grated

Mix cooked rice with other ingredients. Bake 1 hour at 350°. Serves 4 to 6.

Mushrooms and Rice

2⅔ c cooked rice
6 tbsp salad oil
2 small cans mushrooms,
   drained
4 green onions, chopped

2 cans beef consomme,
   undiluted
2 tbsp soy sauce
½ tsp salt

Mix and bake covered at 350° until water is absorbed, no more than 30–45 minutes, without stirring. Serves 6.

Rice Casserole

1 c white converted rice
1 can consomme
1 stick butter
1 can water

salt
pepper
parsley flakes

Put all ingredients in casserole. Cover and cook at 350° for 45 minutes. Stir and cook 15 more minutes uncovered. Serves 4 to 6.

Parsley Rice

1 c cooked rice
1 tsp salt
2 chicken bouillon cubes
2 c water
¼ c sliced green onion

⅓ c diced green pepper
¼ c slivered unblanched almonds
2 tbsp butter
½ c chopped parsley

Combine rice, salt, bouillon cubes and water. Heat to boiling. Stir, cover and cook at very low heat for 14 minutes or until tender. Saute green onion, green pepper and almonds in butter for 1 minute. Fold into freshly cooked rice with chopped parsley. Serves 4 to 6.

Sour Cream Potatoes

1 package sour cream sauce mix
1 c grated sharp cheddar cheese
1 tbsp chopped parsley
½ c fresh buttered bread crumbs

2 c potatoes, cooked (½" slices) and drained
2 tbsp chopped onion or sliced green onion
1 tbsp margarine, melted

Prepare sauce mix as directed on package. Combine with potatoes and cheese and put in 1 quart casserole. Top with crumbs tossed in margarine. Bake at 350° for 35 minutes. Serves 4.

Mother's Scalloped Potatoes

6 medium potatoes
3–6 tbsp butter
2 tbsp flour
⅓ c milk

1 tsp salt
½ tsp pepper
4–6 tbsp chopped onions (or more)

Peel and slice potatoes in circles (⅛" thick). Wash. Place in a buttered baking dish a layer of potatoes. Sprinkle with flour, salt and pepper. Dot with butter. Add onions. Repreat with second layer and third, if small dish. Cover with milk. Bake at 350° for 1 hour. Serves 8 to 10.

Variations: To layers, add 1 or more ingredients: grated cheese, pimento, mushrooms, scallions.

Easy Sweet Potatoes

4 sweet potatoes
½ stick butter
3 tbsp sugar

¼ tsp nutmeg
1 tbsp water

Boil potatoes until you can easily stick with a fork. Refrigerate when at room temperature. When cold, slice and place in a baking dish. Dot on butter and sprinkle with water. Sprinkle on sugar and nutmeg. Place in oven broiler and just brown until potatoes have a crunchy crust on top. Serves 6.

Sweet Potatoes in Wine Sauce

2½ c sweet potatoes
2 tbsp butter
½ tsp cloves

½ tsp nutmeg
½ tsp allspice

Cream together potatoes, butter and spices. In a buttered casserole, form a ring of potatoes. Leave a hole in center. If desired, top potatoes with marshmallows or buttered brown sugar (mixed with 1 cup butter). Brown.

Fill Center With:

1 c brown sugar
½ c butter

1 egg, beaten
½ c orange wine or bourbon

Mix sugar, butter and egg in top of double boiler, stirring constantly. Add wine or bourbon. Stir until thick. DO NOT BOIL. Fill and serve. Serves 6.

German Fried Potatoes

½ c bacon drippings
4 potatoes, sliced and peeled,
   (like for scalloped)

1 onion, sliced same as potato
½ c water
salt and pepper

Heat bacon drippings in skillet. Add potatoes until lightly browned. Add onions. Cook 5 minutes. Add salt and pepper and water. Cover and cook slowly. Turn potatoes occasionally. Cook until tender. Serves 6–8. A welcome change from french fries.

Bacon Noodles

6 slices bacon
1 8 oz package spinach egg
  noodles

3 tbsp butter
3 tbsp olive oil
¾ c grated Parmesan cheese

Cook bacon until crisp. Drain and crumble. Keep warm. Cook spinach noodles according to directions. Turn into a colander to drain. In the rinsed pot, over very low heat, melt butter with oil. Add noodles, bacon and ½ cup of cheese—toss. Remove from heat and mix in remaining cheese. Serve immediately. Serves 8.

Noodles and Cottage Cheese

1 5 oz package egg noodles
1 c cottage cheese
1 c sour cream
¼ c chopped onion
1 tsp worcestershire sauce

dash of hot Tabasco
1 tsp salt
1 c grated cheese (medium sharp)
1 small clove garlic, finely minced
paprika

Cook noodles according to directions on package. Drain. While noodles cook, combine in a small bowl the remaining ingredients except grated cheese. Mix. Stir cottage cheese mixture into hot noodles. Pour into buttered 3 quart casserole. Top with grated cheese. Sprinkle with paprika. Bake covered in 350° oven about 20 minutes. Remove cover and bake 20 more minutes. Serves 6 to 8.

Apricot Bread

1 c diced, dried apricots
1 egg
1 c sugar
2 tbsp melted butter
2 c flour

3 tbsp baking powder
¼ tsp soda
¼ tsp salt
¾ c orange juice
1 c chopped pecans

Soak apricots in cold water for half an hour. Drain and chop. Beat egg, stir in sugar and mix. Add melted butter. Sift flour, baking powder, soda and salt together. Add alternately with juice. Add nuts and apricots that have been sprinkled with flour. Mix. Bake in greased, floured loaf pan at 350° for 1 hour.

Mexican Cornbread

¼ c bacon crumbs
1 large or 2 small cans
   creamed corn
1 cornbread mix

1 c cheese
½ c cooking oil
1 jalapeno pepper, chopped

In a deep dish, mix cornbread mix and corn and oil. Put ½ in buttered casserole. Sprinkle cheese, bacon and pepper. Add remainder. Serves 6 to 8.

Baking Variation: In a bowl, mix all except oil. Heat oil in skillet to hot and pour in corn mixture. Bake at 400° for 25 minutes.

Cornbread

1½ c cornmeal
½ c flour
3 tsp baking powder
1 tsp salt

1 egg
1 tsp sugar
1½ c milk

Sift dry ingredients, add egg and milk and beat well. Pour into well greased *hot* pan (or sticks). Bake at 450° for 20 minutes or 12–15 minutes for sticks. Serves 6 to 8.

Variation: Add ¾ tsp soda to regular cornbread recipe. Use sour milk instead of sweet milk.

Sour Milk Biscuits

2 c flour
3 tsp baking soda
1 tsp salt

2 tbsp fat (Crisco)
1 c sour milk

Sift flour and measure. Add the rest of the dry ingredients and sift together. Cut in Crisco. Add milk and mix well. Pour onto floured board. Pat to ½" thickness or thinner if desired. Cut. Place on greased pan. Bake at 450° for 10–15 minutes. Makes 2 dozen biscuits.

Variation: Leave out soda and add ¾ cup sweet milk instead of sour milk.

Easy Cinnamon Rolls

½ stick butter
cinnamon, sugar mixture

melted Crisco

Follow recipe for making biscuits. Pat or roll dough until about ¼" thick. Add melted butter; sprinkle with cinnamon, sugar mixture (generously). Roll into one large roll, about 2" thick. Cut. Place in greased round pan. Cook 10–12 minutes at 400°. Before baking, baste with melted Crisco.

Icebox Rolls

1 package dry yeast
½ c warm water
½ c shortening
½ c sugar

1 egg, beaten
2 c warm water
1½ tsp salt
8 c flour

Dissolve the yeast in ½ cup warm water. Cream the shortening and sugar. Add the beaten egg, water, salt and yeast. Add flour and mix well (knead). Put in a large, greased bowl and grease top of dough. Put in refrigerator and cover. When chilled, shape into rolls and put in a greased pan. Let dough rise for 3 hours and bake at 400° for 12 minutes. Dough will last over a week and makes 4 or 5 dozen rolls.

Chocolate Mousse

5 eggs
½ lb dark, sweet chocolate

5 tbsp cold water
2 tsp rum

Separate eggs. Break up chocolate and melt in double boiler. Add cold water. Remove from heat. Mix in 5 egg yolks and 2 teaspoons rum. Add 5 stiffly beaten egg whites. Pour into small glass cups to chill for at least 4 hours. Makes 8 small servings. Can be made in demitasse cups and topped with 1 teaspoon whipped, sweetened cream.

Chocolate Tarts

2 squares unsweetened
   chocolate
1 c sugar
¼ c cornstarch
¼ tsp salt

3 egg yolks
2 tbsp butter
½ tsp vanilla
1 c milk

Mix sugar, starch, salt in top of double boiler. Add milk and heat. Melt chocolate and add. Cook to thicken. Add 3 egg yolks and cook to right thickness. Remove from heat and add butter and vanilla. Fill tart shells and add meringue topping and bake 5–10 minutes at 325°. Serve immediately. Serves 8.

Meringue: Beat 3 egg whites until stiff while slowly adding 6 teaspoons sugar and ¼ teaspoon cream of tartar.

Creme Chocolate

1 package chocolate bits
   (sweetened)
5 eggs, separated

4 tbsp cold water
whipping cream

Mix chocolate bits in pan with cold water. Stir over low heat, with wooden spoon (if possible) until blended. Remove from heat and slowly stir in 5 egg yolks, beaten. Mix well. Fold in 5 stiffly beaten whites. Blend well. Pour into after dinner coffee cups and store in refrigerator 6 hours or overnight. Top with small amount of unsweetened whipping cream. Serves 8.

Cherry Buckle

1 lb can red sour-pitted cherries
¼ c butter
½ c sugar
1 tsp sugar
1 tsp vanilla

1 egg (slightly beaten)
1 c flour
1 tsp baking powder
¼ tsp salt
⅓ c milk

Cream butter, sugar and vanilla until well blended. Add egg. Sift together—flour, baking powder and salt. Add to above mixture and add alternately with milk. Pour batter into 10 × 6 or 7 × 11 greased pan or use a round cake pan. Cover batter with drained cherries. Sprinkle with following mixture:

½ c sugar
⅓ c sifted flour

¼ c butter
½ tsp cinnamon

Bake at 375° for 40–45 minutes. Serves 8.

Cherry Cheese Torte in Cereal Crust

4 c Rice Krispies, crushed to make
* 2 c crumbs*
½ c sugar
½ c butter, melted
2 8 oz packages of cream cheese,
* soft*
1½ c milk

1 tsp vanilla
1 tsp grated lemon rind
1 package (3¾ oz) vanilla instant
* pudding mix*
1 can (1 lb 5 oz) cherry pie
* filling*
½ tsp almond extract

Combine cereal crumbs, sugar, and butter. Mix. Press into bottom and sides of a 9″ spring form pan. Bake at 350° for 5 minutes. Chill. Beat cream cheese, ½ cup milk, vanilla and lemon rind until smooth. Add remaining milk and pudding mix. Beat slowly until mixture begins to set, about 1 minute. Pour into crust. Chill until firm. Top with cherry pie filling flavored with almond extract (½ teaspoon). Serves 8.

Margaret Fraser's Lemon Delicacy

2 tbsp butter
¾ c sugar
juice of 1 lemon
1 c milk

rind of ½ lemon, grated
2 tbsp flour
2 eggs

Cream butter, add sugar gradually and cream well. Add well beaten egg yolks, flour, lemon juice and rind. Mix thoroughly. Add milk and fold in stiffly beaten egg whites, very gently. Pour into greased baking dish. Set in pan of hot water and bake in slow oven about 45 minutes. A delicate crust will form on top and pudding will supply its own sauce. Serves 4.

Lemon Crumble

Filling:

¼ c lemon juice
rind of 1 lemon, grated
1 c sugar
2 eggs

1 tsp cornstarch
1 tbsp flour
1 tbsp butter

Cook above ingredients in double boiler until thickened and then cool. Mix crumble mixture: 1¾ cups Ritz crackers (crumbled), ½ cup sugar, ¾ cup flour, ¾ cup butter, ½ cup coconut flakes, toasted, and 1 teaspoon baking powder. Layer: cracker crumbs, filling, crackers. Bake at 350° for 30 minutes. Serves 4 to 6.

Lemon Cloud

1 envelope unflavored gelatin
½ c sugar
½ c water
5 egg yolks

½ c lemon juice
1 tsp grated lemon rind (if desired)
5 egg whites
½ c sugar

Mix gelatin and ½ cup sugar in saucepan. Add water. Heat until gelatin and sugar are dissolved. Beat 5 egg yolks and lemon juice. Pour gelatin mixture over eggs and mix. Stir in lemon rind if desired. Chill. Beat 5 egg whites until stiff. Beat in sugar (½ cup). Fold lemon mixture into egg whites. Pour into meringues or individual dishes. Chill. Serve plain or with whipped cream. Serves 6.

Lemon Starletts

3 eggs
¾ c sugar
⅓ c ReaLemon bottled lemon
   juice

8 3″ tart shells
1 8 oz package cream cheese
⅓ c chopped, salted almonds
   or pecans

Beat eggs until thick and fluffy. Continue beating while gradually adding sugar and ReaLemon. Cook in heavy sauce pan over low heat stirring constantly until mixture is thick and smooth. Soften the cream cheese to room temperature and gradually blend into the hot custard mixture. Cool and fill tart shells. Sprinkle tops with chopped nuts. Serves 8.

Orange Cheese Souffle

1 package no bake cheese cake,
   filling & crumbs
3 tbsp sugar
¼ c butter
1½ c cold milk

¾ tsp orange extract
1 c whipped cream
1 can (11 oz) mandarin orange
   sections

Combine graham cracker crumbs, sugar and melted butter. Press mixture firmly against sides and bottom of 1½ quart casserole. Refrigerate 15 minutes. Combine cold milk and orange extract in small bowl. Add cheesecake filling and beat at low speed with electric beater. Beat at medium speed 3 minutes longer. Fold in whipped cream; then fold in orange sections. Pour in casserole. Chill 1 hour. Serves 12.

Toffee Torte

1 14¼ oz box of chocolate
   covered almond toffee,
   crushed

2 c heavy cream, whipped
1 8" loaf angel food cake,
   split in half, lengthwise

Reserve ¼ cup toffee. Fold remaining toffee into whipped cream. Fill and frost cake layers. Sprinkle with reserved toffee. Chill. Serves 8.

Divine Tart

8 egg whites
1½ tsp vanilla

1 tsp vinegar
2 c sugar

Beat first 3 ingredients until peaked. Add sugar gradually. Spread in 2 cake pans lined with brown paper. Cook at 300° for 1 hour and 15 minutes.

Filling:

1 can crushed pineapple,
   drained well

2½ pints whipping cream
¾ c maraschino cherries

Whip cream and add fruit. Spread between the 2 tarts and on top. Serves 8.

Strawberry Dessert

1 8 oz package Philadelphia
  cream cheese
1 c sifted confectioners sugar
1 tsp vanilla

1 c Half & Half cream
2 c fresh or frozen strawberries
  (sweetened)
whipping cream or Cool Whip

Soften cream cheese. Beat in the blender or mixer. Beat until smooth. Add sugar gradually while beating. Add cream and vanilla. Use fluted cup cake paper cups. Place 1 in each muffin tin. Fill well and freeze. When ready to serve, remove papers from "muffins" and place one in each sherbet dish. Top with strawberries and Cool Whip or whipping cream. Serves 8.

Raspberry Icebox Dessert

1 can Eagle Brand milk
4 tbsp seedless Smuckers Black
  Raspberry preserves
toasted pecans, chopped

2 tbsp lemon juice
2 (½ pints) cream, whipped
crushed vanilla wafers

Mix all ingredients except ½ pint of cream and vanilla wafers. Line a 9 × 11 pan with crushed vanilla wafers. Add mixture. Add a little sugar, vanilla or whiskey to the other ½ pint cream. Spread on top of raspberry mixture. Put in icebox to freeze. Will never harden. Serves 8.

Almond Praline Balls

1 c toasted slivered almonds
  or pecans

1 quart vanilla ice cream

Praline Sauce:

2 c light cream or Half & Half
1½ c light brown sugar

2 tbsp corn syrup
¼ c butter

Scoop large balls of ice cream. Roll in toasted almonds and place in freezer. Make sauce in heavy saucepan. Cook over very low heat and stir constantly until smooth and slghtly thickened (5–10 minutes). Cool, stirring. Serve over almond balls. Serves 6.

Fresh Fig Ice Cream

18–20 figs
1½ c sugar
4 tbsp dry sherry

1 quart cream, whipped
4 eggs
grated rind and juice of 1 lemon

Peel and mash figs as fine as possible. Add sugar and let stand until sugar dissolves. Beat egg yolks. Add sherry and beat well and add to figs. Whip cream until stiff. Add this to fig mixture. Freeze in trays or in electric freezer. Makes 2 quarts.

Velvet Sherbet

2 quarts milk
2 lb (4 c) sugar

2 c heavy cream
juice of 8 lemons

Dissolve sugar in milk, add cream. Put in ice cream freezer and freeze. When partially frozen, pour in strained lemon juice. Freeze. Makes 3 quarts.

Applesauce Cake

2 c flour
1 c sugar
½ c shortening
1 egg
1 tsp soda
½ tsp salt

½ tsp nutmeg
½ tsp cinnamon
1 tsp allspice
1 c applesauce
1 c raisins
1 c nuts

Sift dry ingredients. Cream shortening and sugar. Add eggs and beat. Add nuts and raisins. Add flour alternately with applesauce. Bake in greased pan at 350° for 1 hour and 45 minutes.

Beer Coffee Cake

1 (13¾ oz) package hot roll mix
1 c warm beer
2 eggs
2 tbsp sugar

1 tsp ground cinnamon
¼ c packed brown sugar (light)
¼ c chopped nuts

Soften yeast from package in lukewarm beer. Stir in eggs, sugar and cinnamon. Add dry ingredients from package and beat until smooth. Cover bowl and let rise in warm place until doubled in bulk. Beat dough again and spread in greased 9″ tube pan. Sprinkle brown sugar mixed with nuts over dough. Let rise in warm place until double. Bake in 375° oven for 25–30 minutes. Remove from pan.

Buttermilk Cake

1 c shortening or butter
1⅔ c sugar
4 eggs
1½ tsp vanilla
3 c flour

½ tsp lemon extract
½ tsp soda
1 c buttermilk
½ tsp salt

Cream shortening and sugar. Add eggs, one at a time, lemon extract and vanilla. Add flour alternately with buttermilk in which soda has been dissolved. Beat. Bake in greased and floured pan at 275° for 1 hour and 15 minutes. Turn out at once.

Lemon Angel Food Delight Cake

Using egg beater or wire whip, blend together in saucepan:

6 egg yolks
¾ c sugar
¾ c lemon juice
1½ tsp grated lemon rind
2 envelopes unflavored gelatin
½ c water

¾ c light corn syrup
½ pint whipping cream
 (whipped)
1 medium or large angel food
 cake (bought)
½ pint whip cream

Using egg beater or wire whip, blend together in saucepan: 6 egg yolks, ¾ cup sugar, ¾ cup lemon juice and 1½ teaspoons grated lemon rind. Cook over medium heat, whipping constantly until thickened.

Soak and have ready to dissolve in hot custard: 2 envelopes unflavored gelatin and ½ cup water.

Beat egg whites until stiff peaks are formed. Beat in corn syrup to make meringue. Fold lemon custard mixture into meringue. Chill until cool but not thick. Fold in ½ pint whipped cream.

Tear angel food cake into bite size chunks and place in tube pan, alternate layers of cake and lemon mixture. Gently drop pan to fill any air spaces after each layer. Chill 6 or more hours or until firmly set.

To unmold, run knife around edge, quickly lower pan in pan of hot water and immediately invert onto chilled plate. Ice with ½ pint whipped cream.

Lemon Chiffon Pound Cake

1 package yellow cake mix
1 package lemon Jello
⅔ c oil
⅔ c water
4 eggs

Mix and beat 5 minutes at high speed. Bake in greased and floured pan at 350° for 1 hour.

Cinnamon Pound Cake

1 pound cake mix (box)
3 eggs
1½ c water
½ c chopped nuts
¼ c soft butter
1 tsp cinnamon
⅛ tsp nutmeg
¼ c powdered sugar

Blend cake mix, eggs, water, nuts, butter, nutmeg and ¾ teaspoon cinnamon until moist. Beat 2 minutes. Pour into greased pan (bundt). Bake at 325° for 45–55 minutes. Invert onto serving plate. Combine ¼ teaspoon cinnamon and ¼ cup powdered sugar. Sprinkle over cake.

Cocoa Divinity Cake

Sift:

1⅞ c flour

¼ tsp baking powder

1½ c sugar

Add:

½ tsp soda

1 tsp salt

6 tbsp cocoa

Add:

⅔ c Crisco

1 c buttermilk

Beat 2 minutes; add 2 large eggs; beat 2 minutes; bake in a 9 × 12 greased pan at 350° for 30 minutes. Frost with Minute Fudge Frosting (following).

One Minute Fudge Frosting

1 square chocolate chopped (unsweetened)

1 c sugar

1 tsp vanilla

⅓ c milk

¼ c Crisco

¼ tsp salt

In saucepan, add chocolate, sugar, milk, Crisco and salt. Bring slowly to a full boil (rolling), stirring constantly. Boil 1 minute (by the clock). Let cool to lukewarm. Beat. Add vanilla. If too thick to spread, add 1 tbsp cream or milk. Double the above ingredients for large cake or 2 layers.

Aunt Mae's Cream Cheese Hot Sauce

½ c sugar
4 tsp cornstarch
1 c hot water
1 beaten egg

1 tbsp butter
Philadelphia cream cheese
    (8 oz package)
gingerbread

Combine sugar and cornstarch in saucepan. Gradually add hot water blending until smooth. Cook over high heat. Stir constantly until thick. Reduce heat and continue cooking until clear, 5–7 minutes. Remove from heat and add butter. Use a good hot gingerbread. Slice in half. Place a layer of creamed Philadelphia cream cheese on bottom slice of gingerbread. Cover with other half of gingerbread. Add another layer of cream cheese. Pour sauce over this and serve hot.

Harvest Pecan Cake

2 c butter
4½ c sifted flour
¼ tsp salt
1 tsp baking powder
6 eggs
4 c chopped pecans

1 lb brown sugar
½ c milk
1 tsp vanilla
3 tbsp instant coffee dissolved in
    3 tbsp hot water

Set out butter to soften. Sift together flour, salt and baking powder. Grease bottom of 10″ tube pan. Separate eggs, beat yolks well, egg whites until stiff. Cream butter and brown sugar in large bowl. Add beaten yolks. Combine milk, vanilla and dissolved coffee. Add alternately with dry ingredients and fold in pecans and egg whites. Pour into pan and bake at 325° for 1¼–1½ hours.

Creole Fudge Cake

4 squares unsweetened
  chocolate
1 tsp instant coffee
½ c water
1 c brown sugar (packed)
1 c sugar
¼ tsp salt

½ c soft butter
3 eggs
2½ c sifted cake flour
2 tsp baking powder
½ tsp baking soda
1 c milk

Preheat oven to 350°. Grease and dust with cocoa, 3 layer pans. Combine chocolate, coffee, water and brown sugar in top of double boiler. Heat over simmering water until chocolate is melted; cool, add sugar slowly to butter, beat at medium speed until blended. Add eggs, one at a time, beating well after each. Beat until fluffy. Beat in cooled chocolate mixture. Sift dry ingredients together. Add alternately with milk and egg-chocolate mixture. Divide batter among prepared pans. Stagger pans in oven. Bake 25–30 minutes (8″ pans) or until cake springs back. Cool 10 minutes. Remove from pans; cool on a wire rack. Frost between layers and on sides and top with coffee butter cream.

Frosting:

2 tbsp instant coffee
¼ c hot water
1 c soft butter

2 egg yolks
6 c sifted confectioners sugar

Dissolve coffee in hot water; cool. Blend in butter and egg yolks. Add confectioners sugar alternately with coffee mixture.

Praline Ice Cream Cake

½ c butter
1 pint (2 c) vanilla ice cream,
   softened
2 eggs
1½ c flour
⅔ c sugar

1 tbsp baking powder
½ tsp salt
1 c graham cracker crumbs
½ c sour cream
1 c caramel ice cream topping
½ c chopped pecans or halves

Melt butter in 3 quart saucepan. Remove from heat. Add ice cream, eggs, flour, sugar, baking powder, salt and graham cracker crumbs. Mix until smooth. Pour into greased 13 × 9 pan. Bake at 350° for 30 minutes. Combine sour cream and ice cream topping. Pour over warm cake. Top with pecans. Cool and cut. Serve with ice cream or whipping cream.

Coffee Creme Pie

Crust:

4 egg whites, beat until stiff
½ tsp salt, add slowly

1 c sugar
1 c chopped pecans, blend in

Mix all ingredients. Press into 2 10″ pans (buttered). Prick with a fork. Bake at 250° for 1 hour. Cool.

Filling:

¼ c instant coffee
1 c boiling water
1 lb marshmallows
4 egg yolks

3 (½ pints) or 1 quart whipped
   cream
1 tsp almond extract

Combine coffee, water and marshmallows. Add egg yolks beaten slightly. Cook 3 minutes. Cool. Fold in whipped cream. Add almond extract. Fill crusts and refrigerate overnight. These can be frozen.

Heavenly Pie

Pie Shell:

4 egg whites
½ tsp vinegar
1 tsp vanilla

¼ tsp salt
1 c sugar
½ c quick Quaker Oats,
uncooked

Filling:

fresh strawberries or peaches

whip cream

Add vinegar, vanilla and salt to egg whites. Beat until frothy. Add sugar very gradually about 1 tablespoon at a time. Beat well after each addition. Beat until stiff and glossy. Lightly fold in rolled oats. Place in mound on greased, heavy, unglazed paper on a baking sheet. Using a spatula, hollow out center and build up sides to look like pie shell. Bake in slow oven (275°) for 45 minutes to 1 hour. Cool for a few minutes and then remove from paper. Cool thoroughly and fill with sweetened whipped cream mixed with fresh strawberries or peaches. Refrigerate.

Daddy's Favorite Buttermilk Chess Pie

uncooked pie shell
1 tbsp flour
1 tbsp sugar
2 more tbsp flour
1½ c sugar
1 stick butter

3 eggs
pinch of salt
½ c buttermilk
1 or 2 lemons
3–6 tsp lemon juice
½ tsp vanilla

Prick the bottom of uncooked pie shell with fork and rub a mixture of 1 tablespoon flour, 1 tablespoon sugar into holes (keeps from having a soggy crust). Bake 10 minutes and remove from oven to cake rack to cool. Blend 2 tablespoons flour and 1½ cups sugar. Melt slowly 1 stick of butter. Beat 3 eggs. Add sugar and flour to eggs. Beat. Add butter and beat. Add pinch of salt. Add ½ cup buttermilk and mix. Squeeze 1 or 2 lemons and gradually add 3–6 teaspoons lemon juice to flavor. Add ½ teaspoon vanilla. Pour mixture into pastry shell and bake at 300° for 45 minutes.

Mimi's Lemon Meringue Pie

1 baked pie shell

Lemon Filling:

2 c boiling water
1 c sugar
5 tbsp cornstarch

3 egg yolks
½ stick butter
5 tbsp lemon juice

Mix cornstarch, sugar, and salt. Gradually add water. Add lemon juice. Cook in top of double boiler until thick, stirring constantly. Slowly add small amount of hot mixture to beaten egg yolks. Add this back to rest of lemon mixture and cook 2 or 3 more minutes. Remove from heat and add butter. Pour into baked pie shell and top with meringue.

Meringue:

Beat egg whites and 6 tablespoons of sugar. Add 2 tablespoons meringue in lemon filling. Pour in baked shell. Top with remaining meringue. Bake 10–12 minutes at 350°.

Mimi's Chocolate Meringue Pie

¼ c cornstarch
1 c sugar
½ c cocoa
¼ tsp salt

2 c milk
2 tbsp butter
½ tsp vanilla
3 eggs

Mix cornstarch, sugar, salt and cocoa. Gradually add milk. Cook in top of double boiler until thick, stirring. Slowly add small amount of hot mixture to 3 beaten egg yolks. Add back to rest of chocolate mixture and cook 2 or 3 minutes more. Add butter and vanilla. Pour into baked pie shell and top with meringue of 3 egg whites beaten stiffly with 6 teaspoons sugar added slowly and beaten. Cook in 325° oven until light brown 10 or 15 minutes.

Satin Pie

1 package (12 oz) semi-sweet
  chocolate pieces
¼ c milk
¼ c sugar
pinch salt

4 eggs, separated
1 tsp vanilla
pie shell baked
whipping cream

Combine chocolate, milk, sugar and salt in top of double boiler. Cook over hot water until mixture is blended and smooth. Cool slightly. Add egg yolks, one at a time, beating after each. Blend in vanilla. Beat egg whites until stiff. Fold into chocolate mixture, blending. Pour into baked pie shell. Let set 2 or 3 hours in refrigerator. Serve with whipping cream.

Cracker Pie

20 rich, Ritz crackers, crushed
½ c chopped pecans
1 tsp baking powder

3 egg whites
1 c sugar
1 tsp vanilla

Beat egg whites until stiff, then gradually add sugar and vanilla. Fold in crushed crackers, nuts and baking powder which have been mixed. Bake in greased pie plate for 30 minutes at 350°. Chill for 2 hours and serve with whipping cream and chopped nuts.

Easy Waxy Pecan Pie

2 c brown sugar
1 c white sugar
6 unbeaten egg whites
2 c flour

1 tsp baking powder
3 c pecans
1 tsp vanilla

Add the brown sugar and the white sugar to the 6 unbeaten egg whites and stir (do not beat). Add 2 cups flour mixed with 1 teaspoon baking powder. Add 3 cups pecans and 1 teaspoon vanilla. Bake in slow oven 45 minutes.

Black Bottom Pie

1 envelope unflavored gelatin	*1 c evaporated milk*
¾ c sugar	*4 squares unsweetened chocolate*
⅛ tsp salt	*1 tsp vanilla*
1 egg yolk	*9" baked pie shell or crumb crust*
¾ c milk	*1 c heavy cream*

Mix gelatin, ¾ cup sugar and ⅛ teaspoon salt in top of double boiler. Beat together 1 egg yolk and ¾ cup milk. Add to gelatin mixture. Add 3 squares unsweetened chocolate. Cook over boiling water until chocolate is melted, stirring often. Remove from heat and beat until smooth. Chill until thick. Whip 1 cup very cold evaporated milk and fold into gelatin mixture with 1 teaspoon vanilla. Pour into 9" baked pie shell or crumb crust and chill until firm. Spread with 1 cup heavy cream, whipped and sweetened. Shave 1 square unsweetened chocolate on top.

Strawberry Pie

1 pint fresh strawberries	*1 tbsp lemon juice*
½ c sugar	*dash salt*
1 envelope gelatin	*½ c whipped heavy cream*
¼ c cold water	*2 egg whites*
½ c hot water	*¼ c sugar*

Add 1¼ cups crushed strawberries and ½ cup sugar. Let stand 30 minutes. Soften gelatin in ¼ cup cold water. Dissolve in ½ cup hot water—let cool. Add strawberry mixture to lemon juice and salt. Chill until partially set. Fold in whipping cream. Beat egg whites to soft peaks—gradually add ½ cup sugar. Fold into mixture. Pour in pie shell and refrigerate.

Ella's Apple Pie

5 apples
1 c sugar
1 tbsp cornstarch
2 ~~tbsp~~ cinnamon

tsp.

1 stick Oleo
juice of ½ lemon
4 tbsp water

Peel and slice 5 apples. Sprinkle 1 cup sugar mixed with 1 tablespoon of cornstarch and 2 tablespoons of cinnamon. Dab 1 stick of Oleo, juice of ½ lemon, 4 tablespoons of water over apples. Place in unbaked pie shell, and bake at 350° 45–60 minutes.

Easy Chess Pie

3 eggs, unbeaten
2 c sugar
½ c sweet milk

4 tbsp cornstarch
½ c butter
1 tsp vanilla

Beat 3 eggs very well. Add 2 cups sugar, ½ cup sweet milk, 4 tablespoons cornstarch, ½ cup butter and 1 teaspoon vanilla. Put in uncooked pie shell and bake at 350° for 35 minutes.

Blonde Brownies

1 c sifted flour
½ tsp baking powder
⅛ tsp baking soda
½ tsp salt
½ c chopped walnuts
⅓ c butter

1 c firmly packed light
 brown sugar
1 egg, slightly beaten
1 tsp vanilla
½ c _glazed_ chocolate chips

Measure sifted flour, add baking powder, soda and salt and sift again. Add nuts and mix—set aside. Melt shortening in saucepan and remove from heat. Add sugar and mix well. Cool slightly. Add egg and vanilla and blend. Then add flour mixture, a small amount at a time, mixing well after each addition. Spoon into greased 9 × 9 × 2 pan. Sprinkle chips over top. Bake in moderate oven 350° for 20 minutes. Do not overbake. Cool in pan. Serve with scoop of ice cream topped with fudge nut sauce.

Fudge Nut Sauce

3 squares unsweetened
  chocolate
½ c light cream
¾ c sugar

3 tbsp butter
dash salt
¾ tsp vanilla
½ c chopped walnuts or pecans

Put chocolate and cream in saucepan; cook over low heat stirring constantly until chocolate is melted and mixture is smooth and blended. Add sugar, butter, salt and continue cooking, stirring constantly, 3–5 minutes longer or until slightly thickened. Remove from heat and add vanilla and nuts. Can be stored in refrigerator (covered). Before serving, place bowl of sauce in hot water and stir until smooth.

Cheesecake Cookies

⅓ c brown sugar, packed
½ c chopped walnuts
1 c flour
⅓ c melted butter
1 8 oz package cream cheese

¼ c granulated sugar
1 egg
1 tbsp lemon juice
2 tbsp cream or milk
1 tsp vanilla

Mix brown sugar, nuts, and flour in a large bowl. Stir in the butter and mix with your hands until crumbly. Remove 1 cup of the mixture to be used later as a topping. Place remainder in an 8″ square pan and press firmly. Bake at 350° about 12–15 minutes. Beat cream cheese until smooth with the granulated sugar. Beat in the egg, lemon juice, cream and vanilla. Pour this onto the baked crust. Top with the reserved crumbs. Return to a 350° oven and bake about 2 minutes. Cool thoroughly, cut into 2″ squares. These can be baked the day before serving, cover with plastic wrap and keep refrigerated. Makes 16 cookies.

Butterscotch Squares

¾ c flour
¼ tsp salt
½ tsp baking powder
⅓ c butter

1 c brown sugar
1 egg
½ tsp vanilla
½ c chopped nuts

Mix and sift flour, salt and baking powder. Cream butter and sugar. Add egg and beat well. Stir in dry ingredients. Mix in vanilla and nuts. Bake in greased pan at 350° for 23 minutes. When cool, cut in squares and dust with powdered sugar.

Tea Cakes

1 c sugar
¾ c butter
2 eggs
1 tsp vanilla

2 tbsp milk
2 tsp baking powder
2 c flour (you will need more)

Cream sugar and butter and add eggs, one at a time. Add milk and sifted flour and baking powder and mix. Add more flour if needed (maybe a cup or more) and mix. Roll out and cut into cookie shape. Cook at 375° until lightly brown on edges. These may be rolled, refrigerated and sliced also.

Brown Sugar Cookies

1 c light brown sugar, sifted
1 egg white

1½ c pecans
1 tsp vanilla

Beat egg white stiff. Add sugar, nuts and vanilla. Drop from teaspoon on greased flat pan, giving room to spread. Cook in moderate oven until crisp, or less if you like chewy cookies.

Butter Cookies

4 c flour
2 c powdered sugar

1 lb butter or margarine

Mix together (will be stiff) and spoon by teaspoonfuls on to a cookie sheet (ungreased). Flatten out a little. This will be a fairly large cookie. Bake at 300° for 20 minutes or until slightly brown on edges.

Meringue Cookies

2 egg whites (beat until very stiff)
½ c sugar
1 tsp vanilla

½ c pecans
½ c chocolate chips (if desired)

Mix and place on foil (about 1 tablespoon for each cookie). Bake 35 minutes at 250°. Cool on cake racks.

Blonde Fudge

3 c sugar
1½ c milk
3 tbsp butter
4 tbsp white corn syrup

½ c chopped pecans
¼ tsp vanilla
½ tsp almond extract

Mix sugar, milk, syrup and salt and bring to a boil over moderate heat. Cook to soft boil, stirring. Remove from heat and stir in butter. Cool. Add pecans, vanilla, and almond extract and beat until stiff and loses its gloss. Pour in greased pan and cut into squares when cool.

Peanut Brittle

2 c sugar
1 c Karo
1 c water
2–3 c peanuts

¾ tsp salt
1 tsp soda
1 tbsp butter

Cook sugar, Karo and water to 260° on candy thermometer. Add peanuts and salt and cook to 295°. Add soda, butter and pour on greased surface.

Chewy Pecan Candy

½ c white sugar
½ c brown sugar
1 c white Karo
4 tsp butter

⅛ tsp salt
¼ tsp ginger
2 c chopped nuts

Mix all ingredients in a saucepan and cover. Cook 5 minutes. Remove cover and cook to hard ball stage. Pour into lightly greased pan. Mark in squares. When hard, break apart and wrap candy in waxed paper.

Foamy Omelette

egg
1 tbsp milk

salt and pepper to taste
1 tbsp butter

Separate whites and yolks of egg. Beat white until it holds a peak. Beat yolk in separate bowl with 1 tablespoon milk. Add salt and pepper to taste. Pour yolk mixture into white, folding gently. Add 1 tablespoon butter to omelette pan or skillet. Melt and add omelette mixture. Cook slowly, lifting sides to cook all of egg. When sides are done, fold over for 15 seconds and serve.

Variations: After pouring omelette mixture in pan, add 1 or more of these: grated cheese, sausage pieces, bacon pieces, fresh mushrooms, chopped tomatoes, chopped scallions or hot sauce.

Robert's French Toast

1 c Bisquick
1 egg (beaten)

1 c milk
2 tbsp oil

Mix all ingredients and store in the refrigerator until ready to make french toast. Stir before using. Remove the crust from bread and cut into triangles or halves.

In a skillet, add 2 tablespoons butter and ¼ cup oil. Heat but do not let it burn. Dip bread into batter and put in skillet. Brown on both sides. Remove and drain. Serve immediately with powdered sugar or cinnamon sugar mixture and syrup.

Cinnamon and Sugar Mixture:

1 tsp ground cinnamon

¼ c sugar

Mix.

One cup batter mixture will make french toast for 6 slices of bread.

INDEX

INDEX

Poultry—see Chicken, Dove, Duck, Quail, Turkey

Venison

Please send me _______________ copies of your cookbook "Cuckoo Too" at $9.95 per copy plus $1.55 per copy for mailing. Enclosed is $__________ .

Name ____

Street ____

City ____

State ___________________________ Zip _____________

Make check payable to   Cuckoos
5142 Green Tree
Houston, Texas 77056

Please send me _______________ copies of your cookbook "Cuckoo Too" at $9.95 per copy plus $1.55 per copy for mailing. Enclosed is $__________ .

Name ____

Street ____

City ____

State ___________________________ Zip _____________

Make check payable to   Cuckoos
5142 Green Tree
Houston, Texas 77056

Please send me ____________ copies of your cookbook "Cuckoo Too" at $9.95 per copy plus $1.55 per copy for mailing. Enclosed is $________ .

Name ____

Street ____

City ____

State _____________________________ Zip ___________

Make check payable to   Cuckoos
                         5142 Green Tree
                         Houston, Texas 77056

Please send me ____________ copies of your cookbook "Cuckoo Too" at $9.95 per copy plus $1.55 per copy for mailing. Enclosed is $________

Name ____

Street ____

City ____

State _____________________________ Zip ___________

Make check payable to   Cuckoos
                         5142 Green Tree
                         Houston, Texas 77056